ESSENTIAL STRATEGIES FOR SCHOOL SECURITY

ABOUT THE AUTHORS

Richard A. Haynes, CPP, CPC, is a certified protection professional with backgrounds in both law enforcement and private security. He is a retired Captain with the Charleston Police Department, where he served in various capacities including Chief of Detectives, SWAT Commander, and Deputy Chief of Police. Mr. Haynes has also served as a security consultant for numerous business, industrial, and security organizations. He has consulted on issues involving security management, guard force operations, training, internal theft, executive protection, and various other related matters. In addition, he has written numerous articles regarding protection-related topics and authored the book, *The SWAT CYCLOPEDIA*. He is a graduate of the West Virginia State Police Academy, the FBI National Academy, and West Virginia State College, among others. He is a licensed private investigator, a member of the American Society for Industrial Security, International Association of Professional Security Consultants, and the Council of International Investigators.

Catherine L. Henderson, MA, is a teacher and a free-lance writer. She has taught English, journalism, speech, media, and writing for publication at George Washington High School in Charleston, West Virginia, for more than thirty years. She has conducted seminars and investigated complaints of sexual harassment. She helped form a task force for school security and worked as a liaison for student programs with the Community Oriented Policing Division of the Charleston Police Department. She has written about crime and violence for international, national, regional, and local publications and for fifteen years was a regular writer for a travel magazine. She has authored a long-running column on the business of writing, has taught writing seminars, appeared in a year-long travel feature on PBS, and is the author of *Fairs, Festivals, and Funnin' in West Virginia*. Ms. Henderson received a BA degree in English from Morris Harvey College and an MA degree in journalism from Marshall University. She is a member of the Mystery Writers of America, Sisters in Crime, the Ohio River Valley Sisters in Crime, the Society for Professional Journalists, and the American Crime Writers League.

ESSENTIAL STRATEGIES FOR SCHOOL SECURITY

A Practical Guide for Teachers and School Administrators

By

RICHARD A. HAYNES, CPP, CPC

and

CATHERINE L. HENDERSON, MA

Charles C Thomas
PUBLISHER • LTD.
SPRINGFIELD • ILLINOIS • U.S.A.

Published and Distributed Throughout the World by

CHARLES C THOMAS • PUBLISHER, LTD.
2600 South First Street
Springfield, Illinois 62704

©2001 *by* CHARLES C THOMAS • PUBLISHER, LTD.

ISBN 0-398-07177-2 (hard)
ISBN 0-398-07178-0 (paper)

Library of Congress Catalog Card Number: 00-054395

With THOMAS BOOKS *careful attention is given to all details of manufacturing
and design. It is the Publisher's desire to present books that are satisfactory as to their
physical qualities and artistic possibilities and appropriate for their particular use.*
THOMAS BOOKS *will be true to those laws of quality that assure a good name
and good will.*

Printed in the United States of America
SM-R-3

Library of Congress Cataloging-in-Publication Data

Haynes, Richard A.
    Essential strategies for school security : a practical guide for teachers and
school administrators / by Richard A. Haynes and Catherine L. Henderson.
        p.   cm.
    Includes bibliographical references and index.
    ISBN 0-398-07177-2 -- ISBN 0-398-07178-0 (pbk.)
    1. Schools--Security measures--United States--Handbooks, manuals, etc. 2.
School violence--United States--Prevention--Handbooks, manuals, etc. I.
Henderson, Cathy (Catherine) II. Title.

LB2866 .H39 2001
371.7'82'0973--dc21

                                                                00-054395

To the fallen and injured teachers, students, and staff at Pearl, Mississippi, Paducah, Kentucky, Jonesboro, Arkansas, Littleton, Colorado, and all those we may not know who have been a victim of rampage violence in their school.

PREFACE

School security has become a topic of intense concern for educators, parents, communities, and public officials. With it comes numerous questions.

Certainly paramount is the question: What types of protection are necessary to protect students, teachers, and staff? But equally important are the answers to a second question: What does the campus feel is suitable to protect it and its people from the threats of crime and rampage violence?

Essential Strategies for School Security is a self-help, easy-to-read guide for teachers, school officials, and anyone who is interested in this sensitive issue.

It explores the many factors that are involved in implementing an effective program of protection for schools. It provides direction and answers to the many questions posed by crime and violence in our schools by translating certain principles of security into easy-to-understand applications for the campus setting.

As *Essential Strategies* explains the various protection measures that are required for a thorough, comprehensive security program, it also seeks to correct certain misconceptions about security within schools.

Too often, a security program is perceived as uniformed guards and closed-circuit cameras. Such an error can leave a school dangerously unprotected. *Essential Strategies* stresses the need for a comprehensive program and shows officials how they can provide in-depth protection for their school.

Essential Strategies also confronts the problem of rampage violence. Although schools may be victimized by the typical, everyday criminal events such as theft and vandalism, the threat of rampage violence demands they seek more effective solutions that will protect and prepare them for this spontaneous threat.

Although this text focuses on the secondary school, college and universities will also find this text to be a valuable aid as they develop a new security program or upgrade an existing one.

R.A.H.
C.L.H.

INTRODUCTION

America's schools are in crisis! Not from overcrowded classrooms, a lack of competent teachers, or even drastic budget cutbacks. The emergency is rather from the sudden surge of violent crime that is attacking classrooms, teachers, and students.

In times past, schools were gathering places where young people came together to grow intellectually and socially. They learned and practiced the processes of cooperation, leadership, and responsibility. Teachers concentrated on instruction, and parents felt secure, confident that their children were in a safe, carefree environment. It was a wondrous cocoon of innocence and naivete.

Then something changed. Crime crept into the classrooms, and schools underwent a vast transformation.

Indicators that schools were headed toward this disturbing turning point first appeared in the early 1970s. An influx of illicit drugs gained a powerful and permanent grip on the country and on teens. By the 1980s, street gangs invaded the schools. Their existence, which grew in numbers and force, centered largely on an increasingly lucrative drug trade, which brought with it still another brand of crime.

As if drugs and gangs were not enough of a threat to the already beleaguered schools, the 1990s introduced yet another, entirely new phenomenon—the armed and angry teen, who suddenly turned on classmates and teachers and gunned them down with a vengeance. The nation was stunned. Worse yet, their senseless acts seemed to defy logic. Experts of every sort, even at the White House, scrambled, trying to figure out Why?

Ultimately, the discoveries, such as they were, merely confirmed what most educators had known all along—the answer is not simple. There is no one single reason why crime and violence have attacked our schools, and there is certainly no easy, one-solution-fits-all answer. Schools are a microcosm, a reflection of our society. Today's youth, many of whom grow jaded long before they grow up, mature faster and harder.

Exposure to the Internet, the media, and the world at large has created the best-informed generation of young people our world has yet to see. Propelled into the super-information age, they have become more knowledgeable, more sophisticated, but not necessarily more emotionally mature than any other generation of teens.

Adolescents already scarred by broken homes, behavioral disorders, child abuse, identity crises, socioeconomic disparity, and intense peer pressure receive daily overdoses of movies, television, and video games that blow up, gun down, and annihilate everyone involved, including the player. For the emotionally immature youth who is more child than teen, the combination can be, and has become, a cataclysmic force for expressing personal conflicts and frustrations.

As the 1990s became the "Age of Rage," even violence had its own terminology: "Workplace Violence," "Road Rage," and "Domestic Violence" are but a few of the common phrases that reveal a nation that has not only turned its hostilities on itself but has also blurred the line between tragedy and entertainment.

Consider the phrase "going postal." Initially, the word was coined to refer to the numbers of tragic acts of workplace violence that claimed the lives of numerous post office employees. Teens during the 1990s, however, knew the word as a video game.

Although most people recognize democracy is a privilege and are perfectly content to live out their lives as law-abiding citizens, others view their freedom as an unlimited opportunity to trample the right of others and victimize the unsuspecting or the unprepared. The bad guys, whether adult or juvenile, always have the preemptive option of striking first. They can seize the best opportunity, because when and where they plan to attack is their choice.

The advantage is always theirs, whether the target is a car they wish to steal, a bank they wish to rob, a shopper they wish to mug, or fellow students and teachers they wish to maim and kill. For the perpetrator of crime and violence, there is no greater inducement than the unprotected victim or target.

No doubt Thomas Jefferson was referring to our enemies from without, not those among us, when he warned, "The price of freedom is eternal vigilance." It is a lesson hard learned and always expensive, one that has forced both business and industry to revise their thinking, to anticipate, and to realize that a guard at the front gate and good locks on the doors are no longer sufficient to ward off crime and violence.

Even American law enforcement has had to revamp its philosophy. Historically, reactive in their response to crime, police departments, from small towns to sprawling cities, are establishing a proactive, preventative approach by incorporating programs such as community-oriented policing to combat the constantly changing complexities of crime.

Schools, too, must change. They must reassess their response to the crime and violence that is steadily invading their classrooms and toward those who rape, rob, assault, maim, and kill their students and their teachers.

Logic, it would seem, should dictate that schools, as with business, industry, and even law enforcement, must incorporate protection and must defend their staffs and students with a prescribed, sensible, thorough readiness. In other words, they must develop and incorporate a program of security.

Yet, the country has learned such a shift is far from simple. It is a truth no one knows better than teachers.

As experts, from the genuinely knowledgeable to the self-appointed, argue over the best course of action, those in decision-making positions of authority—school boards, superintendents, administrators, and those in between—often attempt to defend their schools' inadequate preparations against crime and violence. They predict, with all the accuracy of a crystal ball gazer, that it can't happen here. Still others criticize, reprimand, and ultimately refuse to fund the security programs that individual schools or staffs themselves have attempted to develop.

Goldfish swallowing, and even flag-pole sitting were once fads. They faded, then disappeared. Perhaps violence against schools too shall pass. Maybe the mass murders of students and teachers by juvenile assailants will cease. Then again, maybe they won't. And if not, what? Perhaps Pandora's box will not be closed now that it has been opened and evil has been unloosed.

Educators have been reluctant, sometimes fearful, to embrace the idea of school security, primarily because of certain misconceptions about just what a formal program of protection involves than because of actual fact.

Beyond the typical budget constraints, politics, and a reluctance for change is a clash of concepts—that schools that have been characterized largely as free and open cannot successfully join forces with security that would restrict, inhibit, and surely stifle the learning process.

Then there are those who argue security is unnecessary, that national statistics show a decline in crime, and that tragedies such as those that occurred in Paducah, Pearl, Jonesboro, and Littleton are but a fluke, an anomaly.

Most of the major categories of violent crime have indeed flat-lined or are showing annual decreases. Even juvenile crime, at first-glance, seems to be on the decline as well. A closer look at recent statistics reveals that violent crime and homicides perpetrated by juveniles have actually doubled. Decision makers who place great value on statistics not only deceive themselves but also provide a false sense of security to the schools, to the teachers, and to the students—the very ones whose lives hang in the balance.

Even if crime does appear to be on the decline, for the unsuspecting, unprotected victim who is raped, robbed, or murdered, the statistic is 100%. When anyone can become a victim at anytime, Americans must understand that, at best, statistics are indicators of the past. Organizations and individuals must properly protect themselves for the future.

The human mind is unpredictable, capable of creating sonnets and rockets by some, yet fomenting violence and death from others. To predict the future on the basis of what has transpired in the past is surely courting disaster.

Schools must never forget: once a tragedy occurs, the damage cannot be undone. Victims cannot be "un-shot" or "un-murdered." Unlike the untimely death of a popular sit-com hero, lost lives of real students and real teachers cannot be rerun or magically restored with a new program. Those in charge must take every action and must make every preparation necessary to stop or to deter criminal threats, not after the tragedy plays out but in advance, before bombs and bullets can make believers of even the most skeptical. This is the reality, the message, and the mission of security.

Of no less importance is the current-day criminal. More tempted by his own crime than fearful of the police, he runs less and less of a risk of being caught by understaffed, overextended law enforcement and ultimately convicted by a burgeoning criminal justice system. Juvenile criminals fare even better. Although experts disagree and debate just how young mass murderers should be punished, their sentences, so far, vary from juvenile detention to life without parole.

Perhaps last, but not necessarily least, is liability. Schools stand responsible for providing a safe learning environment. It is a debt they owe. Yet educators know the numbers of isolated, lonely, angry teens are growing. Try as they may to reach the troubled child through counseling, peer mediation student groups, and after-school activities such as sports, band, and drama, schools concede the task is overwhelming.

Oftentimes, even the system's best efforts are further complicated by some parents who insist they most certainly do know their own child. Their child is innocent and simply could not have committed the atrocity eye-witnesses claim they saw. Faced with overwhelming evidence, few parents will admit they do not really know their own child.

At present, many teachers conclude that should a tragedy occur in their school, even remotely similar to those at Pearl, Paducah, Jonesboro, Littleton, the *school* will be charged with failing to take appropriate action to intercept the tragedy, the *school* failed to implement adequate safety and security measures, and a *teacher,* not a county, not a state department of education, and certainly not a politician or some armed-chair critic, was negligent to the extreme.

Stripping away all the bureaucratic red tape, personal qualms, misunderstanding, or sheer refusal to recognize the truth, there is one fundamental, undeniable certainty: if you have something of value—cash in a bank vault, a new car in your driveway, nuclear secrets in a national agency, or students and teachers in a classroom—there are those who are more than willing to do whatever it takes, whether they must steal, destroy, or kill, and use whatever means necessary to achieve their violent, criminal ends.

Perhaps, at some future time, we may discover the trigger that once pulled, compels some students to assassinate their peers and teachers. Until then, schools themselves must defend their staffs and students, schools must implement a system or a program that will prevent crime threats, and schools must be ready to respond effectively and efficiently if an incident should develop.

Essential Strategies for School Security is a self-help guide designed to provide answers for educators, school officials, parents, or any lay person concerned about school security. Highly readable and easy to understand, *Essential Strategies* also offers a comprehensive, definitive examination of the various components of protection.

Essential Strategies helps schools assess the security threats that confront them, explains the "what" and the "why" of the security measures they need, then outlines techniques, applications, and strategies associated with modern security.

Essential Strategies dispels the myth that security must be restrictive and it clarifies security's role on the campus. With careful planning, security can be simultaneously effective and livable. Not only can security co-exist with an academic atmosphere, but with a program of protection in place, the business of education can continue because staff and students are reassured their safety is of utmost concern.

ACKNOWLEDGMENT

To Jo Martin and Pete Corbett, two of education's finest. Your professionalism is tireless. In addition to the infinite number of other aspects of your job, you sincerely care about effective school security.

CONTENTS

ILLUSTRATIONS

Disclaimer

The authors and the publisher specifically disclaim any liability for personal injury, death, damage, or property loss resulting from the use, misuse, application, implementation, practice, adoption, misunderstanding, or misinterpretation of any information contained in this document.

ESSENTIAL STRATEGIES FOR SCHOOL SECURITY

Part 1

BASIC SCHOOL SECURITY COMPONENTS: PREVENTION AND DETERRENCE

The foremost mission of any security program is to establish a presence that will stop crime and deter violence *before* it can develop. A school security program must discourage perpetrators to the degree that they realize committing crime and violence at this school is futile and will only lead to detection, apprehension, and punishment. Such an atmosphere is the essence of security.

Chapter 1

DEVELOPING THE SCHOOL
SECURITY PROGRAM

IN RECENT YEARS, business, industry, and many organizations have
expanded their use of security personnel and technology. Their aim has
been to protect their company against theft, vandalism, and product tampering and their employees and their customers from acts of violence. In an
effort to prevent internal rampages of workplace violence, many have also
instituted internal programs.

As violence becomes more commonplace in our society, many institutions, especially schools, still remain unprotected, still continue to learn their
lesson—that no security invites tragedy and that effective security does save
lives.

THE SCHOOL SECURITY FORMULA

Schools continually strive to determine their direction, both academical-
ly and socially, along well-planned, orderly paths. Teachers ask that new
programs first be researched, then introduced with detailed thought and
input from the entire staff. They expect to receive preparation and consideration, because they will be the ones to make any new program work.

Implementing a security program must be no different. Even the definition of school security—a process or system that provides the necessary safeguards to protect the students, faculty, and the premises from harm—should
also be incorporated into the mission statement of every school.

From the outset, teachers and staff, who will primarily control and direct
the security program, must have a clear understanding about how it is to be
formed and how it will work. Because there seem to be so many misconceptions associated with security, misconceptions that can lead planners
down the wrong path, everyone on the school staff needs a thorough and
clear understanding of the concepts of security.

Certainly the most common mistake about security is that one form of
security can be stretched and shaped to cover all the problems that can and

do threaten a school. Both the business and the industrial community have discovered that quick-fix security simply does not work and that popular, fast solutions to security problems cost money but often fail to deter the crime.

Companies that have reacted to a crime with one single security measure such as hiring a guard to stand at the front gate or installing closed-circuit television to warn the premises are under constant surveillance have often and unfortunately discovered their response was haphazard. Not only had they failed to assess the problem before they chose the type of security measure they would use, they also neglected to determine whether the application would be appropriate and if, indeed, one single security measure would deter the crime.

For those who are desperately trying to find hasty solutions to problems and do not thoroughly understand the concepts of security, popular remedies often seem like the right thing to do. Surveillance cameras are often installed because the technology is well known. The same goes for hiring security guards. It is a commonly accepted practice. The list of fragmented, miscalculated security measures is endless.

Schools must realize that guards are not security, nor are burglar alarms, locks, and lighting. Each is merely a component of security. Real security occurs when these parts are carefully arranged into complete protection. The formula then becomes both comprehensive and workable.

As with any structure, a solid foundation is essential. An effective security program is carefully designed and methodically planned. The school must construct its plan around the following two essential components.

Prevention and Deterrence

The essence of an effective security operation is to defeat security problems before they develop.

Interception and Response

If a security problem does develop, measures must be in place that intervene and disrupt threats or loss, that react appropriately to apprehend the perpetrator, and that control damage and maintain order should some crisis result.

In addition to these two fundamental concepts, an effective security program must also meet the following requirements.

Security Must Be Proactive

The fundamental purpose of any security program is to prevent harm or loss and deter the would-be perpetrator. Whether the target is people or property, effective security acts in advance to discourage threats or block them. A school must be absolutely thorough as it reviews and assesses its needs.

The school must carefully study and judge any current threats and especially anticipate those that have the potential to cause harm or loss. Then, well before a security program is put into operation, a school can develop a plan with measures that will intervene effectively should crime or violence occur.

Security Must Be Comprehensive

If a school desires an effective security program, it must consider all the aspects that will be protected—its people, its programs, and its activities. The three P's of protection illustrate this concept more fully and detail the three components, people, procedures, and physical security, that are necessary for a comprehensive security program.

People comprise the first component of the protection formula. Not only must staffs and students be protected but they must also become the protectors. Designated staff members will be the ones responsible for the system of safeguards, and it will be their job to ensure the program is effective and is operating at optimum levels at all times.

The next component of this comprehensive formula involves *physical security*. Physical security includes the necessary hardware and technology such as closed-circuit camera systems, locks, lighting, intrusion alarms, access control systems, and the like.

The third component, *procedures,* completes the security equation. At this point the *people* component and the *physical security* applications merge and just how strong the school's protection program actually is will be determined. Will it remain strong and effective or is it doomed to erode and eventually be forgotten?

Broken locks that are not repaired, burned-out light bulbs that are not replaced, video tapes in closed-circuit camera systems that are not changed, or staffs that are out of compliance with certain security regulations are just a few of the first telltale signs that a security program is failing.

Whenever people become lax or decide to shortcut a particular protection practice, it will soon be circumvented and eventually conveniently forgotten. Only through constant and consistent monitoring can a school maintain an effective security system (see Figure 1).

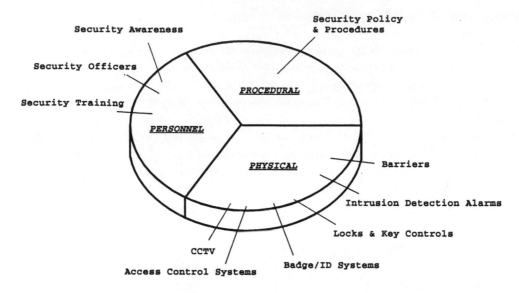

Figure 1. The 3-P's of a Proper Protection Program

Security Must Be Integrated

Although each of the three P's of protection is essential to the overall security program, their real strength lies in their combination. By intertwining the three into a comprehensive operation, each component complements and supports the others. If bricks form the protection program that defends the school, then it is the integration, the mortar between each one, that solidifies a wall and makes it strong and sturdy to keep out harm.

Uniting the various security aspects of an organization's security program into a well-coordinated, cohesive whole also provides overlap, measures that are designed to fail-safe should a crime or threat occur.

OVERLAPPING SECURITY MEASURES

Overlapping security measures provide a series of stopgaps or backup features that are designed to intervene automatically if the primary security measure fails to intercept a threat or if it is somehow circumvented.

Many schools already use some form of overlapping security. When they secure offices, rooms with technical equipment, and computers, not only do they install door locks but increasing numbers of schools are also equipping their building with intrusion alarm systems. Should a break-in

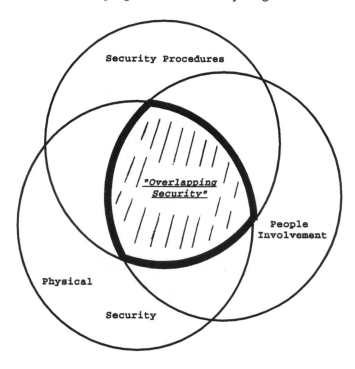

Figure 2. Overlapping Security

occur that bypasses door locks, the alarm system alerts the appropriated authorities (see Figure 2).

THE PROTECTION PROGRAM MUST HAVE DEPTH

Create enough protective insulation around people or property and a perpetrator will discover that it is simply too difficult to gain access to the target. Such is the concept of *protection-in-depth*. By placing concentric rings of protection around an object or a location, the target is insulated.

Consider the bank vault. Made of heavy-duty steel and fabricated to withstand high-impact assault, it would seem to be impenetrable. Nonetheless, banks still protect it with an alarm system, locks on the doors of the facility, an alarm-activated camera system, and countless other measures designed to delay and detect any attempts at theft (see Figure 3).

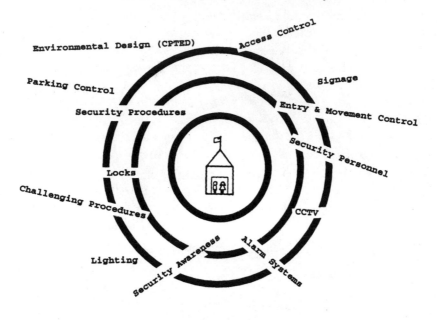

Figure 3. Protection-in-Depth

THE DEVELOPMENT PROCESS

Developing a security program for a school must follow an orderly process, a series of progressive stages or phases. Each must be carefully based on the one before it and lead to a eventual system of fully functioning safeguards that will protect the school, its students, its staff, and others.

It is essential for those who will plan the school's protection to use a sensible approach. For the school with little security other than the standard locks on the doors, the process will take time and money. Both resources are often in short supply at most schools. Caution and careful planning will avoid wasting both.

Step 1: The School's Commitment

Probably the first and largest step toward security is the school's decision it does need a program of protection. Its second is commitment from those who will benefit. They must firmly agree to cooperate and participate. They will need to develop a proper program and keep it operating at optimum levels at all times.

In a school, such a commitment is no small undertaking. Teachers and staff are the ones who will keep the program efficient and effective, yet they are already overburdened. However, they, most of all, more than parents, more than boards of education, or even more than community leaders, see that school security is absolutely necessary.

Even in business and industry where employees have agreed their corporation needed security, many programs have still failed, largely because management mandated or force-fed security arrangements down to its workers. Dictating a security policy rather than seeking input and support from all personnel can doom a program, even when protection is vital.

A successful security program relies on the involvement of all concerned. Employees who are antagonistic toward the newly imposed system can resist what they regard as restrictions on their freedom. Because they do not feel like a part of the program, they may simply fail to report security lapses—a broken door lock, a malfunctioning light in the parking lot, a lost identification badge. Workers may pointedly ignore developing threats that could lead to serious losses.

Step 2: Formulating the School Security Task Force

Organization is the backbone for any successful program. It is a fundamental that schools and especially teachers understand.

During the decision phase, when the school discussed whether to implement a security program, certain staff members most likely expressed their own particular concerns about security. Probably, they more than others urged the school to be more concerned with protection and begin a formal, serious approach to securing its staff and students.

Because those individuals expressed that they were highly concerned about security, they should be more motivated and should make excellent choices to serve on this next phase of making security a reality for the school—organizing a task force.

The *task force,* as the name suggests, is a group whose function is to make security a reality for the school. Unlike a committee whose job it is to serve as a fact-finding body when a course of action is unclear, the task force already has a clear-cut purpose.

The size of the school security team should be kept manageable, large enough to represent the various groups within the school such as teachers, counselors, custodians, cooks, and aides, but small enough for the group to find a common meeting time, to arrive at decisions fairly easily, and to move forward at a reasonable pace.

A task force of about six to ten members is a workable number unless the school is particularly large, perhaps is consolidated and has a bigger than average staff, or it is unusually small. In both cases, the size of the staff would dictate the size of the task force.

Regardless of the number of persons on the task force, most should be teachers for several reasons. Certainly, they occupy most of the staff positions within the school, but teachers are also, by the very job they do, more intimately knowledgeable about the overall setting of the school, its history, and its past problems. They are also in daily, hourly contact with the students, their attitudes, activities, and changing sentiments. Likewise with counselors, who first-hand hear the fears, frustrations, tragedies, and the anger of students.

Maintenance staff must also be represented. Not only do they know the layout of the grounds and the building, particularly the less-traveled areas, they may also possess a special insight into the school's protection, what and where the problems have been in the past, and what might develop and where. Maintenance personnel may know where thefts and vandalism have occurred, where graffiti has been a problem, and which areas of the building are most vulnerable and unprotected.

They may also be able to suggest where lighting could improve visibility and where better locks or other physical changes could improve security. If they become part of the task force, they will also understand what security is trying to do and can help the vendors install the security equipment when the task force reaches that stage.

Heading the task force should be a vice principal, an assistant principal, or another member of the administration, or even a senior teacher who has, or may be delegated, some decision-making authority for just for this one project.

Because the school has decided it does need a security program, no doubt it must have some concerns about the safety of its staff and students. Time is, therefore, of the essence, and appointing the principal to head the task force, especially when principals are often in frequent meetings within the school and even outside the building, may slow the entire process and delay a system that probably needed to be functioning yesterday (see Figure 4).

Schools depend on staff members to do far more than their primary job. From extracurricular activities to special one-on-one assistance, to after-hours, time-consuming fund raising, teachers are expected to do it all. As in any organization that demands so much extra, some staff members readily assume more than their share, are always dependable, and seldom refuse to shoulder one more load. Some schools have attempted to relieve their staff of some of these extra duties and enlisted parent volunteers.

It may, therefore, seem reasonable, as the school begins to form its task force and the faculty and staff recommend their same already overburdened colleagues, to ask parent volunteers, even community leaders, to serve on the task force.

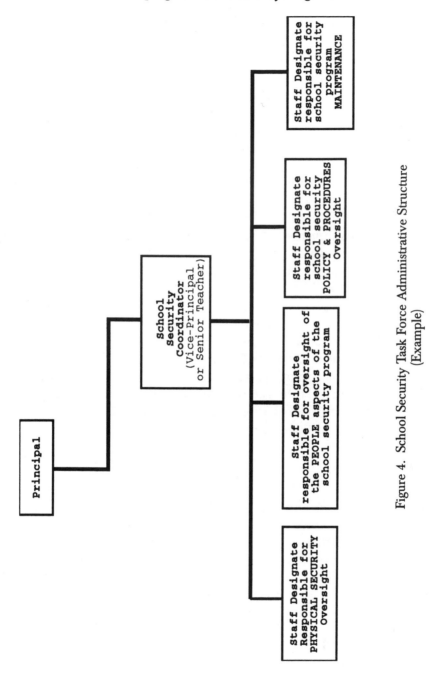

Figure 4. School Security Task Force Administrative Structure (Example)

The school, however, needs to realize that the first step that will be undertaken by the task force will be to assess the specific needs of the building. Before it can plan and then implement an effective security program, it must carefully determine the school's current threats and vulnerabilities and any potential ones. Only the insider, the teacher, the counselor, the cook, the custodian, who works in the school on a daily basis understands and has the perspective that will be most valuable.

Parents can play a far more valuable role by providing support and ultimately assisting with finances, because the security system will probably be beyond the school's budget.

Certainly the task force's primary responsibility is to guide the overall project by developing a comprehensive security program for the school and seeing that it is completed. The task force will also serve as a conduit, a direct channel through which other staff and students can convey their input, their concerns, and their ideas about safety for the school. In turn, the task force can report back to the staff and faculty. This two-way communication will keep everyone informed about how the security program is developing.

Probably one of the most, if not the most, difficult commodities for the task force to find is time. The team must meet on a regularly scheduled basis, but most members will be teachers whose only available time will be planning periods and lunch hour. If the school expects them to develop a security program that will benefit the entire staff and the students, these teachers must be provided some special time away from their regular duties.

It is at this point that the staff must be supportive. They must believe security is important enough to assist their colleagues and help them be a part of the task force. Perhaps task force members could be released from extracurricular duties, club sponsorship, or certain other time-consuming activities that are in addition to teaching.

Step 3: Assessing Security Needs

For any security program to function properly and to defeat the threats that are already known or that may arise, it must be specifically tailored to the school and its particular needs. Thus, the first step toward protecting the school is to assess the facility and its people and to determine through an in-depth investigation exactly what threats and vulnerabilities currently exist and what potential they have to develop.

Step 4: Analyzing the Assessment

Once the assessment has been completed, its findings can be analyzed to determine just where the problems lie. These problems, which are characterized as threats and vulnerabilities, are the adversaries, the challenges to the school's security. A *threat* is an indication of impending harm or danger and is recognized or made immediate when it has an active human sponsor. A gunman is perhaps the most obvious and the most recognizable example.

An offshoot of the threat is the *vulnerability.* Characterized by its susceptibility to a weakness, a vulnerability exposes a person or a location to harm. The individual is victimized or the facility suffers loss because the perpetrator is able to seize an opportunity or gain some advantage and then commit an offense against the school or its people.

Areas of the school that are poorly lighted and where people congregate at night and substandard or malfunctioning locks that are easily defeated and permit illegal entry leave individuals unprotected against robbery and assault and buildings vulnerable to loss and vandalism.

Step 5: Selecting the Countermeasures

After the analysis of the school that identified the various threats and vulnerabilities, the next step is to select the necessary countermeasure that will provide the structure and substance to the security program.

Countermeasures are the different types of security applications, technologies, and procedures that will nullify or defeat the various threats and vulnerabilities that were identified in the assessment process.

The types of countermeasures that are required will depend on the situation and on what problems were identified and analyzed. It may be that a single countermeasure will suffice. Perhaps multiple applications may be needed to ensure proper security.

It is especially in the area of countermeasures that special consideration must be given to the financial aspects of the security program. Security costs money. Many schools may not be able to pay for all their needs at once. They must devise a workable strategy for acquiring the necessary security measures over time and also keep the program moving forward.

The best approach to deal with limited finances and still implement the necessary security arrangements is to *prioritize.* Here, the task force must look at the many security threats that have been identified and list them in order from the most serious to the least serious. Once the list has been established, the necessary countermeasures can be chosen. The most serious needs can be funded first, then each successive item as funds become available.

Prioritizing security needs also draws attention to the urgency of obtaining additional funds so that the program will be completed as quickly as possible.

Step 6: Testing the Security Program

Once the various security problems that threaten a school have been identified and the necessary countermeasures have been selected, the development process of the security program is in no way concluded. Even after the program is in place, its various components must also be tested to determine whether they function properly and appropriately. This testing should evaluate the following two particular aspects.

- Each individual component should be tested. The technical applications, procedures, and people must function as the program intended.
- The overall program should be tested to determine whether all components work in conjunction with and complement one another. They should work together to provide a well-integrated program that is thorough in design and provides in-depth protection as a backup. Making certain that such safeguards are functioning properly will prevent a threat from circumventing or defeating a particular countermeasure.

It is important to point out that this testing phase does not end with just one test. The security program must be checked periodically and regularly to keep it efficient and effective. If any weaknesses or shortcomings are discovered, necessary adjustments must be made to the protection formula.

The ultimate aim of continued inspections is to see that the security program remains capable of providing the desired levels of protection to the school and to the people who work and study there.

Chapter 2

ASSESSING THE SCHOOL'S NEEDS

U NTIL RECENTLY, many schools largely ignored security. Aside from a
few locks, some lights, and an occasional fire drill, they had little need
for much else. Serious trouble was what happened outside the school, exactly where troublemakers found themselves when they refused to straighten
up. By and large, most kids who had problems seemed to be helped with
two C's–communication and counseling.

Even now, other schools, like some businesses and industry, attempt to
incorporate security as an after-the-fact desperation. Only after a large-scale
theft or some act of violence do those in charge become suddenly, thoroughly alarmed. They scramble to install a closed-circuit camera system,
badge identification, or access control systems, whatever technology they
believe will protect people and property. Although they may not be exempt
from the consequences of their previous lack of protection, at least they feel
secure surrounded by technology. That is until the protection system is challenged.

Unfortunately, security, so implemented and that schools believe is so
impervious to attack, will stand a more than even chance of failing. Not
because the equipment itself is faulty, but for essentially the very reason that
the school failed to begin their security program with the first logical, critical
step, an assessment of the entire site to determine, first, what the problems
are, and second, what remedies are required.

Without a thorough assessment of the school facility, its personnel, its
problems, and even its potential for spontaneous violence, security will be
guesswork, a haphazard assembly of measures that may or may not protect.

The *security survey* is the process of assessing the school and its needs. It
is the most important phase in the school's entire effort to develop its security program. This review, particularly in a school where so many lives literally hang in the balance, must be formally organized, directed, and focused.
Most especially, the survey must be absolutely comprehensive.

THE SECURITY SURVEY

A security survey is an in-depth investigation into an organization, its facilities, and its activities. Its purpose is twofold. First, it identifies any threats and vulnerabilities that may expose the school to potential harm. Second, it determines the necessary security measures that will prevent or deter crime or acts of violence.

A thorough, comprehensive survey actually begins with a step backward. It reviews the school's history for at least the last five years. With this perspective, the task force can examine any crime or violence problems, however large or small, that the school has experienced in the past.

The school's security task force should consider the following as it gathers this large amount of information.

1. Review all previous reports of security problems that have been documented and maintained in the school files.
2. Meet with local law enforcement to discuss any past data about crime that involved the school, its students, or its staff.
3. Conduct a formal survey of students through a written questionnaire to obtain their thoughts, concerns, perceptions, or experiences with crime or violence that relate to the school (see Appendix E).
4. Conduct a formal survey of the staff and faculty that asks them to recall any past episodes of crime and violence they observed at the school (see Appendix F).
5. Conduct a walking tour of the entire campus, all of its buildings, and other facilities to view first hand just what security measures are currently in place, what the condition of each is, and what needs to be added and/or upgraded (see Appendix A).

As the task force examines the history of the school for any episodes of crime, it should realize that many such occurrences may not have been documented, often for a variety of reasons. From concerns about the school's image, to community pressures, to misperceptions about what constitutes criminal behavior, all may influence some administrators to fail to report incidents to the police or even maintain records within the school that detail problems that go far beyond disruption and mischief. Such events may, in reality, be actual crimes.

Just because the information was not written down somewhere in some form does not lessen its value, at least, from the security survey standpoint. Long-standing faculty and staff members with their wealth of information will remember. Ask them to jot down any happenings, however large or small, they recall. Even if some of the data are repetitious, it is always better at this point to have too much than too little.

Conducting the Security Survey

Although it might seem that conducting a school security survey is a formidable task, it is not insurmountable, especially if the *survey team* is organized and well prepared.

The survey team does not need to be large, nor does it need to include all the members of the task force. Two members are sufficient.

Before the team actually begins the survey, it needs to review the facts and figures it has collected, which include all of the previous incident reports of crime or violence that have occurred at the school, the results of the interviews with the police, and all the data from the student and staff questionnaires.

From this information, the team can quickly determine the areas where the school is especially vulnerable and which are areas where vandalism, theft, or even chronic disciplinary problems occur more frequently.

Even if the school is fortunate enough to afford the services of a security consultant, it should still have members of the task force comprise the survey team to work with the consultant. Some consultants may be reluctant to take on this arrangement, but for several reasons the task force does need to participate. First, at least one member of the task force will have to act as a liaison for the consultant who will need specific information and an escort around the campus. Second, and even more importantly, at some point the consultant will conclude the survey project.

The job of keeping the program in place and running efficiently will be left to the task force. If they have been actively involved with the consultant as the survey was developed and put in place, the transition will be smooth, eased into place because they understand the workings of a multifaceted security program and are prepared to monitor the program so that it remains effective.

At this point, the survey team is almost ready to begin assessing the campus. However, as one last preparation, they should acquaint themselves with three particular concepts that will assist them as they search for threatening, vulnerable, and potential conditions where crime can occur. These three concepts are the following.

The Threat Triangle

The *threat triangle* illustrates the components of crime with three factors that must be present for any crime to be committed. Remove any one and the crime or violence cannot occur. This formula can provide valuable insight for the survey team as they observe certain problem areas and then later determine what countermeasures will eliminate one part of the triangle.

The first component is the "target" or the object or focus of the threat. The target may be a home the burglar wants to break into, a car he plans to steal, or a school he intends to terrorize. The perpetrator's interest, for whatever reason, from the familiar to the bizarre, is either a person, a place, or an object that will be the target.

"Desire" is the second part of the threat formula and is best explained as the perpetrator's intent, the assailant's strong inner impulse or purpose to undertake and carry out a crime. Just as with the target, there is virtually nothing that can alter or affect this component, at least from the victim's standpoint. There is little that can be done to alter the predisposition of an individual who is determined to commit a crime and has few reservations about inflicting loss or even harm on others.

"Opportunity," the third component necessary for a completed threat, is a situation or conditions that are favorable and encourage the perpetrator to attempt and/or follow through with some wrongdoing. Security can have the greatest impact here. Simply by deterring the would-be perpetrator, a person, a place, or a situation is saved before becoming a target.

The school that implements a comprehensive security program, which integrates physical, procedural and human applications, can greatly diminish the threats against it simply by imposing certain restrictions that will prevent or discourage potential crime.

Conversely, any organization that permits certain conditions to go unchecked, especially those that actually promote threats and vulnerabilities, heightens the possibility that a perpetrator can take advantage of its people or its property (see Figure 5).

As the school analyzes and plans its security, it needs to understand that these three essential components are the adversaries of their security program. Crime is more than a person with some malicious or destructive

Figure 5. The Threat Triangle

intent. It is a three-sided design. Remove a side, any one of the three components, and the threat is incomplete. The crime is deterred.

Today, many schools feel helpless to defend their staff and students, especially against those students who may be plotting some mass shooting or bombing. They will tell you that it is impossible to deter such pending destruction—simply hopeless. Such an attitude is understandable, especially when schools view crime as one dimensional. A threat is simply a kid with a weapon.

However, schools do not need to feel that they are being held hostage. They can protect themselves. By following the crime triangle design as it applies to their school, they can identify and then analyze their particular problem areas that permit threats and vulnerabilities to exist. Countermeasures, appropriate to the school's particular needs, can then be incorporated for a more thorough program of security. It will not only reassure the staff and students that they are protected but will also work properly in a crisis.

The ABC'S of Security

As the survey team assesses the school, it also needs to be aware of the ABCs of security. These factors are expressed in the formula:

$$A + [B + C] = S$$

The *A* of the formula represents the "attack" or the crime that the perpetrator undertakes. The crime may take any form from theft of school property, a student's or staff's personal belongings, or an after hours break-in to a violent act of terrorism that results in casualties.

The bracketed *B* can best be characterized as the "blocking." This barrier halts or intercepts the criminal's threat before the crime can be completed. The *B* is either a procedure, a device, or a combination of both that disrupts the intended crime or violence.

The bracketed *C* represents the "countermeasure" or the component that combined with *B* blocks the attack. A lock on a door might be such a countermeasure, as would be systems that provide layers of protection for the school, such as closed-circuit cameras and intrusion alarms that are designed to back up the school's locking system and provide protection in depth.

The result of this mathematical interpretation is the product, the "security" or the *S* factor that represents the entire protection program. The formula illustrates that the various components of the security program are interrelated and securely joined. Their combined strength and vigilance can stop, deter, or intercept crimes that may threaten the school.

It's a "Black Hat Operation"

Once upon a time, in the old cowboy movies, it was easy to tell the good guys from the bad guys. Good guys wore white hats; bad guys wore black. Perhaps crime is not quite as obvious or as simple as it once was, but the survey team can benefit from the old approach as it reviews the school.

For the moment, the team needs to trade in its white hat and temporarily don the black one—view the school from the bad guys' perspective. Look at the school, its people, and its activities and continually ask, "How can I commit crimes or acts of violence against this school, in this area, at this time, under these conditions?"

Team members should keep the elements of the *threat triangle* in mind, as well as those in the "ABC" formula. In essence, the survey is a fact-finding quest, a thorough search of the campus for weaknesses, however slight, that can promote crime and criminal attacks.

Because this exploration is the most vital, the most important part of the security survey process, the team should particularly look for conditions that permit "opportunity" and points for attack. The team should view its mission as an investigation that will determine the following.

- **The Who?** Who might threaten the school, not only from without, but also from within?
- **The What?** What could harm students and staff? What would a perpetrator stand to gain?
- **The When?** When are the most likely times that crime has occurred and could occur again?
- **The Where?** Where is the school most vulnerable?
- **The Why?** Why is the school more vulnerable in some places than others? Why would someone attack the facility and/or its people?
- **The How?** How would someone who intends to harm the staff or students or steal property enter the building, remain undetected, and proceed to carry out a plan, etc.?

The Site Tour

The site tour of the school is when the survey team will learn first-hand about the campus and about the conditions that pose security problems and weaknesses.

As the team moves about the building and grounds, it should especially search for points of attack or areas where a perpetrator can best strike to cause harm and points of opportunity that are places that permit a perpetrator to strike and go about the crime undetected. The team should ask the following questions, but not limit its answers to the following.

The Local Area

- Are there businesses or locations, i.e. beer taverns, abandoned houses, within proximity to the school that pose a threat to students as they travel to and from the school?
- Are there places near the school that are hangouts for drug dealers and others who may jeopardize or create potential harm for students?
- Has the school met regularly with local police to review any conditions that surround the school and present potential harm? Has the school then requested special enforcement attention?
- Are there special nighttime problems or weekend conditions that pose particular security problems for the school?
- If the campus is open, does it need to be closed?

Barriers

- Does the school have fencing that is used for security or for just boundary line demarcation?
- If fencing is used for security purposes, does it completely enclose the building, facility, or location it is designed to protect?
- If fencing is used, is it a chain-link variety of number 9 gauge fencing fabric or better?
- If a chain-link fence is used, is it of sufficient height (7 feet or taller) to deter easy circumvention by climbing over?
- If a chain-link fence is used, does it have a top rail for stability? Are all line posts set in concrete?
- If a chain-link fence is used, does it need a three-strand, barbed-wire top rigger to prevent an intruder from easily climbing over?
- If chain-link fencing is used, is the fencing fabric between each of the line posts tangent to the ground and anchored into the surface to prevent an intruder from lifting the fencing and crawling underneath?
- If fencing or some form of barrier is not used on the campus, are there certain areas that need fencing or barriers for security purposes?
- Does the fencing enclosure have a suitable gate that is in good working condition? Does it have a secure latching mechanism for a lock?
- Is the fencing or security barrier in good condition?
- If chain-link fencing is used, is the fencing fabric free of all vegetation that can cause corrosion and can also restrict viewing through it?
- Are all segments of the chain-link fence in an upright position?
- Are there concrete "stops" in place along all fenced parking areas to prevent car bumpers from making contact with the fence line and damaging it?

- Who is responsible for fence maintenance?
- Is there a clear-cut strip of at least twenty feet on either side of the fence to provide good visibility along its length and to eliminate any places where an intruder could hide?
- Are air intake vents for the heating and air-conditioning (HVAC) system protected from malicious tampering?

Closed Circuit Television (CCTV) Surveillance System

AUTHORS' NOTE: The following survey questions apply to a CCTV system that is currently in place or is one that the task force is contemplating.

- Does the school have a CCTV surveillance system in place to monitor various areas of the school?
- If a system is in place, does it still provide the observation coverage that monitors potential trouble areas of the campus as it was originally designed to do?
- Does the current system need upgrading by placing additional cameras to cover all locations where observation is needed?
- Does the current system need to be upgraded to better equipment and cameras to improve observation?
- Does the current system have suitable recording equipment for documenting everything the cameras observe?
- Are the CCTV cassette tapes maintained under secure conditions for a period of time in case they are needed later for reference?
- Is the CCTV recording equipment maintained under secure conditions that prevent tampering with and/or destruction of equipment and tapes?
- Are all exterior cameras secured in weatherproof, bullet-resistant housings?
- Are all interior cameras housed in protective domes or similar coverings that prevent easy tampering with or destruction of each unit?
- What exterior campus areas need camera coverage?
    1. Student parking area?
    2. Faculty parking area?
    3. Athletic field?
    4. Student congregation areas?
    5. Outside smoking areas?
    6. All building (four sides) exteriors?
    7. Building entrances?
    8. Specific walkways?
    9. School bus boarding and off-loading areas?

    10. Exterior commons/quiet study area (QSA) locations?
    11. Other designated outside areas?
- What interior areas need camera coverage?
    1. Commons/quiet study area (QSA)?
    2. Library?
    3. Study hall?
    4. Cafeteria/vendeteria?
    5. Main office area?
    6. Teachers' lounge?
    7. Gymnasium?
    8. Auditorium?
    9. Particular hallways?
    10. Entrances and exits to restrooms?
    11. Interior congregation points?
    12. Other designated inside areas?
- If the school has no CCTV surveillance system in use, does it need such a system? If not, why not?
- Are there written procedures regarding the CCTV system?
- Who is responsible for the CCTV system?

Communications System

- Does the school have a system of two-way communications between each classroom and the main office?
- Do teachers and staff members have a means of contacting "911" directly in the event of a sudden terror tactics emergency?
- Are there secure telephones located at strategic locations throughout the school for emergency purposes?
- Does the school have a system of emergency signals, besides that of just a fire alarm, to alert teachers and staff to special security problems that have suddenly developed within the school?
- Are there bullhorns readily available for mass communications in the event of evacuation or other such conditions?
- Has a current directory of telephone numbers for community emergency services been developed? Is it maintained in strategic locations about the school premises?
- Are there written procedures regarding the school's internal emergency or two-way communication system?
- Who is responsible for the school's communications arrangements?

Security Personnel

- Does the school need security personnel or off-duty police to patrol the campus or the building?
- Does the school need the services of a school resource officer who would be stationed on campus during the regular class day schedule?
- If the school elects to incorporate security personnel as a part of its security program, should they be attired in the standard security officer police-style uniform or would the softer "slacks and blazer look" be more suitable to the school atmosphere?
- If security personnel are in use on campus, has each officer received suitable orientation about working in the school atmosphere and about interacting properly with students, teachers, and staff?
- Are security personnel suitably equipped with the necessary communications gear, i.e. walkie-talkies, cellular telephones, for general and emergency purposes?
- Are security personnel sufficiently trained to react properly in the event of emergencies that might occur at the school?
- Are security personnel trained in first aid and first responder operations?
- Are security personnel to be armed in any manner and, if so, are they properly trained with any weaponry they may be assigned?
- Are security personnel sufficiently trained to liaison with responding local emergency services in the event of a crisis at the school?
- Do security personnel receive periodic in-service training that is designed to keep each officer current and abreast of school security operations?
- Are there written procedures regarding the operations and activities of security personnel?
- Who is responsible for the security personnel used on campus?

Security Signage

- Are signs posted about the campus alerting all onlookers to the fact that loitering on campus is a violation of the law (if this is, indeed, a violation of state or local law of the respective jurisdiction) and that all violators will be prosecuted?
- Are signs posted that direct visitors, students, teachers, and staff to their respective parking areas?
- If a closed-circuit camera surveillance system is in use on campus, are signs posted to warn would-be violators that all activities are being monitored and recorded for evidence purposes?

- Has the school posted crime prevention posters as reminders in various locations throughout the school facilities?
- Has the school posted signs that direct all visitors to the main office, or wherever the school has designated, when they arrive at the school?
- Who is responsible for sign maintenance and new postings?

Locking Devices

- Has each door lock been inspected to determine whether it is in proper working order?
- Has each door lock been inspected to determine that each has at least a 1- to a $1^{1}/_{2}$-inch throw (or bolt) that sets into the securing plate on the door facing?
- Has each door been inspected to determine that all exterior door hinges have a set-screw to prevent them from being easily removed for an unlawful entry?
- Have all padlocks in use about the school facility been inspected to see that they are in proper working order?
- Does the school maintain a quantity of solvent that can be used to remove glue and other similar substances that may be used to vandalize locking devices?
- Is there a system of regular inspections made of the school's locking devices to check their proper working order?
- Do all locks used in exterior settings have a protective shroud placed over them to protect them from the weather and corrosion?
- Are all door locks set in doors of sufficient strength that are, in turn, set in door frames of sufficient structural strength to deter them from being easily manipulated, tampered with, or dislodged from their mounts?
- Are any chains used on security gates? If so, are they of sufficient strength to prevent them from being easily cut or pried open?
- Are gates in use about the campus equipped with guide rods and proper security devices to prevent the gates from being pushed apart enough to allow an intruder easy passage?
- Are spare locking units available for quick replacement or repairs in the event a lock malfunctions?
- Are there written procedures regarding the locking system?
- Who is responsible for lock maintenance?

Key Control Systems

- Does the school have a key control system in use?
- Are all keys accounted for at all times?
- Do recipients sign for their keys at the time of issue?
- Does the school use a master-key or grand master key system?
- Are keys retrieved from separating personnel?
- Is a follow-up investigation conducted for all lost keys?
- Does the school use card keys for access to certain locations?
- Does each key issued have "Do Not Duplicate" stamped on its bow?
- Are keys ever issued to students?
- Who is assigned master or grand master keys and is each key accounted for?
- Are there written procedures regarding the key control system?
- Who is responsible for all key-related matters?

Inventory Control System

- Does the school mark equipment and other property that is used on campus?
- In addition to obvious identification tags that may be used on assets, is there a hidden identification number or mark also inscribed on equipment?
- Is a record maintained of all the school's equipment and property?
- Does the log record the:
  1. Item's nomenclature?
  2. Model number?
  3. Department issued to?
  4. Serial number?
  5. Purchase price?
  6. Location of hidden identification number?
  7. Date item was received?
  8. Other necessary data?
- Does the school report all lost or stolen property and equipment to the local police?
- Are there written procedures regarding the school's inventory control system?
- Who has responsibility for inventory controls?

Badge Identification System

- Does the school use a badge identification system?
- Are all students, staff, faculty, and visitors required to wear badge identification on outer clothing during all the time they are on school grounds?
- Is each badge made of tamperproof material? Does it contain a picture with additional necessary information about the respective wearer?
- Does the badge identification system incorporate life safety data on the badge for emergency purposes?
- Are there written regulations regarding the badge identification system?
- Who is responsible for the school's badge identification system?

Lighting System

- Do the entire school premises have sufficient lighting that provides suitable visibility during nighttime or early morning periods?
- Are all entrances to the school buildings sufficiently illuminated to provide good visibility?
- Are all walkways leading to buildings sufficiently lighted?
- What lighting units were found to be malfunctioning or burned out?
- Does the exterior lighting scheme enhance the CCTV system as it views and documents activities?
- Are the control units to the school's lighting system kept secure at all times?
- Is sufficient interior lighting left on to assist local police patrols as they observe the school buildings?
- Is the lighting system on automatic timers? Have these been adjusted for the annual time changes?
- Are there unique environmental or climactic conditions i.e., fog, smog, that require special adjustments to the school's lighting scheme?
- Is the entire lighting system maintained and inspected regularly to ensure that it functions properly?
- Who is responsible for the maintenance of the lighting system?

Alarm Systems

- Is the school's fire alarm system in proper working order?
- Does the school use an intrusion detection (burglar) alarm system? Is it in proper working order?

- Are all sensors, wiring, and control units for each of the alarm systems properly protected from tampering?
- Does the intrusion alarm system have an audible sounder unit to ward off intruders?
- Does the intrusion alarm system immediately alert local police to an unauthorized entry?
- Are rooftops to all buildings equipped with sensors to detect unauthorized entry by a "roof job"?
- Have all underground access points to buildings i.e., tunnels, passage ways, been equipped with sensors to detect unauthorized entry?
- Does the school use any form of duress alarm to notify police in the event of emergencies?
- Are doors equipped with "prop" alarms to notify the main office when a door is left open or propped open?
- Are all alarm lines "supervised" to immediately detect any compromise or tampering?
- Does the school's alarm system have a history of false alarms?
- Is the school being assessed penalty fees for excessive false alarms?
- Are the alarm systems tested on a regular basis to see that they are functioning properly?
- Are interior locations suitably equipped with motion sensors to detect persons who may hide inside the school before it closes?
- Who is responsible for the school's alarm system?

Computer Equipment Security

- What locations throughout the school contain computer equipment?
- Has there been any loss of computer equipment?
- Is each location properly secured to prevent loss of computer equipment?
- Have the serial number, nomenclature, and all other descriptive particulars been recorded for each piece of equipment?
- Has each piece of computer equipment been inscribed with a hidden identification number or other markings to specifically identify the equipment as belonging to the school?
- Has each piece of computer equipment been secured in place by security cables or by anchoring the item to a table or counter?
- If laptop computers are used, is each kept secured when not in use?
- Are passwords used to secure computers from unauthorized use?
- Are passwords changed periodically to ensure proper security?
- Are there written procedures regarding the security of the school's

computers?
- Who is responsible for the security of the computers?

Visitor Controls

- Are there exterior signs that inform visitors where to park and to report when they arrive?
- Are visitors required to register at a central office before proceeding to their destination within the school?
- Are visitors issued a "visitors" badge to be worn on outer garments at all times while on campus?
- Are visitors required to return to the registration point to sign out and return their badge?
- Are visitors escorted to their destination within the school?
- Is the visitors' log kept for a period of time for future reference?

Parking Controls

- Does the school issue parking stickers to be displayed on all student and staff vehicles that are parked on campus?
- Are parking areas for staff, students, and visitors separate and plainly marked?
- Are all parking areas enclosed with a fence?
- Are all parking areas observed by a CCTV camera system?
- Are all parking facilities sufficiently illuminated at night and early morning for safety and security purposes?
- Are periodic security or police patrol checks made of the school's parking areas?
- Are sufficient security signs in place to warn onlookers of "No Loitering," and "Violators Will Be Prosecuted," and "Do Not Leave Valuables in Plain Sight Inside Vehicles?"
- Are parking facilities situated away from buildings?
- Are speed bumps situated throughout the parking lot lanes to deter speeders?

Money Safeguards

- Is cash kept on the school premises?
- Is all cash kept secured at all times when not in use either in a safe or another security container?
- Are all funds accounted for at the close of the school day?

- Are all vending machines emptied of all funds at the end of each day?
- Who has central responsibility for all school cash and its accountability?
- Does the school deposit cash periodically in some sort of bank account?
- Who handles these bank deposits?
- Does the school maintain only a minimum level of cash at the school before it is deposited?

Chemistry Laboratory Security

- Does the school have a chemistry laboratory on site that is used in education courses?
- Has the school consulted with the Drug Enforcement Administration or the local police department to determine whether any chemicals that are stored in the laboratory may be used to manufacture illicit drugs?
- Are the chemistry laboratory, chemicals, and all equipment kept secured at all times when not in use?
- Are chemicals and all laboratory equipment carefully accounted for?
- Who is in charge of the chemistry laboratory?

Cafeteria/Vendeteria Security

- Are all food and equipment used by the cafeteria kept secured at all times when the school is closed?
- Has the cafeteria experienced any loss of supplies?
- Is all money collected in the cafeteria kept under secure conditions and properly accounted for?
- Do security cameras monitor the cafeteria?
- Who is in charge of the cafeteria and/or the vendeteria?

Security Reporting System

- Does the school have a dedicated security report form that is used to document all school security-related incidents or problems?
- How long are security incident reports maintained on file?
- Who is in charge of the school reporting system?
- Are there established criteria that specify when school personnel are required to complete a security report?
- Are staff and students made familiar with and oriented to the school

security reporting system—how it operates and what conditions will be reported?

Records Security

- Are all school records maintained in security file cabinets that are kept secured when not in use?
- Is access to school records kept closely restricted?
- Does the school use shredders to destroy discarded documents?
- Are there clearly written procedures regarding the use, handling, and disposition of all school records?
- Are computers that contain school records carefully secured with passwords and maintained under secure conditions at all times?
- Who is in charge of the school's record-keeping system?

Office Security

- Does each office have sufficient door locks and window locks?
- Are offices alarmed to detect unlawful entry?
- Are CCTV cameras in place to monitor all traffic within the office area?
- Does the school have a "clean desk" policy when the respective office is not in use?
- Are offices kept locked when not in use to prevent theft and/or unauthorized access and telephone use, etc.?

Personnel Screening

- Does the local school handle any personnel screening procedures or is this matter conducted at the local school board level?
- Are nationwide criminal background checks conducted on all applicants for school positions in addition to credit checks and driving history reviews?
- Are the credentials, background work history, and references reviewed and confirmed on all prospective applicants before they are hired?
- Who conducts background investigations on applicants?

AUTHORS' NOTE: The aforementioned survey questions have been prepared from the standpoint that the school may or may not have certain aspects of a viable security program in place.

As the survey team goes about its site tour and sees that certain security components are missing, the questionnaire information about that particular segment can be used to remind the team to address that vulnerability when the school begins to implement its security program.

Night and Weekend Tours

To produce a thorough survey, the survey team should not limit its tour of the school site to just daytime hours. The school is also subject to threats and vulnerabilities during evenings, nights, and weekends when many school facilities are used for evening classes, community meetings, and numerous other activities. Although numerous groups not directly associated with the school may use the facility, it is the school itself that is responsible for security.

Buildings that are used extensively must analyze and then tailor their program to include the particular needs that these additional activities may generate. Not only can an effective daytime security program be compromised if the facilities are left unprotected during the evening hours, but security must also be extended to those individuals who are on school premises during the evening hours.

The survey team should visit the school during the evenings when classes or meetings are being held and note the areas of the building that are being used. The team should record which classrooms are involved. If only a few are needed, then perhaps it is unnecessary to open the entire building.

Can a wall be built with only one door that would cordon off this section? Individuals would enter and exit through this one door. Because they would be restricted to this particular area, they would be unable to move freely through other parts of the building.

School grounds are often congregation areas for kids who want to use the ball field or the track or who just want to "hang out." Likewise, school parking lots often become the area of choice where young people gather to drink alcohol and drag race. Sometimes their "harmless fun" results not only in a public nuisance but also in vandalism to the school. Graffiti can be sprayed on the building, on walls, and sidewalks, and the building can be burglarized.

These activities can cost the school, obviously for damage and loss, but also for liability. Legal actions could hold the school financially accountable if an injury or death occurs and it has not taken adequate measures to discourage such behavior.

Although the team may generally know, or think they know, what activities occur at the school during the evening and night hours, after hours, and on the weekend, tours will reveal the specifics. An effective security program must take into account not only the authorized school activities but all those other spontaneous, social gatherings, all of which may present certain protection problems for the school.

Tools of the Trade

Conducting a security survey can be hard work. It can, however, be made much easier by using certain equipment. The following list suggests some items that the survey team might find useful as they conduct their survey. These include, but are not limited to:

CAMCORDER/VIDEO CAMERA. After the survey has been completed, videographic footage can serve as an invaluable aid for a later review.

NOTEPADS AND PENS. Each team member, who will keep individual notes, needs plenty of these most basic supplies with them as they tour the site.

SECURITY SURVEY FORM. Each team member will need an individual copy of the survey form to make individual entries and notes. Later, when the team is ready to develop the program, members can compares notes to refresh their memories about what they found (see Appendix A).

FLASHLIGHT. As the team conducts a night tour of the facility, each member needs a flashlight for personal safety and for viewing locks, fences, etc.

MAGNIFYING GLASS. A magnifying glass is useful for viewing close-up detail such as suspicious marks on a lock or door knob that may indicate attempts to pry or jam.

35-MM CAMERA. The team may want to take still photos of certain conditions they observe on the site, in addition to videographic footage, or especially if a camcorder is unavailable.

TAPE MEASURE. A tape measure of at least six feet is suitable.

WORK GLOVES. Team members will need general-purpose gloves to protect their hands.

UTILITY CLOTHING. Team members will need old clothes or work apparel that can withstand such activities as climbing onto the roof or other out-of-the-way areas of the school.

HAND TOWEL. A hand towel will permit the team to wipe dirt and grease from their hands.

SMALL TOOL KIT. The team may need a small tool kit, i.e., pliers, screwdriver, to remove or loosen certain coverings to view switches, wires, etc.

LADDERS. Team members may need to view inside acoustical ceilings or on the tops of buildings.

The survey team might also wish to take a careful look at the areas they will tour before they start the survey so that they can identify any special tools or other equipment they might need.

Outsourcing for Assistance

As schools undertake a security program, they will select their task force from faculty and staff. The team will obviously be experienced in education but will most likely be novices to security. Their next most logical move is to enlist the help of an outside source, usually a consultant.

Money, which is almost always the first and often the foremost obstacle in a school, will be the first major hurdle. Perhaps the school may find a security professional who is willing to donate this service simply for goodwill or community spirit, but more than likely the work will have to be paid for.

How the school will pay and how much the security consultant charges present the second major barrier. The number of security consultants and, in this case, those who are particularly knowledgeable about school security, is limited. Not only must they know about metal detectors and security cameras, but they must also understand philosophies about education, teenagers, staffs and faculties, and communities. In other words, they must be familiar with the total package that constitutes a school.

Before a school hires a security consultant, the task force should examine the prospective consultant's professional credentials and background. The task force should know the following.

- Whether the security consultant specializes in school security?
- How long this individual has been involved with school security?
- Has this individual conducted security surveys for other schools?
- Is the individual willing to provide a list of the other schools he or she has served?
- How versed is this individual in the various aspects of school security? In other words, does this person "specialize" in schools by providing advice and counsel on physical security, policy, and procedures, or is the expertise limited to just one particular aspect?

All too often, schools with limited budgets and pressing security concerns jump into a program without the benefit of a survey or a consultant. They hope a closed-circuit camera system, for instance, will solve their problems. The result may be that either the company or the salesperson who supplies the technical equipment becomes a consultant of sorts. Although the vendor is no doubt perfectly capable and knowledgeable about the equipment, his or her expertise most likely ends there. The security capabilities do not extend to the overall school setting.

The task force should look for an *independent security consultant,* one who does not represent any products or services beyond the consultation. These professionals do not take on a project to sell equipment or any other service beyond advice and counsel (see Appendix C).

If, however, the school determines that its budget cannot stretch to hire a security consultant, the task force can contact another source.

At present, American law enforcement is changing its approach to crime. Police agencies nationwide are adopting community-oriented policing to meet the changing dynamics of the trends in crime. As part of their overall effort, many have also revamped their crime prevention units. Some offer well-trained crime prevention specialists to work with community businesses and property owners at no charge. These officers suggest ways to improve the security on commercial or private property.

Although these crime prevention specialists may also provide some valuable assistance to the school that will not require financial outlays for their services, the task force does need to recognize, well in advance of the security project, that there are limitations to this arrangement.

Crime prevention specialists usually neither have the experience or the time to conduct a total security survey. However, they may be able to assist the task force with physical security such as choosing what type of hardware or technology that will provide some security for the school.

They may also offer suggestions based on the Crime Prevention Through Environment Design (CPTED) such as eliminating certain exterior arrangements such as shrubbery that an attacker may use as concealment.

Again, just as with the security consultant, it is the specialist's experience and depth of background that determine just how much assistance the officer can lend.

For the school with no more security than locks on the doors and perhaps a burglar alarm, a security program will be neither cheap nor quick. Most things of value seldom are. But even if the school can manage to afford the services of a security consultant, the task force must still spend much time working with the consultant to see that the security program the school expects is indeed the program the school gets.

With so much time and money invested, the task force needs to make certain, well before a consultant is ever hired, that everyone understands the steps that must be taken, the money that will be spent, and the type of program that will be implemented.

Chapter 3

STRUCTURING THE SCHOOL SECURITY PROGRAM

Once the school determines that it needs and wants a security program, it has crossed the first major hurdle toward protecting its staff and students. At the second phase, that of development, the school determines just what it needs, decides what countermeasures and procedures are necessary, then puts in place what appropriately protects the school, its staff, and its students.

With all these steps completed, it would seem the school has given adequate attention to security. Everyone can now return to the business of education. However, the school's security program and its operations are far from concluded, rather they are just beginning.

The school must not assume that once everything is in place and functioning correctly that security requires no further attention. The program will not function on its own. It must have ongoing direction and oversight. Just as the football team needs a coach and the band needs a director, so must the security program have a *coordinator.*

Too often, especially in corporate settings, this essential element, this role of overseeing and directing, has been downplayed and often completely disregarded. Such a decision, which is usually due more to cost-cutting than a lack of understanding, can be a fatal mistake for any security program, especially one within a school.

The best approach to managing and controlling a security program is to establish a structure and either select or appoint a particular individual to oversee the security program. Only with such specific leadership can the school ensure that its protection activities will stay on course and remain effective.

STRUCTURE

At best, most school systems employ only an adequate number of people to handle everyday activities. There is little, if any, extra in the way of personnel, finances, and resources to commit to long-range projects. For each school to hire a director to manage the various tasks associated with security is generally out of the question.

Nevertheless, a plausible alternative is possible, one that will ensure that one person with authority and responsibility will continuously monitor the program and keep it in working order.

If the school created a task force to oversee the development of its security program, this group can be an excellent foundation on which to build this coordinating structure.

Certainly those persons who have been involved in the development of the program will know the most about it. It is, therefore, only logical to assume that they may also be willing to continue and assume some of the ongoing duties that will be necessary to structure the program.

This is not to say that these same persons are the only ones who may be needed to direct the program. No doubt, in time, many other staff members will also be needed, but this core group can serve as a nucleus to coordinate all the necessary activities and guarantee that the program remains efficient and effective (see Figure 6).

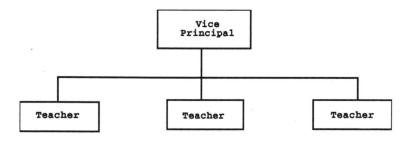

Figure 6. Basic School Security Task Force Structure
(Example)

Most likely, when the school put together its task force, the entire staff, or perhaps just the task force itself, selected a leader who was an assistant principal, a vice principal, a senior ranking teacher, or another school official who not only had decision-making authority but also dealt directly and regularly with the principal. Perhaps this same leader may be willing to continue and now assume the position as coordinator.

Although the position carries certain responsibilities, it does not need to be simply one more full-time job with no pay. Hopefully, those staff members who served on the task force will continue to be involved and will assist the coordinator with various tasks. Duties that are essential to keep the program running can be parceled out. Small tasks can be performed by most everyone so that the entire weight of the program will not rest on the shoulders of just one individual.

Staff members who recognize that an effective security program directly benefits them and their students usually feel that exchanging a small bit of time for increased safety is more than a worthwhile trade.

In addition to saving money, using in-house personnel to oversee the program's coordination also allows the program to proceed without interruption and without loss of time or momentum, which could easily develop during the period when the school searches for an individual to hire into this position.

FUNCTIONS

The coordinator of the school's security program will oversee a variety of tasks, most of which will be delegated to other staff members, who will then, in turn, monitor their part of the program. Maintenance employees, for instance, will periodically inspect lighting units and door locks to ensure they are in good working order. Another member may provide security updates, and still another can conduct security awareness training programs. The main point here is that one person will be responsible for each component. That particular person is then directly responsible for making certain that one particular item or area is in proper working condition and for reporting any problems to the coordinator.

Creating a program with this tiered structure doubles a school's security. First, because the coordinator is at all times fully aware of the status of the security program and, second, because this form of communication, from each person to the coordinator, establishes an early warning system. Should a problem develop that could cause some vulnerability in the school's security, it will be detected more quickly. The coordinator can then make a prompt decision that will remedy the trouble before, not after, the school, staff, or students suffer a loss.

Essentially this system of checking and reporting involves the three primary components of the security program, previously listed and described as the three P's of protection. The coordinator should:
- Monitor the assigned area or aspect of the security program to ensure it is working properly.
- Note any new or developing security problems that need to be remedied by upgrading equipment and/or revising policy and procedures.
- Arrange for any repairs to and/or replacement of security equipment

as needed.

- Report any deficiencies that are found in the current protection arrangements.
- Monitor any changes in the school's activities, in renovated facilities, in campus additions, or in any other outside factors that may require alterations to the school's protection arrangements.
- Liaison with outside agencies, e.g., police, fire, and schedule frequent follow-ups to ensure full and knowledgeable cooperation between the school and each agency. This combined effort can put plans in place that ensure both groups are adequately prepared for both emergency and nonemergency situations.
- Continue to reinforce the security mission and message to students and staff with periodic awareness briefings. Maintaining such emphasis encourages everyone to continue their support of and participation in the program.
- Develop and update all security policies and procedures that relate to the program.
- Document all activities of the security program and forward progress and status reports to the appropriate superiors within the school system.
- Establish a follow-up system that investigates the circumstances of a crime on campus, its resolution, and its disposition.
- Establish a reporting system that documents all threats or any victimizations that occur on campus or affect the school in some way. Make certain to document the follow-up response and the final disposition of the incident.

All these tasks are vital for an effective security program. But it is not enough for them to be completed. Each must be concluded in an orderly and a timely manner.

The coordinator is the one responsible for establishing a schedule, which should use a specific timeline or form of reference to list each task and specify when it is to be performed and who is responsible.

By knowing what is to be done and when, the coordinator can continuously monitor the entire program and prevent any breakdowns, some of which could occur because of nothing more than a simple oversight.

POLICY AND PROCEDURES

Developing written policy and procedures for the school security program is one of the coordinator's most important functions. The importance of clearly defined, well-written policy and procedures that outline the purpose, activities, functions, responsibilities, and all other aspects of the school's protection program cannot be overstated.

Simply put, the guidelines define and distinguish a school's security. They shape the program and mold it into one that protects it or dooms it to nothing more than mere existence.

Policy and procedures define the parameters within which the program will operate, fix the responsibility and accountability for a properly operating program, and provide a basis of understanding for everyone who is concerned with or affected by the school's security.

As schools emerge as larger, easier targets, caught in the crossfire of escalating lawsuits, clear, thorough, policies and procedures provide vital guidelines when situations and issues arise that involve alleged liability.

Moreover, well-thought-out, soundly enforced policy and procedures demonstrate the school's sense of "fair play" and show that it has provided suitable safeguards to stop or deter potential crime threats from harming students, staff, and others who may be associated with the school.

It is not unusual for institutions and companies to spend large amounts of money and time developing, installing, and putting a security program in place only to have it falter and fail because of inadequate or no policy and procedures.

Far too often, persons involved in instituting a security program concentrate all their efforts on getting everything in place and making certain things are working correctly. Once these tasks are accomplished, security is considered complete. The job is pronounced "done!"

Policy and procedures essentially set down, in writing, all aspects of the security program. From periodic security awareness training for staff and students to the inspection and repairs of equipment to the emergency procedures that must be followed in the event of a shooting or a bombing, policy and procedures remove the guesswork from what to do, when to do it, and how to do it.

Although policy statements are often designed to be administrative declarations, they should also include a sufficient number of all-inclusive statements that provide an "umbrella" of guidance and help everyone understand the goals and objectives of the school's security program.

Creating policy and procedures for security should begin with a *mission statement,* a concise, to-the-point introduction that describes the purpose of the school's protection program. An example could be: "It is the intent of this school to provide a safe and secure environment in which students, staff, and faculty can work to make learning a reality."

Policy and procedure statements follow the mission statement. Examples of such statements can include, but do not need to be limited to, the following:

- To endeavor to suppress or eliminate crime on campus
- To observe all laws, school board regulations, and the rights of individuals in the course and conduct of the security program
- To work with all law enforcement agencies, prosecuting attorney's office, and the court system, which will assist the school with its goal of controlling crime
- To seek assistance and input from parents, civic groups, community organizations, etc., for the ongoing improvement and success of the school's security program

Policy statements expand and enhance the mission statement. They explain the "why" of the program. Why it operates as it does and why it uses the particular activities it uses.

However, these statements must be flexible and adaptable enough to accommodate the school environment, which is in constant change as are the problems that threaten it daily.

The coordinator and staff must, therefore, remain vigilant to new and developing conditions that may require that the security policies for the school be changed.

Policies come to life once the necessary procedures have been formulated and put into operation. Procedures are the rules and regulations, the "nuts and bolts" of "how" the security program is to be conducted.

Much more specific than policies, procedures spell out the specifics, such as the disciplinary actions for violating the rules of the school's protection activities. Procedures also detail how infractions will be handled, from the small—such as a student who refuses to wear an identification badge—to the serious, perhaps a fight or a theft that is caught on a surveillance camera.

Procedures reduce confusion. Not only do students feel secure knowing they are protected, but they also realize that security, just as with any other program, whether it is an academic, a social, or a sports activity, is only effective and efficient when it operates by rules.

Such rules are well defined and put in place as the program develops, not when a violation occurs. As a camera system, a badge identification program, or an access control process for visitors is added, written procedures should be developed at that time.

For most schools, just the financial constraints alone may mean that it will take some time to incorporate an entire protection program. Waiting until the program is fully in place and then writing procedures will not only make the task of writing monumental, but it will also permit students and perhaps even outsiders to challenge each phase of the program as it is implemented.

Parameters of tolerance—what is considered a violation and what the consequences are—need to be introduced right along with each new phase of the program. Policy and procedures should be devised for:

- All technical equipment applications such as a CCTV system, a lock and key control system, and lighting
- A reporting system
- A badge identification system
- Barriers
- Security personnel or off-duty police officers that patrol the school, etc.
- A security maintenance program
- Emergency procedures
- Law enforcement liaison
- Duties and roles of the school personnel in school security activities
- Theft/loss reporting
- Parking controls
- Access controls
- Conducting searches
- Confiscating contraband and other prohibited items
- Disciplinary actions for violating the regulations of the security program

Once the school establishes the policies and procedures for its security system, the coordinator should review the guidelines. They must be specifically tailored to the school.

"Borrowing" policies and procedures from other schools is not recommended. From size, to programs, to community attitudes, to regions, just to name a few differences, schools are probably more dissimilar than similar. A major caution: one-size-fits-all security, won't fit.

As policy and procedures are being developed, the coordinator must pay particular attention to any state laws or school board regulations that may affect the school's security program. In particular is there any legislation, or, as the case may be, lack of it that pertains to teachers and school officials in their professional roles and responsibilities?

In today's atmosphere of sporadic episodes of school violence, lawmakers and other authoritative bodies are seeking to enact laws that will assign certain obligations to teachers and staffs for their conduct during such events.

By virtue of their employment, school employees may be held liable for what they should have done and did not as well as what they did do. Teachers, county or district officials, teachers' associations or unions, and the school board attorneys should carefully scrutinize all such legal requirements to make certain that the language, the intent, the consequences, etc. are, first, thoroughly understood, then, second, factored into the pertinent security procedures.

Likewise, before the school implements any security procedures, the coordinator should submit the entire document to the school board attorneys, or any other appropriate legal advocacy contingent, for a review and approval.

Again, this step shows that the school exhibited a sense of fair play that may help it avoid any legal pitfalls should an unforeseen conflict develop between an adopted security practice and a law or a legal doctrine.

This additional legal consideration is especially important for matters such as locker searches that use drug detection dogs, confiscating contraband and/or drugs, and stopping and detaining students who are suspected of concealing weapons underneath their clothing or in bookbags. Higher court decisions, which are constantly being rendered and overturning previous ones, such as with the issue of lockers, can affect the procedures that school officials themselves must follow when they conduct protection activities.

Soliciting a review from the appropriate counsel not only lessens the potential for future legal complications, but it also provides certain legitimacy to the school's protection procedures and, in turn, to the total program package.

BUDGETS

Most major programs that schools undertake today, regardless of how important they are, still require financial support from sources other than the school's appropriated budget. The sobering fact is that security programs, like practically everything else, are not free. They do cost money sometimes more than the school has.

School systems are governmental organizations. They must depend on annual appropriations to conduct business and often end the year barely able to balance all their accounts. Usually little to nothing is left over, especially for projects such as security. After all, the school can operate, can open in the fall without a security system, but it cannot function without supplies.

Schools that have so far escaped some violent occurrence continue to hope the unthinkable is not going to happen. Many believe that the trickle of money from fundraisers is more urgently needed to replace outdated computers, upgrade underfunded libraries, or pay for one of a thousand other needs from a long list that never seems to get shorter.

Yet, times are changing. Everyday, violent acts from hostile individuals threaten the school scene and the people there. Staffs and students who never thought they would be victims of crime or violence are rethinking, reconsidering that perhaps security in the school is a must after all and that the lives and well-being of staffs and students are at least as important as computers, laboratory equipment, or new desks.

Just because most school budgets cannot bear such a burden all at once does not mean that staffs who recognize that they and their students need protection should be discouraged or permit their efforts to be stifled.

The good news is that with some rethinking, careful planning, and scheduled implementation, a suitable security operation is possible.

Whether school security will be left to each local school, its particulars are legislated by school boards and lawmakers, or the final result is a combination of both, financial commitment must obviously be addressed first.

As the school begins to formulate a budget for a security program, it needs to consider certain major categories for expenditures. These costs are essentially built around the three P's of protection: the people, the physical, and the procedures. Included in this list, but not limited to, are the following:

- Capital outlays that are generally one-time expenses usually associated with startup, such as purchasing equipment (CCTV camera systems, access control systems and other technology), paying security personnel or off-duty police who may be used, and any outsourcing for consultants or other security planning specialists
- Maintenance fees to keep-up or replace equipment, etc.
- Revolving expenses that recur every year such as ongoing security training programs
- Any other expenses that are required to keep the school's security in proper working order

Within each of these major categories would, of course, be the various subheadings for expenditures within that particular group. However, because changes are sometimes necessary within the program, the budget needs to remain flexible enough to adapt to and accommodate any necessary upgrades.

REPORTING

An especially vital component of any security program is a reporting system. Although it will serve a variety of purposes, a reporting system's primary functions is to document all activities and occurrences that relate to protection.

Second, a reporting system provides a basis for determining the strengths and weaknesses of the school's protection arrangements by documenting not only where losses or crimes have occurred but also what upgrades are needed to "plug any holes in the dike."

Reporting also allows the coordinator to communicate the progress and status of the security program to all upper levels of administration.

Finally, in cases that involve the school in litigation or some other legal action, a written report provides essential information of the incident and documents what transpired on the part of all parties concerned.

Similarly, if an incident results in police prosecution of an offender for a criminal matter, an aftermath report will be helpful to the investigation.

As the reporting system is developed, the coordinator should make certain it allows for documentation of all the different aspects of the security program, including:

- Incidents of criminal activity occurring at the school
- Follow-up inquiries conducted on security-related problems at the school
- Status reports concerning the progress or changes in the school's security to be reported to higher levels in the educational system
- Repairs and/or maintenance of equipment
- Reports of threats or other possible harm that may occur
- Lost or missing school property
- Any other information that the school's administration believes is necessary.

The information should be documented on a form that is dedicated and used for security-related matters only. It should be designed to provide certain details of the matter that is being reported. These include:

- Name and contact information of the person completing the report
- Date and time of the incident
- Date and time the report is completed
- Topic or subject of the report
- Location of the incident
- Narrative of the actions involved or taken
- Name, description, and other identifiers of the perpetrator
- Any other details deemed pertinent (see Appendix G)

Certainly an integral part of any filing system is a retrieval feature. Reports that have been completed and need to be held for future reference should be assigned a designation code that permits pertinent data to be retrieved quickly and efficiently.

Chapter 4

PLANNING THE SCHOOL
SECURITY PROGRAM

Effective security does not just happen. Each phase, each purchase, and the accompanying activities for each step must be carefully planned. Some goals for a comprehensive security program will be relatively distant, determined largely by time and money. Others, such as certain types of awareness training, can be immediate.

Essentially the program design should be a series of major goals. Each is then subdivided into smaller objectives. This methodical approach is especially important for the smaller school, the school that is financially limited, or the school that has had no security program and is just beginning to implement certain features.

Such organization will also benefit the members of the task force. Because their duties on the task force are in addition to their primary job within the school, the complete security plan, laid out in sequential steps, will help them stay focused. They can see, at a glance, how the program is progressing, and they can also analyze any problems that have developed and delayed the completion date for a particular phase.

THE FUNCTION OF SECURITY PLANNING

The *security plan* is a scheduled and orderly progression of events and activities that lead to a fully operational security program. Not only does it allow all members of the task force to have regular input into the course and direction of the program, but it also functions as a check and balance system to ensure that there are no oversights or omissions. In essence, it becomes one more safeguard for the school.

Planning allows the school the necessary time to adjust to certain security measures. Even the most security-resistant school can be transformed into a well-protected campus if measures are implemented smoothly and logically.

Staff and students who are provided with a direction and know what to expect from a protection program will be less resistant to security measures.

The process also helps the task force to identify any potential pitfalls or shortcomings. Experienced members of the task force will know ways to anticipate and avoid certain problems. Sudden or unexpected budget constraints, staff changes, or even administrative shuffling within the district can sidetrack, or even derail, the school's security program before it ever gets started.

However, even the best-intended security plan is of little value if it is not implemented within a reasonable time. Certainly nothing can be achieved overnight, but violence can strike at any minute. It is simply prudent to have the security program in place and operational as quickly as possible.

FORMULATING THE SECURITY PLAN

It is not enough for the task force to draft a security plan that covers the major steps of a complete protection plan. It needs to determine just what components will comprise the school's final security program. It also must determine the smaller steps that will get the program to that phase.

Are major goals of the plan to install a CCTV system, metal detectors, or a badging system? Each component should represent a major phase. Then each phase should be subdivided into smaller related steps. This way, no essential segments will be omitted that would leave the total program weak or limited.

Adding a CCTV camera system can serve as one example. Many schools have learned from frustrating, sometimes costly experiences that purchasing the system, then having it installed and fully operational took far longer than they anticipated.

More precise planning can help the task force keep to their schedule. However, they must begin their timeline as soon as they make their decision to implement cameras.

Obviously, their second major step will involve funding. How will the school pay for the cameras? Can they install only a few cameras at a time then add to the system as more money becomes available, or can they install a complete surveillance system now?

To set reasonable time limits, the task force should work with the company to understand the extent of the work and amount of time that complete installation should require. Among other information, the task force should know:

- Whether the company will need to pull wires through acoustical ceilings
- Whether the company can work on this phase of the installation dur-

ing the school day or must it wait until evenings and weekends
* Whether exterior cameras must be installed on poles
* Who will provide the poles?
* Who will set the poles in place?

Individual schools often do not employ their own electricians, carpenters, painters, etc. Their custodial staff is responsible only for general maintenance, cleaning, and small repair work.

Large jobs such as installing light poles are handled by specialized workers who are dispatched from the central office or district and may not be available on short notice. The task force needs to factor in these workers' schedules and their availability.

Oftentimes, when attempting to schedule county or district maintenance workers, what first appeared to be a relatively inconsequential step turned into a major obstacle and delayed the entire installation.

With a project such as installing cameras, a schedule change on the part of the school may force the installation company to move on to other previously scheduled jobs. It may be days, even weeks, before the contractor is able to return and complete the school's system.

Phases of the program that have been timed for a certain completion date, but must extend beyond a deadline because of unexpected delays, can threaten the security of the entire school. A hardware phase that is postponed means that staff and student orientation must also be postponed.

Ultimately, parts of the security program may be operating, but the school's population is essentially unfamiliar with the new system. New rules and regulations may still be unexplained or unclear.

In the final analysis, security can be seriously compromised not because the total program is weak but because of the way it was implemented or, in this case, the way it was not implemented. Essentially, the school's security is perceived as unorganized and haphazard.

The school's final security plan should be developed through a series of steps that include:

Step 1

The task force should begin with a security survey (see Chapter 2). The results of this survey will reveal any threats and vulnerabilities that can become security problems. The survey will also indicate the different forms of countermeasures that will be needed to offset or deter any problems.

For example, if outsiders come into the school and wander the halls unchecked, this threat can be halted with an access control system. Congregation points about the campus that permit dealing drugs, drinking alcohol, or fighting may need to be monitored with CCTV cameras.

Once the task force reviews the survey, then it can determine each type of problem and decide which measure will best correct it. The group is then ready to plan the school's protection.

Step 2

The next step is to determine which components will be included in the final program, such as metal detectors, access control measures, CCTV cameras, identification badges, or any other measure. The task force needs to remember a crucial point–keep the security plan flexible; it may need to be adjusted.

As the program begins to take shape, certain conditions may change. New threats may even develop within the respective school or at schools in other districts or even in other states.

Step 3

The third step should establish the sequence of events or the schedule for incorporating each component. This phase decides *when* each particular countermeasure will be added. Schools with more financial resources may be able to complete their security program quickly, perhaps within a year. Schools with limited economics may be looking at a plan that will take them several years to complete.

If the task force's school is the latter, it may, at this point, need to consider *priority-based planning*. Here, two particular factors are used to gauge the overall program. "What" measures will be added and "when."

First and foremost, the task force should consider the school's threat-based factors, then rank them beginning with those that pose the most immediate danger down to those that present the least. The task force should consider whether each is an actual or a potential threat and give priority to the most serious first.

They should ask: Is this a clear and present danger or is it a lesser possibility that gives no particular indication that it presents any immediate harm to the school?

For example, if the school has seized a number of weapons from students or the number of fights has increased, the task force may determine that the need to incorporate metal detectors, security officers, or off-duty police officers is immediate and try and remedy this problem.

On the opposite end of the spectrum, when the potential for a crime is low, is the possibility that the school may be burglarized or vandalized. However, the security survey has not found either type of crime to have been a problem in the past because the school has always maintained good outside security on its building. Because exterior security is already in place and effective, the task force has one less area to consider.

Many schools implement their security program by adding expensive, large-scale technical equipment on a *component-based timeline.* They install their security system component-by-component as funds become available.

Sometimes, however, schools receive an unexpected grant, an appropriation from a local or state agency, or even a donation from a private benefactor. Without question, a sudden windfall is a decided advantage. However, the task force still needs to adjust its security implementation schedule to avoid confusion or omission of a vital step.

Conversely, the same can be true if the original plan designated that a certain piece of equipment was to be installed at a certain time, but the funding source is suddenly no longer available. Certain types of equipment may even be currently unavailable. Regardless of the situation, the task force should return to its timeline and make the necessary adjustments.

THE TIMELINE

A particular aid for the entire school and community, as well as the task force, is a *timeline.* The timeline is a graphic representation of the sequence of events and the projected date when each is scheduled to be implemented from beginning to end. It shows what has already been completed and what must be accomplished.

Not only is this simple linear illustration particularly beneficial to the task force for keeping its own activities on track, it can also serve as a quick, convenient, and easily comprehensible visual aid. Many schools need to raise money to complete their security program. The task force can use their timeline to illustrate their progress.

Parents and community members can see at a glance what has been done and what still remains. Those who are asked to contribute can recognize that the program is not some hastily assembled, knee-jerk response to a shopping list of potential threats but rather a thoughtful and detailed security plan that is thorough and reasonable on the basis of what a security survey revealed the school needs (see Figure 7).

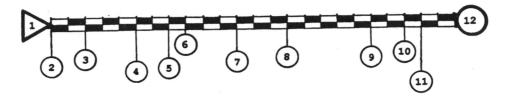

1. Week 1 - School security program development initiated.
2. Weeks 1-2 - School security task force appointed.
3. Weeks 4-5 - Security survey conducted.
4. Weeks 6-8 Security survey completed and recommendations
   (countermeasures) determined.
5. Weeks 6-8 - Countermeasures selected for the school's
   security.
6. Weeks 9-12 - Meetings scheduled with security equipment and
   service vendors.
7. Weeks 12-20 - Physical security upgrades completed.
8. Weeks 12-20 - Security procedures implemented.
9. Weeks 20-21 - Security awareness training sessions held with
   staff and students.
10. Week 22 - Security briefings held with parents.
11. Week 23 - Mock crisis drills conducted.
12. Week 24 - School security program completed and in full
    operation.

Figure 7. Example Time-Line

Chapter 5

HARDENING THE TARGET

LITTLE MORE THAN A DECADE AGO, most schools, like the rest of the nation, had not yet heard the term "soft target." Those few who had did not yet realize the definition applied to them. Violence-prone adolescents knew better.

With virtually unrestrained, unlimited opportunities, rampage killers began to demonstrate the terrifying lesson they had never learned in the classroom. They now knew how to inflict maximum tragedy.

Ultimately, a few were forced to stop. Some turned their guns on themselves. Others, for whatever reason of their own, spent their fury and laid down their weapons. It came as a national epiphany. Schools were essentially unprotected and defenseless against violence.

Yet, schools realized then, just as they understand now, they simply cannot become armed encampments. They are, first and foremost, centers for learning.

However distressing, the facts do remain. To limit the possibilities of rampage violence, or any form of violence, schools must change their protection posture. They must "harden the target." They must institute security measures that make it tougher for someone to commit such violence, and they must prevent or deter the potential assailant.

However, should the unthinkable happen and one or even several perpetrators gain a foothold, then the necessary measures will be in place to intercept, control, and minimize their violence.

This coordinated response of people, procedures, and physical applications working together is the three P's of effective security. It is what the school's safety mission is all about.

Until now, this text has focused on laying the foundation for the school security program by concentrating on the people component, the first of the three P's. In-depth presentations have shown the school how to assess the various threats and vulnerabilities that could cause it harm, or have the potential to cause harm, and explained why a strong program administrator is necessary to keep its security operating at the desired levels of protection.

At this point, the school is actually ready to select the necessary technology and determine which procedures will round out its security program. It is ready to "harden the target."

This chapter will focus on the remaining two P's of security—*procedures* and *physical*. Data here are not to help the school explore sales information but to assist the task force as it decides which technical applications and procedures will offer its staff and students the best protection. The notation in parenthesis acquaints the task force with each component, whether it is a physical or a procedural element (see Figure 8).

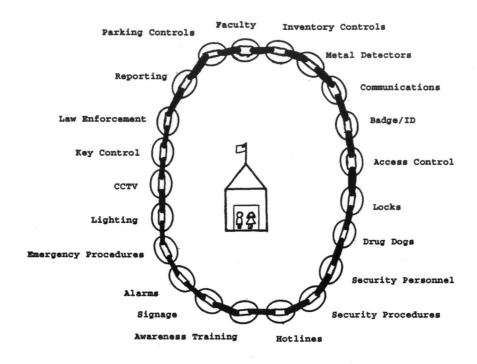

Figure 8. The School Security Chain of Defense

Access Control Systems (Physical/Procedural)

Access control systems are basically designed to prevent or limit access to a particular area. Locks and keys are the most popular and most frequently used form because they are cost-effective. They do, however, have their limitations. When keys are lost or the system for tracking them is faulty, control of the entire key system is then quickly lost.

Science and technology have recently made monumental strides in the field of security. One of the beneficiaries of such development has been in access control, especially in what is known as card-key systems. These systems include the card-swipe and the card-insertion method, both of which use a credit card-size device that is passed through a reader unit, which, in turn, activates the door release.

A variation of this concept has also been developed in the form of proximity readers. These units will activate when specially devised cards are simply brought within their "proximity." Convenience is obviously the advantage here, and because the sensitivities can be adjusted to read through certain materials, the person carrying the card does not even need to remove it from a wallet or a purse.

Another more versatile variation of the proximity system now includes a small fob on a key ring that replaces an electronic card.

There are some unique advantages to the card-key access control system. One of the most valuable is its integration with a personal computer to monitor all activity. The computer can add and delete card keys as needed, a decided advantage over the lock-and-key system. Lost keys or those that belong to a former employee can be deleted easily. A second particularly desirable feature is this system's ability to program card keys that will admit only certain individuals into authorized areas or restrict their movement to designated times.

The computer also provides a complete audit of all access transactions that the system has monitored. All persons who use their card key or other similar devices leave a record of the entrance they use, the time they arrive, the length of their stay, the time they leave, and the exit they use.

All these data are especially valuable if the school needs to determine who might have been present during a specific time when some questionable activity occurred.

The school can enhance its card-key system by incorporating a keypad and assigning each cardholder a personal identification number (PIN). The PIN must be used along with the card to gain access. It also provides added security if the card is lost and a period of time elapses before it is reported and deleted from the system.

Card keys should not display the school's name or its logo. Without such specific information, a lost card can not be traced to its origin and used by an unauthorized person. Card keys can be used in a variety of places: teachers' lounge, staff restrooms, computer rooms, record rooms, or any location that requires limited access.

If the school decides to use a card access system, it should select a system that:
- Is durable
- Is user-friendly
- Is flexible and will accommodate add-on features for future expansion
- Is affordable

- Provides replacement cards that are affordable
- Has user-friendly computer programming for tracking entry/exit data and for audit trails
- Includes reasonable maintenance and warranty contracts.

Alarm Systems (Physical)

An alarm system is fundamental to any security program in any setting. Not only does it serve the life safety role of detecting fire, but it also performs the equally important function of spotting any unauthorized individuals who may enter the facility.

An intrusion-detection alarm system (IDS) is most frequently installed to alert law enforcement to after-hours break-ins that are usually of two particular types. Theft is the first and most obvious. Computers and audiovisual equipment have good resale value on the "streets" as "hot" property. Vending machines contain money, and the cafeteria usually stocks plenty of food.

However, oftentimes, what began as a burglary results in considerable vandalism and property damage from thieves who do not find what they want or who just want to leave the school a "message."

Because both of these types of criminal threats place a heavy burden on the intrusion alarm system to be efficient, dependable, and reliable, the task force should specify exactly what the system will be expected to do. Being precise is especially important if the system must be submitted for bid.

However, if the system is to be a sole-source purchase, the task force should seek out an alarm dealer who is known to be especially reputable.

Features of an intrusion alarm system that the task force should be concerned with include the following.

1. All windows, doors, and any other openings that are 96 square inches or greater are places that an individual could crawl through. Each should be equipped with an appropriate sensor that will activate when an entry is made or is attempted.
2. The system should be outfitted with an audible alarm sounder unit that will alert the intruders that the burglar alarm has been activated. The premise here should be the objective of any IDS system. First, it reduces the thieves' time-on-target. Second, it diminishes their window of opportunity for theft and vandalism.
   a. Many forms of interior sounders are available. From just the simple siren to the more sophisticated prerecorded message that tells the thieves the alarm has been triggered and the police are in route, the object is to motivate the intruders to hasten their departure.

b. The alarm system should also incorporate an exterior communication unit. Although a silent alarm might seem to be more appropriate, an audible signal is actually more practical, because the sooner the invaders are out of the building, the less they can steal or destroy.

3. The IDS alarm should also send an immediate signal to local police. This method of monitoring alarms is actually a service and requires a periodic fee. The task force must figure these charges into the security budget.

4. All alarm lines should be "supervised" so that they warn of any tampering attempts.

5. Access points located on rooftops or underground such as through tunnels should be secured. Entry points should be equipped with alarm sensors.

6. If the school has several buildings on its property, each structure should be "zoned" or identified. Police units that respond to an unlawful intrusion can then proceed to the exact location where the break-in occurred.

As an optional feature to a school's alarm system, the task force may want to consider adding a manually operated panic alarm or a medical alert. This "panic button" will summon emergency medical personnel without having to call "911" and can be strategically located in the main office. In the event of trouble when the police are needed on the scene quickly, simply pushing the panic button immediately activates the alarm.

Badge Identification Systems (Procedural)

Determining just who belongs on a campus can be a formidable task. Even in small schools, not every administrator, sometimes not every teacher, knows every student. In large schools, staff members may not know volunteers, part-time staff, substitute teachers, or visiting specialists.

Schools also tend to be accessible to anyone and everyone. Just as many workplaces have done, all schools, large or small, should incorporate a badge system to identify staff, students, visitors, and any other authorized personnel.

An ideal badge is one that can be clipped or pinned to outer garments or worn on a lanyard or wrist bracelet. It should specifically and readily identify the wearer with the person's photograph, identification number, pertinent bar coding, school logo, and any other particulars that are necessary. The badge must also be tamperproof to resist any alteration that could circumvent the system.

Current technology has produced badge identification systems that are both cost-effective and user-friendly. These two factors are essential for the school's protection and where badges must be produced in mass. Certain systems, which include a basic camera unit with a laminating function, create a card-sized unit that is typically $2^1/4$ by $3^1/4$ inches. With the personal computer and a closed-circuit television (CCTV) camera, the photo and other identifying data can be entered to produce a quick, efficient badge. The information and the picture can be stored and later updated or accessed to replace a lost badge. Even visitors can receive photo identification within minutes.

Badges can be further enhanced by color. Backgrounds in certain shades not only distinguish the wearer but can also make alterations or even replications more difficult. Specific color-coded backgrounds for different groups can distinguish one class from another and identify faculty, maintenance workers, volunteers, and visitors.

Although more and more businesses and organizations require employees to wear identification badges, students sometimes resist. Their reasons range from vocal declarations about being labeled to the "I lost it" or the all too familiar, "I forgot." Their resistance may be passive, yet it is resistance nonetheless.

Some of their objections can be countered through awareness training. By simply and truthfully pointing out how significant the badge is to school security, especially if there have been any recent episodes of intruders onto the campus, most students and most staff will be convinced. Staff must be especially supportive, because it is up to them to set the example. They must be willing to adhere to the identification badge rule. They must wear their badges daily and at all times.

Oftentimes, students object merely because "It's a rule." To reduce the sting of yet one more school law and maybe even endear the badge to its wearer, life safety information can be listed on the reverse side. This vital information, which has less to do with security than saving a life, can include emergency medical data such as blood type, allergies to medications, family physician, next of kin notification, and telephone numbers.

In the event of a tragedy or even a student or staff's own personal medical emergency, having such critical information readily available can literally make the difference between their life and their death. Such immediacy is a most compelling reason for everyone to wear their badge.

An additional selling point is to incorporate a bar code on each card. As more and more school cafeterias process students by computer rather than cash, this feature can speed up long lunch lines and make records and billing more accurate. Students and staff merely swipe their ID through a scanner, which works much like a check-cashing card. The same procedure can be used to check out library books and any number of other activities within the school that are, or can be, computer monitored.

Visitors pose another problem for badging. All visitors must be properly identified as persons who are not routinely authorized to be on campus. Their presence is temporary, for a particular purpose, and for a specified amount of time. Visitors passes, however, are usually generic, only display the school's logo and a large, easily recognized number, and are not always easy to control.

Far too often, these badges are also difficult to retrieve, especially if the school does not have a specific procedure that makes the visitor accountable for checking out and returning the badge.

The task force can handle this problem in several different ways. They may wish to incorporate a system that takes a photo of the visitor and creates a badge within minutes. This system is quick, efficient, and highly effective, but it can cost several thousand dollars.

Another possibility is the temporary badge that self-destructs after a certain period of time. The inexpensive card-sized unit is constructed of paper and has an adhesive back that sticks to clothing. After a few hours the surface turns black and the badge is rendered invalid for any further use.

Although the badge does not need to be retrieved, the school should still have an official exit procedure. All visitors should return to the registration office to check out and record their exit time (see Figure 9).

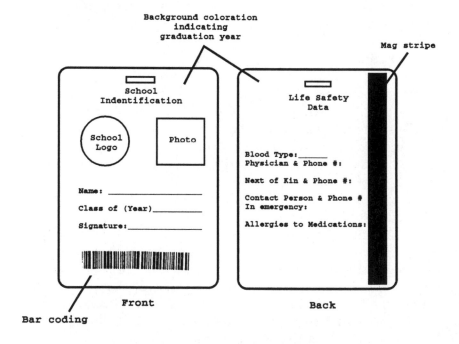

Figure 9. School Badge Identification for Staff and Students
(Example)

Biometrics (Physical)

Recent developments in technology have produced some amazing, highly sophisticated electronic sensory equipment and hardware that can strengthen a facility's security. One of the latest of these innovations, dubbed "biometrics," has become quite reliable and affordable.

Essentially, biometrics uses scanning technology to read certain human characteristics, either physiological or behavioral. It determines an individual's identity, that the person is who he or she professes to be, and permits that person to have access to a secured area.

To date, biometrics includes the following types of scanning systems for security applications:

- Voice identification
- Hand geometry
- Retina identification
- Palm reader
- Signature identification
- Facial image verification

Although the technology associated with biometrics is beginning to gain acceptance as a viable application for security, the future will, no doubt, see the development of other such scanning capabilities.

For the present, biometrics is technology worth considering. The task force might wish to investigate this field of protection if their school has the available funds.

Book Bags (Procedural)

In the younger world, book bags have become an essential. Many are very expensive, monogrammed, and fashionable. Students regard them as necessary as a notebook and as stylish as jeans. School officials, however, often view them quite differently. Book bags may afford their owners a convenient carryall, but they can also present serious security problems for the school, primarily because they can conceal contraband, drugs, and weapons.

The problem is further compounded by the issue of students' rights. Can the school legally search book bags? Do such searches violate a student's right to privacy?

The task force must determine whether permitting book bags into the school also admits more serious potential problems? If the decision is to allow the bags, the task force must ensure that procedures, which are in accordance with local school boards and state laws, are in place in case bags must be searched. If, however, the bags become an identifiable problem, particularly if they are found to be concealing weapons, fashion statement or not, they must simply be banned.

In a effort to be reasonable, some schools, especially those with metal detectors, require students to pass through the scans, then take their book bag directly to their locker. Bags are not to leave lockers nor may they be carried into the classrooms. Other schools ask students to leave their bags outside the classroom doors in the hallways. Some schools hope just to limit the bags to the front of the classrooms. It is not uncommon in many schools, particularly those with no firm policies on book bags, to see all of these practices, as well as no procedure at all, exist within the same building.

Another compromise to the popular canvas or nylon material has been a see-through style, which comes in a clear plastic or fishnet fabric. Students who have been forced to carry either this style or no book bag at all are quick to point out that the practice is not foolproof. Weapons or contraband that can be seen through the outer material can be shielded and concealed by the contents of the bag.

There is, however, one positive note in the book bag issue. In the event of a shooting or a bombing incident, a book bag can serve as a makeshift shield to protect the student from bullets or flying shrapnel. Obviously, this technique, because of the variety of the contents inside the bag, may not totally protect a victim, but it still may help to reduce injuries.

Closed Campus (Procedural)

Despite continuing crime and violence involving juveniles, many secondary schools continue to keep their campuses open. Students may walk or take their cars off campus for lunch, for breaks, or for numerous other reasons, depending on school regulations. It is a practice that should be terminated. The potential for harm and danger far outweighs the benefits.

Although administrators or staffs may believe the privilege of an open campus encourages students to be responsible, in reality it may have just the opposite effect. If the school allows its students to come and go at will, it is also, in turn, permitting those who have no connection to the school to come onto the campus to sell drugs or maybe settle a score. The result can be violence. Participants and innocent bystanders alike can be injured or killed.

An open campus makes determining who is in the building and who has left campus particularly difficult. If an event occurs that makes it necessary for the school to account for every person in the building, such uncertainty can quickly become a significant safety issue.

Rescue efforts at a fire, an explosion, or a gas leak can be hampered, and lives can be endangered or lost if the school cannot determine exactly who is in the building and who is not.

Car wrecks, which occur during the school day can pose a special liability for the school, especially if numerous teens are passengers in the car and their parents were unaware of their child's activities.

An open campus places a tremendous and unnecessary strain on the school's security program. Monitoring students as they come and go, to say nothing of simply processing the extra traffic through metal detectors and inspecting bags and packages, demands extra personnel or critically over-loads the existing staff.

To those schools that have an open campus and plan to institute a secu-rity program or upgrade an existing one, closing the campus will not be easy. However, it can be done and done successfully *if* restrictions are phased in gradually.

If this caution appears to contradict previous information in this text that urges thorough and immediate security arrangements, readers should remember the unsuccessful experiences of business and industry with secu-rity, primarily because they mandated security to their employees.

Responses from the students in schools that have an open campus may well be just as unreceptive. To them, an open campus spells freedom. Regardless of the risks involved, it is a freedom they will not relinquish eas-ily. Abruptly closing their campus in the name of security, a protection they may neither want nor feel they need, can lead to protests that will seriously jeopardize the security program and its future.

Implementing a major change will proceed more smoothly if it is started at the beginning of a school year, especially for those schools that attempt to close a campus that may have been open for years. Each fall, schools nor-mally start off with general orientation. Beginning security awareness train-ing at this time can address parents about this new direction of closing the campus. The task force needs to be aware that some parents may be as unhappy with this change as their child is.

At the start of a new school year, students expect some changes, but even then, when both staff and students are still enthusiastic, optimistic for a suc-cessful year, restrictions should still begin gradually.

Systems that evaluate students for good grades, regular attendance, and punctuality and then reward them with permits to take their cars off campus have the best chance for increasing responsible student behavior while simultaneously closing down the campus.

Closed-Circuit Television Systems (CCTV) (Physical)

As school buildings and student populations have both become larger, administrators and teachers have discovered they cannot supervise hallways, cafeterias, libraries, computers rooms, and parking lots, to name only a few places, at all times. They need assistance. A CCTV surveillance system can provide the extra eyes the school needs to know what is happening through-out the building, on the outside campus, and in the parking lot.

Over the last several years, schools have begun to realize just how prac-tical CCTV systems can be in protecting their staff, students, and building. The application has gained considerable acceptance by helping administra-tors monitor certain trouble spots or activities that have the potential to cause harm.

Placing cameras at strategic spots inside and outside the building also offers the additional benefit of a "scarecrow effect." Often the camera's mere presence deters those who would otherwise perpetrate some act of crime or violence. No one about to commit an illegal act wants his or her picture taken.

As cameras become more cost-effective, they can be placed virtually anywhere to provide a more detailed coverage of the entire school. It is not uncommon to see students who congregate with the idea of causing some type of trouble or disruption suddenly dissolve and move on when they dis-cover they and their activities are being filmed and recorded by a camera.

For those schools that already have an existing system but have new trou-ble spots, the best solutions is to add cameras to provide greater coverage. Moving units will only chase the crowd from one place to the next. Once students realize the camera has been removed from their original hangout, they will return. Continuing to move cameras is far more time-consuming and costly for the school than it is threatening to unruly students.

Camera screens should be monitored for any questionable activities. It is this video evidence that makes a CCTV system especially valuable. However, if it is not possible for a person to monitor the cameras at all times, a video recorder, incorporated into the system, will record and preserve all activities. In the event an incident does occur, the school will have the pro-tection of proof on videotape.

If a CCTV system is to benefit a school's security, it must include a vari-ety of features. The task force should think of the overall camera system as a compilation of components in five basic subsystems, which are as follows.

- Camera units
- Cable transmission lines
- Monitoring system
- Recording system
- System accessories

The cameras are the eyes of the CCTV surveillance system. These extensions view the critical areas inside and outside the building for any questionable activity. What they see needs to be absolutely as distinct and clear as possible. Resolution must be a primary concern. Cameras have become more affordable and their prices still continue to drop, but the task force needs to make certain it does not sacrifice quality for cost. What the cameras must do in relation to the conditions under which they must perform is far more important. As the task force selects a camera system, it should consider the following conditions for outside units.

- Will they operate in low light?
- Will they tolerate hot and cold temperatures?
- Will they withstand dampness and moisture?
- Are they protected from vandalism or wanton destruction?
- What is their field of view, the area that they are expected to cover?

Essentially the camera unit is composed of two elements. The first is the lens. This optical component determines the quality of the image. The second element is the camera itself. This mechanism converts the image and communicates it to the monitoring and recording components.

Modern technology has produced what is now known as "chip" cameras. Simply put, chip technology is advanced electronic circuitry that greatly improves the camera's ability to define color, sharpen details, and extend its life beyond the old tube models. Chip units also add flexibility by helping cameras function more efficiently under special conditions such as low light.

Although the specific characteristics for each camera vary according to the conditions under which it will operate and the expectations it is to fulfill, the task force should be aware of certain general features.

Each exterior camera unit should be protected in a bullet-resistant housing and placed as far out of reach as possible from unauthorized persons. Cameras that are pole mounted need to be placed on metal poles as opposed to wooden poles, which can be cut down. Outside cameras may also need a heating unit in their housing to eliminate humidity that can fog the lens. Interior cameras should be protected by a dome or other covering that reduces the potential to destroy or tamper with them.

Security cameras are usually thought to be in a fixed position. Although true of some models, current capabilities can pan-tilt-zoom(PTZ). A mere movement of the control mechanism changes their viewing area, and the flexibility to pan an area or zoom in for a closer look can be a valuable feature.

However, vital coverage can be lost at certain times, maybe even crucial periods, because someone changed the camera's viewing position and forgot to return it to its original setting. If numerous people have access to the controls and each arbitrarily alters the viewing area, the school may end up sacrificing vital coverage of a problem area.

Because cameras can be moved so easily, viewers may be tempted to "play" with the cameras and the system, adding even more wear and tear to the equipment and necessitating more repairs or even premature replacement.

The task force may, therefore, conclude that a CCTV system of all, or at least most fixed cameras, is more economical and ensures the school of more consistent performance. Simply adding a few more fixed cameras, rather than relying on a system of a few PTZ, can provide equally thorough coverage at a lower cost, both in purchase price and maintenance. Answers to such comparisons will help the task force select their vendor.

As the task force explores the various uses for the CCTV system, it should also explore a feature that could be particularly life saving during an episode of rampage violence.

The camera system that is selected should have the capability to be switched to an "emergency mode." During this time, each camera that would be zoned to cover its immediate area would relay its images to dedicated television monitors or computer monitors in classrooms or other locations on the campus. Teachers and students could check the hallways outside their door and to the nearest exit to avoid running into a line of fire.

This same principle of coverage can also be extended to local law enforcement. The task force should enquire about the availability of software that law enforcement can use to view real-time video within the school. During a crisis, the police could assess the situation and be prepared before they arrived on the campus.

AUTHORS' NOTE: Installing a CCTV system often raises the issue of dummy cameras. These cameras only appear to be active. Some schools may believe they can get the price of two for one with this scarecrow effect. They can install cameras that appear to provide surveillance and, simultaneously, save the school a few dollars.

Such a tactic may actually jeopardize the system's effectiveness. Once the word leaks out that some of the cameras are phonies, it will not take students long to figure out which cameras are which. Many of the staff and even some of the students themselves will end up losing confidence in the system.

Adequate lighting also poses special conditions for cameras. As the task force considers where to place units, they may conclude that additional illumination is necessary to provide sufficient visibility for the cameras during nighttime or inclement weather. The task force should also anticipate such factors as glare from flat surfaces.

Ice, which results from standing water, in parking lots for instance, may not have been a condition when cameras were installed but can seriously diminish the quality of the image. The maintenance segment of the security program must periodically check all sections of the program, especially during unexpected or harsh changes in the weather that can alter the system.

Images that the camera observes become electronic signals that are transmitted by a variety of methods. Coaxial cable, hardwire cabling that connects the components, is the most common, primarily because it is more economical.

However, installing the system can be especially difficult if the school is old, especially large, or has some unique structural design. Each camera must be connected to the coax, and the cable must be pulled throughout the buildings and run to all the exterior locations.

If the task force is facing these or any other difficult conditions within its building, it should be sure to review the costs of all the different transmission systems.

Recent wireless innovations are being used to communicate the CCTV camera signal, such as radiofrequency (RF) transmission, microwaves, and fiber optics. Although each has a valid application within its own right, the task force should review each system and compare bids from several vendors on initial cost, maintenance costs, potential for malfunction, etc.

Television units display what the cameras see. Several features can enhance the system's observation and its recording ability, one of which is a screen splitter. This multiscreen capability permits a viewer to watch simultaneous several areas that are being covered by the cameras.

Another such feature for the CCTV system that uses multiple cameras is sequential switching. Here, the system automatically provides a few seconds of observations from each camera, then moves on to the next picture. The operator, however, can stop the switching at any time to concentrate on the view from just one camera.

Combining the screen-splitting feature with sequential switching can greatly enhance the system's flexibility, but the combination of more cameras and continually changing images makes close, careful monitoring more difficult.

Another consideration for selecting monitors is color as opposed to black and white. Although both systems provide good imaging, color, which can delineate shades of hair, skin, or clothing, can make identifications of individuals easier and much more reliable.

A CCTV surveillance system is of little value if it does not have a recording and reviewing capability. Even if the school has sufficient personnel to continuously monitor the screens, and if someone witnesses a problem, and if there is enough response time to reach that location and intercept the incident, the school still needs to record the incident. Video documentation is extremely valuable if it is needed later as evidence.

The camera's observations can be documented either by continuous or time-lapse recording. The task force should view the quality of each to determine just which system they want for their school. Continuous play requires more video tapes, and the tapes need to changed more frequently.

Time-lapse may conserve tape space, but because it only tapes a few frames at a time, it projects a jerky movement rather than a continuously smooth action when it is replayed. Regardless of the system, video tapes should be changed periodically to maintain good recording quality.

CCTV equipment should be secured at all times. All cables should be concealed in protected conduits that limit sabotage. Recording and monitoring units should be housed in secure cabinets, and access to the equipment should be limited to just those persons who are responsible for its operation.

An important point to remember is, if the office area were taken over by a siege, there should be a way to disabled or secure television monitors. Perpetrators should not be able to use the system to view the outside and see responding police units arrive, nor should they be able to view the inside of the building and watch rescue teams who may be attempting to advance on the perpetrators or reach any trapped staff and students.

Exterior locations about the campus where closed-circuit camera units may be required include:

- Parking areas
- Building entrances
- Walkways
- Building(s) exterior sides
- Commons/courtyard area
- Athletic fields
- Student congregation areas
- Smoking areas
- School bus loading/off-loading areas

Interior locations for camera units include:

- Commons area
- Library
- Quiet study area (QSA)
- Cafeteria/Vendeteria
- Teachers' lounge
- Gymnasium
- Auditorium
- Hallways
- Entrances to restrooms
- Main office
- Interior student congregation areas

Computer Security (Physical/Procedural)

Today, computers serve vital functions in most every aspect of our lives. For schools, however, they serve a dual role. As a teaching instrument, computers educate our youth to meet the high-tech challenges and careers of the twenty-first century. As an administrative tool, they facilitate, often control, more and more of the daily business of running a school. They store records, bill for lunches, and link classroom to classroom and classrooms to the main office. Computers can even be integrated into the security program to monitor the various technical subsystems and help maintain the school's desired levels of protection.

As with any technology that is so essential and so complex, computers are especially vulnerable to two threats. Obviously, loss, either from damage or theft, is serious, but the second, compromised information within the system itself, can spell disaster for a school. The task force must address both areas as it designs its security program.

To protect the physical computer equipment from theft or vandalism, the task force should consider the following:

- All computer equipment that is kept in classrooms and/or offices should be secured at all times when the area is unoccupied.
- All manufacturer's serial numbers, models, nomenclature, and any other identifying data should be recorded and maintained separately for ready reference in the event of theft.
- Computer equipment should have hidden serial numbers etched into its housings to identify the school as the owner in the event of theft.
- Security or anchoring cables should secure computers to their respective desk, table, or work station.

Information is often lost to or compromised by persons who enter restricted areas where they simply have no authorization. However, far more damage is often done by individuals who are permitted access to a certain location or may even use certain computers and then override the restrictions that were designed to protect sensitive records or programs.

Special procedures must be established to maintain the integrity of any such data and deny access to "hackers" or anyone who wishes to alter information.

To counter this threat, the following measures should be incorporated.

- Provide passwords to just those persons who should have access to certain computer units.
- Change passwords periodically.
- Keep computers off-line, except when they need to be on-line, to prevent off-premises "hackers" from manipulating or stealing school data.
- Promptly report all "hacking" activities to the appropriate law enforcement authority for follow-up.

Crime Prevention Through Environmental Design (CPTED) (Procedural)

Crime may have many causes, but opportunity permits it to occur. Often, however, just by altering the surroundings of a vulnerable area or its environment, crime threats can be reduced. Such is the concept of CPTED that relies principally on designing physical layouts that minimize isolated spots and make all persons more visible at all times.

This generalized form of "surveillance" prevents individuals from becoming victims because they can see all about an area and assess the location before they enter.

The task force should be aware of and correct the following CPTED conditions.

- Shrubbery or other vegetation that is located too close to doors, entrances, ground-level windows, etc. and can conceal a perpetrator
- Land contours that block observations
- Dark stairwells
- Poorly lighted entrances and exits
- Parking areas that are out of the line-of-sight from buildings or people traffic
- Blind spots created by corners of buildings or interior hallways
- Darkened corridors
- Areas of the campus that are out-of-sight and away from people activities
- Isolated locations on the campus
- Light switches that are not located at the entrance to a room
- Chain-link fencing that has considerable vegetation growing on it and limits visibility through it
- Atmospheric conditions such as fog or smog that limit observations
- Conditions that limit the CCTV system's capability to observe as it was intended

Using the CPTED concept to further protection, the task force should:

- Make certain trees are well away from the structure or trimmed back so that they cannot be climbed to facilitate an upper-level break-in
- Make maximum use of signs on the campus to direct access, travel, parking, speed controls, etc.
- Ensure that all signs are fully visible and free from any obstruction
- Make certain that all campus boundaries are clearly defined to provide obvious separation from surrounding private or public property
- Take advantage of any and all natural surveillance to provide an atmosphere of safety and security
- Make certain all areas where students tend to congregate are in full view and easily observed by all persons
- Identify all isolated areas or locations throughout the school, on the campus, and in additional facilities so that natural or electronic surveillance can be increased

Emergency Communications System (Physical/Procedural)

In the event of an act of school violence, such as a rampage shooting, a bombing, or any effort to create mass casualties, an emergency communications system within the school is essential.

Every room in the school where personnel are present, classrooms, teachers' lounge, cafeteria, main office, maintenance areas, must be equipped with a two-way intercom that is connected to the main office.

Telephones (standard land-line models) should also be situated in strategic locations throughout the building. However, if staff members are unable to contact the main office through the two-way intercom for some reason, or the main office is under siege, or perhaps several teachers need an immediate response from medical or law enforcement personnel, they must be able to dial "911" directly.

A word of caution concerning cellular telephones during a crisis. Because they are so popular, odds are that at any given time in any given classroom most of the students and probably most of the staff will have a cell phone in their possession. The school should have a firm, frequently communicated security procedure about cell phones during a school crisis.

The first rule should be that at the very first sound of whatever bell or signal announces a crisis, all cell phones must be turned off immediately.

Bombers sometimes use radio frequency (RF)-controlled detonating mechanisms to set off an explosion, and because cellular telephones operate by RF transmissions, one could accidentally trigger such a device. The second rule should be that no one is permitted to use a cellular telephone to make any emergency calls either to police or to parents.

During a crisis, the tendency is for many to panic, and those with a cell phone may believe they are helping if they call "911."

In reality, a flood of calls can actually hinder emergency procedures by overloading the switchboard and jamming the circuitry. The task force should frequently review and emphasize these two procedures. They should explain each one thoroughly and clearly during security awareness training for all staff and students.

Probably one of the best pieces of equipment for those trying to regain control during such an emergency is the standard, sometimes legendary, bullhorn. It is reasonably priced, already available in most schools, requires no electricity or RF, and can effectively raise a leader's voice above the din of panic. The task force would do well to see that several are available and placed in strategic locations throughout the school.

Entry and Movement Controls (Procedural)

The daily business of a school involves a large volume of people moving in and out of the facility. From vendors to service representatives to parents, and even to other educators, most have a specific legitimate reason to be in the building. They pose no threat, nor do they intend to cause harm.

However, no one should be permitted to enter the building and wander about freely. Everyone, including parents, should sign in, receive a visitor's badge, and announce whom they have come to see. Then that individual, such as a teacher, should be contacted by intercom. After the teacher acknowledges the appointment, the parent or visitor should be escorted to the teacher, or the teacher should come to the sign-in area and accompany the visitor to a designated meeting spot.

Schools should also consider establishing a policy for parent-teacher meetings. In our current educational climate, teachers are regularly chastised and verbally, sometimes physically, assaulted by enraged parents who appear unannounced at the teacher's classroom or office area and with no appointment demand an immediate conference.

Not only are teachers unprepared, they may be unable to stop whatever they are doing at that moment and have a meeting. Such confrontations are certainly inconsiderate. At best, they waste everyone's time. At their worst, they can be dangerous.

The task force should establish certain procedures for such meetings and communicate them to staff, students, and parents during security awareness training. Such meetings should be:

- Held in designated areas only. Ideally these areas should be monitored by security cameras.
- Attended by at least one other school employee such as a guidance counselor, assistant principal, department head, or even a member of the task force in addition to the designated teacher.
- Scheduled with enough advanced notice that permits everyone who is involved to attend.

Even if the visitors are parents who are recognized by a receptionist or the office staff, they still should not be permitted to bypass this method. The office staff or registration person does not want to be placed in the position of making judgment calls.

Anyone who allows some visitors to bypass regulations but requires others to adhere to them, is, in essence, judging who may be a threat and who may not be. These days, when even the most lethal rampage killer can be someone we know and who appeared "fine" just before he unleashed a fury, such an error can be fatal.

Rather than viewing these procedures as unnecessary or bothersome, most parents will believe their child is especially secure, because any and all unauthorized persons who seek to come onto the school property for ill intent or criminal purposes are also being closely monitored.

The school should consider anyone who is neither staff nor student an unauthorized person. As such, all individuals must abide by restrictions that prevent them from entering freely and moving about the building unmonitored. Procedures to control the movements of visitors should include the following.

1. CCTVs are placed to observe locations such as entry roads, parking lots, walkways, interior hallways, the commons, and any other inside and outside locations where students congregate.

2. Signs are properly positioned to advise all persons who arrive on campus they must report to a certain office and register as a visitor. Signs should be situated so they plainly indicate the route from the visitor's parking area to the designated office.

3. A registration log records visitors' names, whom they plan to see, their arrival and departure time, the organization they represented, and any other information the school may require. One individual should be on duty and responsible for the log and should see that all visitors register properly.

4. A badge should be issued to each visitor who must wear it on an outer garment at all times as long as the visitor is on campus. The badge is retrieved when the visitor departs or the badge self-destructs and can be discarded by the office staff.

5. Visitors should remain at the registration office until the person who expects them comes to this designated office arrives and escorts them to the meeting location. At no time should any visitor be permitted to move about the school unescorted.

6. Staff and students should be instructed to promptly report anyone they do not recognize and who is not wearing a student, staff, or visitor's identification badge.

7. Staff and students should be advised there are proper challenging procedures for persons who are not wearing a badge. The challenge can be as simple as asking the individuals if they need directions to the visitors' registration office. Although the procedure is meant to be helpful and courteous, it also conveys the message that everyone in the school is acutely attuned to the presence of unknown or unidentified individuals.

Fencing (Physical)

Of all the natural and man-made barrier systems that can be used for protection, the chain-link fence is perhaps the most popular. Many schools leave their campuses open for easy access and to accommodate all the varying schedules of school activities.

Consequently, any fencing they may have is primarily for little more than aesthetics or boundary line demarcations.

However, if a school has chain-link fencing that it intends to use for security purposes or plans to incorporate such protection, the task force should be aware of certain facts about this style of barrier when it is used for security.

1. A fence that is designed for security purposes needs to completely enclose the area that needs to be protected.
2. The fence should be at least seven feet high.
3. The fence line should use a top rail that runs its entire length for greater stability.
4. Depending on the level of protection desired for the area, a three-strand, barbed-wire top rigger can be attached to the top of the fence to deter anyone from climbing over. Such an attachment should also be included on the gate.
5. The bottom of the fence line must be tangent to the ground at all points.
6. The fence should be free of all vegetation and undergrowth that can cause corrosion and can also limit visibility.
7. If the fence line is in close proximity to a parking area, concrete stops should be placed to prevent vehicle bumpers from making contact with the fence and damaging it.
8. The fencing fabric should be pinned into the ground with concrete at all midpoints between line posts to prevent intruders from lifting the fence and crawling under.
9. The fence should have a suitably strong gate with the necessary locking device attached to it.
10. The gate should have vertical guide bars attached to it that can be set into the ground to prevent an intruder from pushing the gate apart and gaining entry.
11. In places where the fence line abuts a building, the space between the fence post and the structure should not exceed three inches.
12. A clear-cut strip should run along all points of the fence line to keep it free of vegetation.

Hotlines (Procedural)

Student hotlines are not a crystal ball, nor are they always reliable. However, student hotlines, used carefully, can provide an early warning to administrators about some pending or planned act of violence.

Hotlines, which are simply dedicated phone lines and toll-free numbers, provide students with an anonymous means to tell authorities what they know, because they are the ones most often in direct contact with school violence.

Although the concept may seem sound, school officials should not be fooled. Hotlines are not a panacea for school violence, nor are they an easy answer to security. They should never replace a well-coordinated arrangement of security measures. Administrators should also be fully aware that unless they proceed carefully with such information, tips from hotlines could actually pose a serious liability to a school.

As with anything worthwhile, hotlines can be abused. False information is one such possibility. Certainly an incorrect tip can divert officials' attention and waste their time by sending them in the wrong direction. It can have an even greater danger.

Certainly school administrators must heed every warning and take every precaution they can to avert an act of violence, but they must also proceed carefully with names and accusations. False information can be offered for countless reasons. Everything must be considered.

Pranks may merely tie up the system or, at worst, cause confusion. The caller may, however, have more sinister motives such as exacting revenge on someone or attempting to ruin a reputation.

Whether the information is precisely true, only a rumor, or totally false with the intent to malign another student, it raises certain sensitive issues for security planners and for school officials about how to approach, manage, and follow-up on the information.

Any and all information that is received through a hotline involves two primary issues: (1) handling the information and processing it for follow-up and (2) confronting the accused or the suspected student.

Hotlines are primarily attractive to students, because they allow the caller to remain anonymous. They can pass along unconfirmed, incorrect information that names students who may be entirely innocent.

On the other hand, the tip can be a vital one that should be followed up. It just may intercept a plan and save many lives. Either way, it is a difficult call that no administrator should make without some guidelines.

School boards, administrators, and even legislative enactments need to consider outlining a structure for responding to hotline information. The primary concern of such procedures should be to demonstrate fair play on the part of all concerned yet balance the current trend for rampage violence against the right and privacy of individuals who may be singled out.

Outside contractors for commercial hotline services are responsible for relaying any information they receive to school officials. In turn, it is school officials who must evaluate the report and determine a course of action.

How serious is the information? Does it demand immediate intervention? Are several students cheating on tests, spreading rumors, smoking in the bathrooms, or does the caller identify someone who is vandalizing school property, dealing drugs, or carrying a weapon?

Perhaps the information is urgent. It says that an assault is in the making or plans for a bombing or a rampage killing are being drawn up.

Deciding which reports merit which response can place school officials in a difficult position. To overreact, especially if the report has been vague or turns out to be erroneous, may create unnecessary trauma, personal anguish, or simply embarrassment for the accused student.

If the information is found to be a purposeful lie, well-meaning school personnel could find themselves threatened with legal actions from the students' parents. On the other hand, to dismiss the information or attempt to minimize, even rationalize, threats about a rampage killing or simply to assume a "wait-and-see" attitude could be disastrous.

Because such information is directly referred to school leaders and any and all decisions are ultimately their responsibility, they may need to establish a system of handling and processing such data. Perhaps they might wish to work with a team of counselors who have more of a personal contact with students. Team members, of course, must be available after school hours.

Once the school officials receive the information, they must decide how they will confront the suspected student. They should be guided by specifically defined policy and clearly written procedures that state:

- Are the student's parents to be present?
- Is more than one school official to be present?
- Are counselors and/or psychologists to be involved at this initial stage?
- Is law enforcement to be involved at this point?
- Was more than one student named, and should all be questioned together or separately?
- Should other school personnel be present to document the conversation?

As school leaders devise a system of how they will handle a hotline tip, they, of course, must keep in mind any current legislation regulating a child's rights. Does such sensitive hotline information fall under the current purview of state and federal laws regulating a child's right to privacy?

Above all, school leaders want to make sure they have a system in place for handling hotline tips. They should make certain to have any and all of their questions answered by their local school attorney before they receive feedback from a hotline tip and before they must make such critical decisions, not after.

There is no question that hotlines can make a valuable contribution to school security. They can warn schools about existing crime and potential violence, but they must be more than a phone number and recording equipment. Tips from a hotline are highly sensitive and they, just as with all other aspects of the school's protection program, must be handled fairly and responsibly.

Integration (Physical)

In previous sections, integration has been presented as a method that combines the different protection features into a cohesive, well-coordinated security system.

However, in the field of security, "integration" has another application. It also refers to the use of personal computers to provide an overall system of monitoring the various technical subsystems of the program. With this technology, systems can be interfaced to provide more complete coverage for the school. These systems include, but are not limited to:

- Closed-circuit television system
- Access control system
- Parking controls
- Lighting
- Security officer tours
- Communications
- Badge identification
- Intrusion detection alarms
- Fire alarms

As schools continue to update their computer systems and rely on technology, the task force should become fully acquainted with computerized integration. The group needs to see how it can provide a more in-depth control of its security system regardless of whether the facility is large or small.

An attractive feature of the computer-integrated system is its ability to expand and manage the entire facility. In addition to monitoring all technical security systems, it can be extended to include other nonsecurity systems such as inventory control, time and attendance checks, and heating and cooling units, to name a few.

Inventory Controls (Procedural)

Schools contain a substantial amount of equipment, much of which is often used by several people. To reduce the possibility that items are lost or misplaced and to avoid replacement costs, the task force should implement mandates that provide consistent inventory controls. Such a program should:

- Document all equipment and materials received
- Record the equipment's nomenclature, serial number, model number, purchase price and date, date of receipt, and department or person to whom it was issued
- Etch a hidden identification number on the item and maintain the number in a log
- Attach an asset identification sticker or tag to an obvious spot on the equipment that specifically identifies that the item belongs to that school
- Promptly report all missing items to the police
- Establish an assignment log that documents who signs out equipment and where the equipment will be maintained
- Secure all valuable items when not in use, especially those that are portable
- Document and report any damaged equipment

Key Controls (Procedural)

One of the most difficult aspects of securing a school is key control. Regardless of how elaborate a security program may be, it is only effective if the system that is responsible for keys is absolutely efficient.

Essentially, a system for key control is a set of procedures that limits the number of keys that are issued, that restricts keys to authorized persons only, and that keeps track of each key at all times.

Because key control is absolutely crucial to effective lock security, it is usually the first security measure to erode. Key control is particularly difficult in a school for several reasons. Because so many persons need keys to so many areas that must be secured, schools often tend to issue an excessive number of keys. Oftentimes, a staff member, who is given a key may only need it for a short time or even a one-time use, forgets to return it and there is no follow-up effort to retrieve it.

In some schools, teachers travel. They do not have a stationary room, and without keys, they simply cannot manage locked doors, cabinets, and storage rooms. For these staff members, lost keys present a serious problem, especially if the school must rely on a central division that handles any locksmith service requests.

Replacements can take days, often weeks, and for those schools that have no one to follow-up, to provide temporary keys, and to secure a replacement, the choices are limited.

Teachers may have a duplicate key made by a local locksmith, but, unless they are authorized by an administrator, one more unrecognized, untracked key is entered into the system. On the other hand, they can either find another staff member and borrow a key or leave doors, file cabinets, storage rooms, or whatever area unlocked. For the sake of time and convenience, the choice is unfortunately obvious. Security will be sacrificed.

Never discount even the smallest detail. We remember that the battle was lost "for the want of a nail. . . ." It takes only one such scenario, nothing more than one lost key, to seriously threaten an entire security program.

Good key control procedures require periodic updating. To stay flexible and acceptable to the school and its personnel, a basic program of key controls should involve the following aspects.

- Assign one person to the school's key control program. This individual will be responsible for issuing and tracking all keys.
- Require all recipients to sign for their keys.
- Require staff to promptly report all lost keys and document their loss. A follow-up investigation should determine the circumstances of the loss and whether the locking device needs to be replaced to prevent that secured location from being compromised.
- Avoid, or at least minimize, the use of master keys or grand master keys that open many locks throughout the campus facilities.
- Retrieve all keys from departing personnel.
- Account for all keys at all times by maintaining a log that documents which recipients are in possession of what keys.

Laboratory (Chemistry) Security (Physical/Procedural)

Chemistry laboratories are not often regarded as a security risk. In today's world, however, of homemade bombs and clandestine laboratories that manufacture illicit drugs, the availability of equipment and chemicals within a school can pose a significant threat.

A protection program must provide special measures that nullify any efforts to steal materials or even to sabotage the school with an in-house explosion. The task force should consider the following.

- Contacting the local office of the Drug Enforcement Administration (DEA) or the local law enforcement unit and conferring about any chemicals that may be available in the school laboratory and that may be a target for clandestine laboratory operators. If any such chemicals are found, they should then be placed in extra-secured cabinets, closets, or other arrangements that lock to lessen the potential for their theft
- Installing a CCTV unit to monitor the area at all times
- Conducting regular audits of all records and orders for chemicals and equipment and being alert to any irregularities

Lighting Systems (Physical)

Not so many years ago, schools opened their doors each morning, then closed and locked them each afternoon as staff and students left the building. Today, many schools have extracurricular activities, night classes, and meetings that continue through the evening and often well into each night.

Consequently, an important component of the school's protection program is an effective lighting scheme. First, it must provide enough light so that people can see where they are going. They must be able to walk safely and observe any one else in the immediate area. Second, lighting should be sufficient to illuminate all dark areas and discourage those who may wish to hide and wait for an unsuspecting victim. Last, lighting is especially vital when the school has closed for the day. It permits security patrols or police to view the exterior grounds and interiors of the building more easily and detect any unlawful intruders.

Essentially, there are three types of lighting. *Incandescent lighting,* perhaps the simplest and best known, is the basic light bulb style used in homes, offices and general types of settings. Although inexpensive, its use is limited, particularly outdoors, where large amounts of illumination might be required. Incandescent lighting is good for entrances, stairwells, and other interior locations that are sheltered from harsh weather conditions.

Fluorescent lighting, also quite popular, is used in a variety of businesses and industries. This elongated tube-style bulb can be mounted singularly or in a series, is economical to operate, and provides good visibility and color rendition. However, it functions best indoors, because cool or cold temperatures can directly diminish its illumination output.

The third category is the *high-intensity discharge* (HID) unit. This more rugged form of lighting, which consists of mercury-vapor and sodium vapor, is primarily suitable for outdoor use. Combining the two HID systems produces an efficient and an economical system for wide-area illumination.

As the task force chooses the proper lighting systems and units its school needs, it should view the overall lighting scheme as two separate categories, exterior and interior lighting, and consider the following factors.

- The projected length of life for the lamp or bulb. How long is it expected to last in service based on industry standards and findings?
- The efficiency of the system's operation. How long is its start-up time or the time it takes for the system to come to full brightness?
- The system's capacity to tolerate weather. Can it operate effectively in cold or harsh climates?
- The system's capacity to be glare-free.
- The system's capacity for wide-area coverage. Do each luminary (lighting) unit and the extra illumination of spill lighting, which occurs when all units are combined, provide adequate coverage?

- The economy of the system's operating costs.
- The system's visibility and color rendition capacities.
- The maintenance costs and ease. Are bulbs readily available and are they easily replaced?

Various technical designations recommend proper levels of illumination for certain situations. However, the layman's best guide is simply: Is the lighting in an immediate zone and its surrounding areas adequate so that individuals who are moving into that section can fully observe the location before they enter?

Planning the school's lighting arrangements also means considering the cost of providing suitable night lighting. One economical method is to use timers. These popular devices can shut down certain lighting units when they are not needed. As activities for a school come to an end each night and the people activity ceases, it may be unnecessary to keep all areas of the parking lot lighted.

Rather than keeping personnel on duty for this shut-down operation, a timer can accomplish the same task and save the school tremendous costs of leaving lights on all night.

The task force should review all areas of the campus where such reduction in lighting can be made without reducing the effectiveness of the overall protection levels. Athletic fields and other such outside areas may be such places.

Interior lighting plays an important role in protecting the building after all persons have gone for the day. Sufficient amounts of lighting must always be left on so police patrols can easily spot any unlawful intruders. Such interior areas should include:

- Ground-level classrooms and offices
- Entrances and exits
- Dock and loading areas
- Rooftop areas where land contours, i.e. hillsides, are contiguous to the building and can enable an intruder to climb onto a roof
- Hallways

Lighting is a form of protection that many organizations often overlook or underrate in their overall security formula. Mainly because most operations and activities occur during the day, most security planning is done with just those circumstances in mind. However, the task force must be sure to give equal consideration to nighttime conditions.

Locking Devices (Physical)

A long-standing tool for protecting valuables and property has been the basic lock. Developed centuries ago, it has evolved into many advanced technical forms, but it still remains one of the most recognized symbols of security.

The most commonly used lock today is the mechanical lock, which requires a metal key to operate or open it. For a school, the mechanical lock usually takes two forms, the padlock and the door lock. The padlock is attached to a chain or a hasp, which in turn is attached to the door. The padlock may also be used to secure a gate. As the task force evaluates locking devices, it should determine the following.

1. Is the door that is to be secured sturdy within itself? Will it resist battering? Applying a locking mechanism to a flimsy door unit simply means that intruders can easily circumvent the lock by destroying the door.
2. Is the door-frame in which the door is situated sturdy enough to withstand rough treatment?
3. Are locking devices that are to be used outdoors or in exterior locations properly protected with a metal shroud that covers them and prevents them from being damaged by weather and corrosion?
4. Do door-locking devices that use a bolt throw have at least a one-inch length that sets into the strike plate of the securing door frame?
5. Is the strike plate made from a durable metal?
6. Does each door-locking mechanism have a metal shield that covers the space where the bolt throw sets into the strike plate to prevent an intruder from prying or manipulating the bolt? A good practice is to see that each does.
7. Does the school have a quantity of solvent on hand to dissolve any superglue that may be squirted into the keyways of any locks?
8. Do all doors that use external hinges have a set screw that secures the hinge pin and prevents it from being removed? This set screw arrangement should be required on all doors so constructed to prevent an intruder from circumventing the door by removing it and its locking device.
9. Does the school have a well-regulated key control and issuance program, which is one of the most important aspects of effective key-operated locking devices?
10. Are any chains used with locking devices? Metal links should be strong enough so they cannot be cut or severed with bolt cutters, hack saws, etc.

Another type of mechanical lock is the push-button model with a numbered keypad. This style of lock opens when a specific sequence of numbers is pressed. It is somewhat handier than using a key, especially on those doors that are used frequently.

However, this access method has one distinctive flaw. Unless it has periodic maintenance, certain numbers on the keypad will begin to show obvious traces of wear. Oil and grease from so many hands will help a keen-eyed perpetrator to narrow the combination of ten possible numbers to three or four. If the lock face is enamel, constant use can be even more obvious when the paint on certain numbers wears off or chips. Other numbers continue to look new.

Maintenance of push-button locks is, therefore, especially important. The face and keypad should be wiped clean periodically to prevent oil and grease from building up on three or four specific buttons. Second, the combination should be changed intermittently. New codes not only distribute the wear over all ten buttons but they also lessen someone's ability who has seen the code to use it later.

Metal Detectors (Physical/Procedural)

As guns, knives, clubs, even explosive devices continue to appear in schools, many officials have turned to extraordinary measures to curtail this weapons threat. Metal detectors lead the list.

News accounts that involve school security routinely analyze and debate metal detectors. Are they all effective? Do they address the problem? Would they have saved a shooting victim's life, prevented a stabbing, or stopped a bombing?

Unfortunately, the real problem of focusing on one measure is that although it may not be any more effective than numerous other security measures, it becomes popular. Far too many metal detectors are currently being used as the primary means of ridding schools of weapons, not because they are more foolproof but because they are more promoted. They are a visible, obvious tactic in the war to make schools safe.

Meanwhile, other measures that are crucial for adequate protection are being obscured, even ignored.

Metal detectors most certainly bring a viable component to the school's protection formula. Clearly, they can deter students from carrying weapons into the school. However, they are not a panacea.

Metal detectors will not eliminate all of the threats that a school faces daily. Without substantial accompanying procedures, the hardware, in and of itself, cannot provide the school the protection it needs.

Before the school decides to implement metal detectors as part of its security program, the task force should answer the following questions.

1. At which entrances will the metal detectors be set up to scan staff and students as they arrive?
2. How many metal detectors (walk-through units and/or hand-held units) will be needed to process all of the student body each morning?

3. Who will operate the metal detectors? Faculty members? Security personnel? Others?
4. What is the transaction time that is necessary to process one person through the scanners? How will this procedure affect starting the school day on time?
5. Who will man the scanning units throughout the day to screen others who arrive after the school day begins?
6. What procedures will be involved if an individual triggers a metal detector? What if the individual refuses to submit to a further search of his or her person and claims an invasion of privacy or voices other objections?
7. What procedures will be used to dispose of contraband that is discovered by the scanners?
8. At what point will law enforcement be brought in when illegal devices are detected?
9. How much training is required to operate the metal detectors? Who will receive it?
10. How will dangerous items such as guns be handled by scanning personnel who may not be skilled at or feel comfortable with weapons?
11. What measures are needed to ensure that scanners will not be used to discriminate against any particular student or any group within the school?
12. What are to be the pat-down procedures for persons who trigger a metal detector? Will male personnel be available to search male students, likewise with female students? Are there any regulations about searching a student's clothing? Are there limits on such a search or are there guidelines stating how such a search must be conducted?

A particularly important issue the task force must also consider and plan for is transactional time. Processing every student and staff member through metal detectors takes time. Attempting to scan hundreds of students through only one setup or even several during the morning rush can, without adequate planning, cause major delays and confusion. If the alarm should be triggered and a closer inspection is necessary, the delay increases.

Obviously, the larger the school, the more scanning units and personnel are needed.

Before the task force decides to implement metal detectors, it must also assess the security of the rest of the building. Ground level windows that can be opened and exterior doors that are left unlocked, propped open, or can be used as routine exits, render metal detectors useless.

Unless windows and exterior doors are monitored by CCTV cameras or equipped with sounders that signal when a door or window has been opened, students quickly realize they can bypass the front door screen. Simply by propping a door open or having a student on the inside admit others, or even hand off contraband, a main entrance metal detector can become a security joke.

The same consideration must be given to evening security. Schools that carefully monitor their security during the daylight hours but permit their building to stand open in the evenings, for whatever reason, undermine their own efforts.

If bombs, guns, or other weapons can be carried into a building at night, undetected, they can easily be hidden in countless places until they are needed.

It is vital for the task force to work out the many issues surrounding metal detectors and to understand that weapons scanners are only effective if they are a component to an overall security scheme. They cannot be the school's total form of protection.

Money Protection (Physical/Procedural)

Schools collect varying amounts of money from athletic events, fundraising activities, vending machines, various petty cash transitions, and a myriad of other sources. Oftentimes, deposits are not made at the end of each day, and cash remains in the main office or in other areas of the building. Schools should implement policies and procedures to protect any money, even when the amounts may be small.

Not only will thieves break in to steal any unsecured cash, but they often cause extensive vandalism. The following measures or upgrades should be implemented to ensure good money protection.

- All monies should be collected at the close of each school day and secured in a well-protected location such as a safe or other security container.
- Vending machines should be emptied each day of money, which is then secured in a proper location.
- All monies should be carefully accounted for at the close of each day.
- A designated school official or an alternate should make all necessary bank deposits. Deposits should be made frequently but on different days at different times to avoid establishing a pattern.
- Staff members should be instructed to secure all purses and other items that contain money.
- Signs should be posted in strategic locations to advise all persons that no money is maintained on the premises.

Parking Controls (Physical/Procedural)

Parking can present some formidable problems to the school protection program. Not only can the cars themselves be targets for theft and random vandalism, but vehicles that belong to staff and teachers can be targeted and damaged by students who are angry over grades, discipline, or any number of issues.

Cars can also provide students with a place to use drugs, drink alcohol, or engage in various risky behaviors. Vehicle traffic can injure student pedestrians and other teen drivers. Certainly most dangerous, cars can conceal those who have driven on campus to commit some form of crime.

Regulating parking lots, especially in schools in which a large number of students drive their own cars or campuses are fairly open, is often one of the administration's biggest headaches. As the task force plans security arrangements, it should consider the following suggestions for its parking lot.

1. Staff, student, and visitor parking areas should be separate. Each should be clearly posted with the appropriate sign that identifies it as "Staff Parking Only," "Student Parking," and "Visitor Parking Only."
2. All parking areas should be observed by CCTV cameras.
3. All parking areas should be enclosed within a chain-link fence of sufficient height (at least seven feet) to limit access.
4. Staff and teacher parking areas should be situated away from easy or general access that could expose vehicles to unnecessary vandalism and damage.
5. All staff and students who drive should be issued a parking sticker with an identification number and expiration date. Stickers, which can be color coded to differentiate the driver's status, should be displayed at a designated space on each vehicle.
6. All parking areas should have sufficient overall lighting. Persons who use the lot should be able to easily see all areas and any persons who are present from all directions.
7. All parking areas should be posted with appropriate signs that warn: "No Loitering in Parking Areas," "Do Not Leave Valuables in Plain Sight Within Vehicles,""Violators Will Be Prosecuted," etc.
8. Parking areas should be situated away from buildings.
9. Police patrols should be requested for all parking lots.
10. Security personnel who are employed by the school or other designated school officials should make frequent but irregular patrols through all parking areas.
11. Parking areas should be situated to inhibit flow-through traffic.

Heating, Air-Conditioning, Cooling (HVAC) Systems (Physical)

A vulnerable location is the HVAC system, which provides the necessary fresh air and temperature control for the building. This system depends on a centralized unit that can be a tempting target for pranks and danger. If the unit is unsecured, an aerosol device could be tossed in and the system could pull foul odors through the facility.

Smoke bombs or stink bombs are usually nothing more than unpleasant or irritating, but, in and of themselves, seldom dangerous. However, such a vulnerable system could show teenagers, or anyone else who may be intent on some type of chemical or biological terrorism, just how the entire school can be attacked.

Because HVAC intake ducts are located on exterior sections of the building to permit an influx of air, they need to be protected. The task force should:

- See that the intake duct locations are boxed in. This precaution will deny an easy access to a perpetrator who wishes to throw or place something in or near this area.
- Erect an overly high (twelve feet and above) chain-link fence. Position it well back from the immediate location of the HVAC and cover it with a material that denies direct access to it.
- Cover the opening of the intact ducts with a grating or other protective screening to prevent something from being tossed into the unit.
- Position CCTV cameras to monitor this location at all times and document through video recording any activity that may occur.
- Restrict the area around or near the HVAC equipment. Do not permit it to be a hangout or a congregation point for students when they are not in class.
- Have security personnel include frequent patrols around this equipment as part of their daily activities (if the school uses security personnel).
- Post signs to inform all persons that this is a "no loitering" area.

Personnel Screening (Procedural)

Personnel screening is a vital feature of any security program and particularly so for a school. Most counties, regions, or states routinely run a background check on prospective employees, yet, schools themselves often hire individuals for temporary or limited status positions. They also frequently depend on the assistance of numerous volunteers.

In this mobile age, prospective employees or volunteers for a school may be new faces in a community. It is imperative that administrators know the

professional and personal backgrounds of everyone, from custodians to educators, in their building. However, if the county or district has not run a background check on a prospective employee, it is the administrator's absolute responsibility to do so. Information to be checked and verified includes but may not be limited to the following.
- All information contained in the job application is accurate.
- Listed references have been verified and interviewed.
- A driving history review reveals no drug or alcohol abuse.
- A criminal history check has been done on a nationwide basis. A local background check may never reveal the applicant's criminal activity in other parts of the country.
- A credit history review reveals no fraudulent behavior nor pattern of financial abuses.
- Educational and professional credentials have been verified.
- Drugs screens are negative.

Confirming the information on a job application may require an extensive effort, but it is essential. Effective school security also means that personnel, both employees and volunteers, are trustworthy. Most importantly, they are who they say they are.

Signage (Physical)

Signs play an basic role in the security of any school. They communicate special messages about the types of conduct and activities that are acceptable or are forbidden while on the site.

Signs placed in strategic locations eliminate confusion and expedite the movements of those who may be unfamiliar with the area. Signs also help establish an atmosphere that says "these premises are protected and the facility is alert to crime and crime prevention."

Although there are many types of signs, the task force should consider the following recommendations. A basic system of exterior signs should:
- Indicate staff, student, and visitor parking.
- Indicate the campus has a closed-circuit camera system (if it does). All activity is monitored and recorded and will be provided to the police for law enforcement purposes.
- Advise that loitering or trespassing is prohibited and unauthorized persons will be subject to arrest and prosecution.
- Direct all visitors to the place where they should report when they arrive on campus.
- Communicate that the school is a "crime-free zone."

An additional consideration is night lighting. Once signs are in position, they should be sufficiently lighted so that they are easily visible. Interior

signs and placards should:
- Continue to direct visitors to the designated area where they must sign in.
- Encourage a high level of awareness to crime and violence among staff and students through strategically placed posters about crime prevention.

Drug Detection Dogs (Procedural)

Drug detection dogs have become a popular method for searching schools for contraband such as drugs. Whether the school has used or is contemplating using such a practice, the task force must consider the following.

1. Creating specific written policy and procedures that delineate the use of drug dogs within the school.
2. Signing a statement of understanding with the agency or organization that provides the dogs. This statement should clearly outline the role and the responsibilities of both the school and the agency.
3. Offering an awareness program for staff, students, and parents that outlines the need for drug detection dogs. The program should use the "fair play" approach and warn everyone that drugs will not be tolerated. It also serves public notice that random inspections will be conducted.
4. Having all policy and procedures reviewed by the school's legal counsel before any searches are held.
5. Keeping the date and time of an upcoming inspection strictly confidential. Only those personnel within the school who absolutely need to know should be informed.

CAVEAT EMPTOR

Buyer beware is certainly a sensible warning about any purchase. It is especially pertinent to the task force that is charged with deciding about vendors.

Which ones will provide the most prompt and efficient service, the most dependable maintenance, and the most reliable technology for CCTV hardware, access control units, badge identifications systems, and metal detectors?

Such decisions are both weighty and costly. They require insight and knowledge about security technology and above all, they require extensive time, a commodity most members of the task force, who already have ample professional duties, simply do not have.

Faced with such constraints, the task force can be left to the mercy of those businesses that profess to be protection experts and offer themselves as suppliers.

Certainly, many dealers attempt to work with schools. An occasional representative will even candidly point out the shortcomings of his product, but obviously, there are charlatans.

Far too often, unscrupulous dealers peddle hardware and prey on the unwitting customer. Schools end up being dissatisfied with their security equipment, not so much because the equipment is faulty or that what it would do was misrepresented, but primarily because of the standard explanation for many of life's unsatisfactory results: "You didn't ask that."

This section is designed to point out some of the various considerations for the task force as they search for professional vendors who will provide a quality, worry-free service to the school.

But even this section cannot be, by any means, the end-all source. Each purchase must still be made with common sense. Coupled with adequate time, all contracts, goods, and services from each vendor must be carefully reviewed.

Equipment Vendors

Security equipment is constantly changing. Current products are improving even as new ones are being developed. To help the task force keep pace with the expanding field of security technology and to guide them in making the best decisions about equipment for their school, members should consider the following guidelines for purchasing security equipment.

1. Be fully knowledgeable of your situation before you contact an equipment vendor. Determine, in advance, just what tasks and functions you want the hardware to perform.

2. As you determine your protection needs, do not think only in terms of the present. Consider add-ons and expansion. For instance, a camera system should suit not just the current layout, but it should accommodate future locations where camera units may be needed. Ask any potential vendors about the system's capability for add-ons and about additional costs to do so.

3. Visit other schools that have similar security arrangements. Ask to see demonstrations of the equipment. Inquire about prices, the system's strengths and shortcomings, and particularly about the school's opinion of the supplier.

4. Shop around. Talk to other security companies and review their literature. Study the language in the brochures so the task force is

informed when vendors talk their trade. If the jargon becomes too complicated for common, easy understanding, get a complete and immediate clarification.

Remember, you as a task force member are responsible for the security arrangements for your school. Failing to understand what type of equipment is best for your building may lead to a later weakness in the protection program.

5. If purchasing must go through a bidding process, make sure that bid specifications are specific. State in precise, well-written terms what features the task force has decided are necessary in these systems. Make certain nothing is omitted or overlooked.

6. Check out the vendors before signing any contracts. Review their history of business activities and operations. Have any complaints been filed against them with the better business bureau or consumer protection offices?

   Visit their physical location to confirm they actually exist as a legitimate business. Contact licensing bureaus and government divisions that monitor corporations to verify the business is actually authorized.

7. Obtain references from prospective vendors and contact them about their dealings with the supplier. Have other schools or businesses been satisfied with the supplier's services? If at all possible, actually visit the reference's location and look at the work that was done.

8. Carefully examine all warranties and their coverage well in advance of concluding the transaction. For instance, a CCTV system may contain various component subsystems such as cameras that are manufactured by one company, whereas the video cassette recorder is made by another company.

   The crucial question here is: does each component within the overall system have an individual warranty for repairs and service? Does the vendor also provide a warranty for the total system in addition to the warranties on each component?

   If the task force is confused about any warranty or any part of one, it should not hesitate to submit the documents to the school board attorney for clarification.

9. Are personnel that will maintain and repair equipment locally based or must they travel a great distance, even from another state? Inquire about maintenance fees. If there are any, must they be paid in advance or are they paid at the time of the service call?

10. Confirm the timetable for installation and completion. The task force may want to include a stipulation that if the company fails to initiate and conclude its work in a timely manner, which is not the

school's fault, then the contract becomes null and void.

Do not dance with the contract vendor. Far too often, once the agreement is signed and a portion of money is paid, the vendor suddenly has another, more pressing job or is unable to begin or finish the installation for a variety of reasons.

Schools are number one priority. Vendors who have put schools at the top of their preference list only to substitute a bigger customer once the contract is signed have established a reputation that is hard to hide.

Such delays are unprofessional, annoying, and could possibly be life-threatening. Strike them from your list. Simply do not do business with unreliable companies. School security is too vital.

11. Have school board attorneys review all contracts before they are signed. Any and all questions should be resolved at this time.

12. The task force needs to consider when the security system will be installed. Many schools close down for summer vacation from June through August. Some teachers travel. Others take additional jobs. Although there may be some maintenance people or other staff who may work at the school during this period, most likely the task force will be gone.

    Thus, making a contract to install equipment too near the end of the school year may mean the work will be completed after key faculty members are gone. Other arrangements need to be made because the task force should be available to inspect the work and confirm that everything has been done correctly.

    Equipment that has been installed over the summer and has not been checked or approved may not be ready to go when school begins in the fall. If the contractor has gone on to other jobs, it may also be difficult to get installers to return and make any changes.

13. Task force members should also actually view the system, component by component, as each piece arrives, but before any are installed. They also want to verify that each part that was ordered is the actual equipment that is going into the system and that certain components have not been replaced or substituted for other less expensive items.

RESIDENT LAW ENFORCEMENT OFFICER

Some districts provide housing for a law enforcement officer to live on school premises. The idea is that the mere presence of an officer living on the school grounds will discourage burglars, vandals, and general after-hours loiterers.

Although the technique certainly may repel some potential trouble, it is far too often used as a panacea. An officer's presence cannot be a school's single form of protection. An officer's working day will not be spent on the school grounds, but at assigned daily duties elsewhere. Portions of an officer's off-duty time will be spent sleeping and attending to other personal chores of daily living that will take him or her away from the school. Even those schools that arrange for an alarm to sound within the officer's on-site quarters are not completely protected.

Alarm systems are not totally foolproof, and because burglars who target a school are often students or former students, they can know how the alarm system works, where it can be penetrated, where the unprotected areas are, and how it can be overridden.

Chapter 6

INVOLVING EVERYONE

A N EFFECTIVE SECURITY PROGRAM, whether it is for a corporation, a top secret government installation, or a school requires a wide variety of features–hardware, procedures, and policies–to make it work.

But merely having the best or most elaborate security equipment or a security officer posted at the front entrance, who checks students through a metal detector, is not a security program.

Effective security must be a blending, an interweaving of procedures, policies, and people into one whole protection unit. Unquestionably, each component is a vital piece of the security program. However, as essential as each is, it is the human involvement, the "people" factor of the three P's, that is the most significant.

From the outset of the program, everyone, not just the task force or the administration, but all staff, including maintenance people, cooks, and bus drivers, as well as students and parents, must be involved in the protection process.

In any organization, regardless of its resources, effective protection must be a shared responsibility. Support and cooperation must be genuine.

Organizations that involve the beneficiaries of the program and make them feel, from the beginning, they have input and the program is designed for them and their safety will not only begin an effective program but keep it effective.

Many corporations and industrial operations have installed expensive hardware and elaborate security programs only to see their protection program fail, not because the equipment was faulty but usually because they instituted programs as retaliation or as punishment against the employees. Perhaps the company had been victimized. Maybe management was embarrassed or infuriated over the incident and decided to incorporate a security program that would show "just who's the boss."

Whether the failure was by design or simply through their naivete, management learned that such heavy-handed tactics by a company generate more hostility and alienation from employees than any positive identification with the organization's security program.

The final result is that the most important aspect of the company's security effort—its acceptance from employees and their cooperation—is replaced with contempt, not only for the company, but also for its security arrangements as well.

The second error companies have made is implementing the security program first, then briefing employees. Employees know little about the new program and have little identification with it.

Companies must *inform* employees in advance, well before the program is adopted, just what security measures are being implemented, why the company needs the program, what security is all about, and most importantly, what role the employees will play.

Although such awareness is an essential part of security and is the pivotal point upon which the program will either succeed or fail, it is, without exception, the single most ignored, most omitted factor in the final protection formula.

WHAT IS SECURITY AWARENESS?

Regardless of what the world may show us or what we may often tell ourselves, we are our brother's keeper. In a school, we must be.

Few situations call for such a commitment as much as a school's security program. Here, where protection is essentially everyone watching out for everyone else, every student and every staff member becomes a stakeholder, regardless of how slight their participation may be, in an atmosphere that is totally designed to keep everybody safe and where, each person, in turn, helps maintain a program that works effectively and efficiently.

However, the day-to-day reality is not everyone may be quite so highly motivated to make safeguards a priority, especially in education in which even routine demands on staff, both in time and energy, are relentless.

Periodic awareness presentations, which can be designed to keep the issues and areas of concern fresh in everyone's mind, can also be times to make a subtle appeal, especially to those who are less concerned with the school's protection.

Even if they are not directly involved, it is crucial they do not hinder the security activities. They should be assured that merely reporting a suspicious person on campus or spotting a malfunctioning or burned out light is a great help to the overall effectiveness of the program.

Likewise, it is also important to impress on them that these types of involvement are really not options. They are requirements for protection if the program is going to function at optimum levels.

The process of *security awareness* or orienting others to the school's security program to its intentions, and to its goals before it is implemented, should be designed so that both students and staff have more than just a casual understanding that a program is in place. Beyond the obvious protection of locks, lighting, and cameras, everyone must be knowledgeable about the overall protection designed for their school and understand why it is so important.

Once staff and students are familiar with the program, they then need to become willing participants. It is this step, this willingness, which is the first essential part of security awareness, and the one that is most often overlooked.

Unless the task force makes a special effort to introduce, to familiarize, and to solicit participation from both staff and students, an otherwise effective security program will be weakened.

A good place for the task force to begin to involve staff and students is with the causes and conditions that prompted the school to incorporate a security program in the first place.

Here the task force can stress that awareness is not suspicion or paranoia but is rather a heightened state of vigilance, both to crime and to the various acts of violence that could threaten the school. The point is to open people's minds, to acquaint them with the possibility that the crime and violence that are so prevalent in our society today can occur within the school and can cause harm and loss.

Awareness places everyone on alert, before a situation can materialize into a full-blown incident, by informing them just how crime can be reduced or averted and by acquainting them with the measures the school has in place for detection and prevention.

Ultimately the goal in security awareness is for staff and students to recognize and understand the safeguards that have been established to protect them, to willing accept the program's attempt to stop crime and violence on campus, and to actively assist in their own protection.

THE SCHOOL SECURITY AWARENESS PROGRAM

As the task force begins to plan its approach to awareness for both staff and students, it must begin with two fundamental but distinct concepts of the security program—*crime prevention* and *violence intervention.*

First, the task force must clearly and carefully articulate the primary goal of any and all security—to prevent crime, to deter the criminal, and to save the building from loss or its people from harm.

Second, the task force must also stress there is no guarantee all crime and violence can be stopped completely. There is always the possibility that violence can occur, but with each person's input and participation, the chances for curtailing violence are obviously much greater.

If, however, an act of violence does erupt, the security program has special safeguards, carefully designed measures that can be activated to help maintain order and contain the panic and confusion that often accompany any crisis.

The overall aim at this point is to prevent a potentially bad situation from becoming worse.

It is crucial for the task force to stress that although some incidents have resulted in bloody massacres, there have also been cases in which individuals, who were planning a carnage, were intercepted and stopped because someone was alert and notified authorities of the situation in time to prevent another tragedy.

As the task force begins to orient staff and students to the program and to define the part each will play in both prevention and interception, presentations should include the following.

Teacher and Staff Awareness

If the security program is to meet with any success, it must enlist the full and total support of the faculty. Obviously their daily, hourly contact with students, can go a long way in helping to influence and recruit student support.

Most critically, it will be teachers who will be the first line of defense should a crisis occur. Teachers, not students, will be in positions of responsibility, and teachers will be expected to respond immediately and appropriately to a threat.

This particular burden of making critical decisions rests squarely and specifically on classroom teachers and makes it especially crucial for them to be familiar with each part of the program. Any security orientation for faculty and staff should include the following.

AN EXPLANATION OF THE MISSION AND GOALS OF THE SCHOOL SECURITY PROGRAM. From the outset of a security program, faculty and staff need to be informed. Most likely, although not always, it was their own concerns that caused the school to consider implementing a security program. However, the task force should still be committed to keeping their colleagues informed of the progress.

Presenting the mission statement and goals early in the program's development gives everyone an opportunity for input, to understand the protection is for them, and to voice any concerns or serious objections.

AN INTRODUCTION TO AWARENESS AND AN EXPLANATION OF JUST WHAT CONSTITUTES VIOLENCE. Security awareness is far more than just a concern for violence. Some conditions that exist within the school are often fostered by attitudes that schools have tended to ignore such as long-term bullying or teasing. Both have been cited by some student assailants as part of the reasons for their rampage violence.

All too often schools, just as our society, recognize violence only after it has become a serious problem or has erupted into the extreme and final stages, such as assaults, shootings, and bombings.

Staffs need to take several steps back to realize that our society tolerates violence in many forms. Certainly most staffs intervene when they see obvious contact violence–slapping, punching, biting–but physical violence can also be acts that intimidate or frighten someone, such as blocking their path.

Violence can be verbal–demeaning words, taunts, and mimicking; it can be social–isolating, shunning, or excluding others. It can also be against property–destroying, defacing, or playing "keep away" with another student's possessions.

Many of these behaviors begin early. Even primary grades for some students turn into a daily chamber of horrors, a reality more and more feel they can correct with a gun.

The task force should begin their orientation for faculty and staff with a session on the types of violence. Counselors can help by providing handouts and questionnaires that heighten awareness about the types of violence.

Numerous publications are currently on the market although the task force may want to write their own questions to address certain attitudes or certain types of violence they believe is in their own school.

Questions such as: "I believe this school fails to admit the extent of violence problems to protect the school's image" or "I believe this school is more willing to tolerate violent behavior from advanced or 'gifted' students" permit the staff to examine their own responses to lower levels of violence and determine whether they are inadvertent enablers.

A THOROUGH REVIEW OF THE OVERALL COMPONENTS TO BE INVOLVED IN THE SCHOOL SECURITY PROGRAM. From the time the security program begins, the task force should schedule regular sessions during monthly staff meetings, staff development times, or whenever they are appropriate to demonstrate each new feature of the security program as it is implemented.

If cameras, for example, are added, all staff members, including maintenance personnel, cooks, office personnel, and even parent volunteers need to be familiar with how the system works, what can and cannot be seen, how the system will be monitored, and all other features of the system.

AN EXPLANATION OF THE FACULTY'S ROLE AND RESPONSIBILITY IN THE SCHOOL'S PROTECTION ARRANGEMENTS. Each staff member needs to understand that effective security requires everyone to be vigilant and to report any broken, malfunctioning lights, locks, or any problems they see developing.

Everyone needs to be encouraged to suggest improvements, to have opportunities to offer their suggestions, and not to turn a blind eye to security issues.

A CONFIRMATION, IN THE EVENT OF AN ACT OF VIOLENCE, SUCH AS A SHOOTING OR A BOMBING THAT INVOLVES THE ENTIRE SCHOOL, THAT FACULTY MEMBERS ARE IN CHARGE OF THEIR RESPECTIVE CLASSROOMS OR GROUPS OF STUDENTS. During security orientations, students must understand and the administration must reinforce the message that if a crisis occurs, staff members are knowledgeable and trained to deal with the emergency.

Unless evacuation by any means or by any route available is critical, students must wait, follow instructions from the teacher who is present, and not "take matters into their own hands." Decisions such as fleeing a classroom without first checking to see whether the hallway is safe could place students directly in the path of danger.

A COMPLETE EXPLANATION AND REGULAR PRACTICES OF ALL EMERGENCY PROCEDURES TO BE USED BY THE SCHOOL IN THE EVENT OF AN ACT OF VIOLENCE. On the basis of the security components that are in place, the task force should prepare an extensive list of procedures to be followed.

Just as fire drills are practiced, so should security drills be done. Teachers and students must know to wait for a code over the intercom that will advise them of the situation, whether doors to rooms should be locked or unlocked depending on the emergency, whether lights should be on or off, and whether all televisions (if the school has a camera system that permits classroom monitors to view the entire school) should be turned on or remain off.

Staff members must also know where first-aid kits and emergency supplies are located, to turn off all cellular phones, and a lengthy list of numerous other procedures.

AN OUTLINE OF THE CHAIN OF COMMAND IN THE EVENT OF A VIOLENT INCIDENT ON A MASSIVE SCALE. Staff members need to know a chain of command has been established. Someone is in charge at all times.

If an act of violence occurs and the principal, the vice principal, or even both are out of the building, there is a next designated individual who is in charge and knowledgeable about handling the emergency.

Understanding that a chain of command does exist and the individuals so named are prepared to assume their role prevents confusion. Too many attempting to take charge can be as detrimental as no one, especially when everyone is uncertain just what should be done and in which order.

A BRIEFING OF THE VARIOUS PROCEDURAL AND TECHNICAL APPLICATIONS THAT ARE INCLUDED IN THE SCHOOL'S PROTECTION PROGRAM AND EXPLANATIONS ABOUT WHY THEY ARE NECESSARY. The teaching staff in many schools, unless they have a direct involvement with a particular issue or student, is often unaware of the amount and the types of crime and violence plaguing the school.

Administrators, however, routinely deal with such problems, often on a daily basis, and many simply do not realize their staff knows very little about the thefts, assaults, or confiscated weapons within the school, that is, until a major tragedy results.

Other administrators foolishly believe they are protecting their staff, whereas some simply believe teachers' business is to teach. They do not need to know the day-to-day threats against the school.

To control certain behaviors, some schools have installed metal detectors along with certain dress codes to rigorously prohibit certain types clothing.

It is every staff member's right to know weapons are coming into their school; that oversized coats and baggy clothing can conceal multiple guns; that drug use and gang activities are a threat; and particular colors, symbols, and articles of clothing denote gang membership.

THE DISCIPLINARY ACTIONS FOR NONCOMPLIANCE TO SECURITY RULES AND REGULATIONS. Teachers realize certain attitudes among teenagers, particularly rebellion, are contagious. Teens may espouse individualism, but most secretly abhor being different.

More often than not they follow the leader, especially certain leaders who refuse to follow procedures that they view as coming from the "establishment." Such student leaders may or may not be model students; some may actually be the school's biggest discipline problems.

By and large, schools view most student protests as "business as usual" and believe most are relatively harmless. However, certain types of defiance, such as refusing to wear identification badges, can threaten everyone's safety and seriously undermine the school's security program if they are not fairly and consistent handled.

A BREAKDOWN OF THE SCHEDULE FOR IMPLEMENTING THE VARIOUS COMPONENTS OF THE SECURITY SAFEGUARDS. Staffs need to know their school is concerned about their safety. They can work more effectively when they believe they are protected. They also have a right to be safe and feel safe from harm.

Informing staff members of plans before they are implemented fosters a spirit of professionalism, of participation, and of inclusion in the serious matters of the school.

THE INTERCOM AND OTHER SPECIAL SIGNALS DESIGNED TO ALERT STAFF AND FACULTY TO A THREAT THAT IS IN PROGRESS AT A PARTICULAR LOCATION WITHIN THE SCHOOL. *No room in a school building, especially a classroom, should ever be without a two-way intercom system.* Whether the emergency is a potential hostage situation, a fight, or even an accident, teachers must have direct communication with the main office to summon help immediately.

The task force should also develop a signal system to alert staff and students to dangers that require everything from caution, to evacuation, to a lockdown. Posters should be placed in strategic spots throughout the building and in all rooms to remind everyone of the code.

Not only should each section or color of the code be practiced at regular intervals to familiarize everyone with the procedures, but in the beginning stages, especially while the school is learning each phase of the code, evaluations should always follow-up each drill and be carefully and specifically communicated back to the staff and students.

FACULTY SENATE OR STAFF MEETINGS CAN ENCOURAGE STAFF TO MAINTAIN VIGILANCE ABOUT EXISTING OR DEVELOPING SECURITY PROBLEMS BY DESIGNATING A PERIOD OF TIME SPECIFICALLY FOR THEM TO VOICE THEIR CONCERNS. The president or the security coordinator should open the floor for the staff to report any current security threats they may have observed or problems that may be developing. Even what appears to be the most insignificant matter could be an indication of a potentially serious problem.

Certainly, it is important for teachers to communicate their concerns to superiors anytime they uncover certain problems. In turn, administrators or the task force can use these observations for broad-based discussions to help reinforce the need for everyone to participate.

Awareness and cooperation are especially important as state laws and boards of education continue to place special responsibilities on teachers and their actions in the event of a school crisis. The task force should watch for the following.

- Incidents of students reporting to class under the influence of drugs or alcohol
- Chronic or abnormally high incidents of students hurt in accidents on campus that may indicate their use of controlled substances
- Stalking incidents against teachers or the families of teachers who may have had a confrontation with a particular student and now find themselves followed, intimated, harassed, or threatened with an attack by that same student or by a group of the student's friends
- Incidents of, or an increase in, vandalism against teachers' personal vehicles, property, or their homes
- Increased incidents of fighting or arguments between students

Student Awareness

Once awareness training has been completed with the faculty and staff, the focus should shift to student awareness.

Just as with the faculty and staff, student awareness should begin with a look at just what constitutes violence–how violence can be nonphysical and physical, can be against property and people, and can be both verbal and social.

Interestingly enough, many students who have endured been "picked on" by other students, or have been teased, or called names, feel vindicated when they realize the hurtful behavior they have suffered does constitute violence and, although adults may have ignored or dismissed the treatment as "kids being kids," it is unacceptable.

Oftentimes, students, far more than the school may realize, see violence on a daily basis, at home and among their friends. Many know which of their peers are involved with drugs or guns and can name several they fear who are capable of serious violence.

In the past, students relied on the school, on teachers, and on administrators for protection while they were in the school building. Now students need to understand they will be part of the school's protection program. Because they greatly outnumber the staff, it stands to reason they will be in more places to see and hear happenings that could threaten the school.

Numerous large-scale acts of violence have been averted, often because students were aware and reported what they knew. Vigilant students can greatly increase the early warning potential for the entire school.

As counselors or members of the task force develop a student awareness program, they should concentrate on presentations and discussions that help students look beyond the more obvious indicators of crime and violence. These sessions should include the following.

An Overview of the School Security Program and the Reasons for its Implementation. Young people, although they know we live in a violent atmosphere, often view security as restrictions, more rules just at a time when they resent the ones they already have. Many teens, because of their age, feel invincible. Violence is something that happens to someone else.

Presenters, therefore, need to level with students and be honest without divulging confidential information or without being overly dramatic about the crime and violence problems the school has experienced. Often, the students' biggest surprise is not what problems are actually going on within the school or perhaps outside the school that involve certain students, but that the staff actually does know the extent of drug and alcohol abuse, theft, and numerous other crimes.

Students, just as staff, must understand security is not just a program on violence or even just a system of policies, procedures, and technology. It is a total approach to keeping everyone safe. The people involvement, students and staff, is by far the most crucial aspect of the system.

Specific sessions on student awareness can be conducted by the task force, certain staff members, or counselors. However, the task force should make certain that if everyone, homeroom teachers, for instance, is to conduct student awareness training, those teachers must convey information that is factually accurate and according to the spirit of the program's intent.

An Explanation of the Mission and Goals of the School's Security Preparations. Again, students should be dealt with honestly. They need to hear, within reason, that certain problems at the school made the staff decide to begin a security program that will help keep them safe. Students should be familiar with the mission statement and should know what the school's goals are concerning security and why the school is moving toward this direction.

A Review of the Various Security Procedures and Technical Applications that are Incorporated into the Security Program. Students need to see how some technical applications work, and they also need to know the "why"–why the procedure or the hardware was added and why it is important.

Security cameras are an example. In the school that has had little security, some students often regard new cameras with great suspicion, a contemporary Orwellian version of "big brother."

The reality is few schools have the inclination and certainly none have the time, and considering the expense, all have far more serious reasons to install video surveillance than to "spy."

More than a few students in schools where camera systems are new have discovered, much to their satisfaction and sometimes relief, that a camera has recorded the theft of their purse or bookbag, caught some act of vandalism against their car, or captured a presence in the school of someone they fear.

Young people, far more so than adults, resist change, even when it is for the better. The familiar is more comforting, and their school should stay just as it is, even if the rest of the world is changing rapidly. Yet new procedures, such as wearing identification badges, can be introduced effectively if they are thoroughly explained.

Once again, presenters should stress that certain crimes and episodes of violence have necessitated these particular procedures. Security is not punitive. It is the school's sincere effort to keep everyone safe.

Expectations from Students in Their Responsibilities to the Security Program. Students need to understand that, just as with other programs in the school and even in the world at large, everybody must be responsible and do their part to keep the school safe. That includes following the rules and abiding by the policies and procedures designed to protect them.

An Overview of the Types of Threats each Student Should Watch for and that Should be Promptly Reported to School Officials. Burned out lights, broken or defective door locks, intruders in the building, or knowledge about some act of violence that may be pending are all crucial threats to the school's security.

Students need to be made aware, first, that they should actually take notice of the broken light and, second, that they should understand it is specifically their responsibility to report it. Better ten students report a dark hallway than no one, because everyone depended on the maintenance crew who is in charge of the entire building and had not yet realized the problem.

Students regularly move through hallways, in and out of the building, and through commons areas or the cafeteria. They are more likely to see a threat or hear about an act of violence that may be pending than a staff member. Students must be told, directly and clearly, to report what they see and what they hear. They must understand that such dangers could be serious even life-threatening.

"Ratting on your friends" ceases to be an issue when one or perhaps many lives could be at stake.

DISCIPLINARY ACTIONS FOR NONCOMPLIANCE WITH SECURITY PROGRAM RULES AND REGULATIONS. Certainly, students should not be threatened with policies and procedures. The objective of security is for everyone to help keep everyone safe. Obviously, the plan works best when presenters start security awareness training by emphasizing the need for cooperation and participation.

Most students are no different than most adults when it comes to logical, reasonable requests for compliance. After all, agreement is a daily part of their school experience.

As certainly as the sun will rise, there will be those few who will refuse to wear their identification badges, who will challenge the school with complaints that badges infringe on their individuality, and who will protest any dress code because they believe it violates their rights to free expression.

The task force must have policies and procedures firmly in place well before students have the opportunity to challenge the system. Schools routinely communicate expectations to students, including defined provisions for violators.

Rules about security must be no different. They must be clear, simple, up front, and fair. They must also be firm.

Educators recognize the difference between misunderstandings and flat out defiance. They also know if some students are permitted to ignore one rule, before long most everybody will be ignoring all rules. At that point, the entire security program will be in jeopardy.

THE ROLE OF TEACHERS AND STAFF IN THE EVENT OF A SHOOTING, BOMBING, OR OTHER SCHOOL CRISIS. Students must be told, specifically and directly, that in the event of a crisis, teachers, not students, are in charge and their instructions must be followed. Students must understand they cannot simply react, nor may they make decisions they may be unprepared to make.

Although presenters must be firm about this directive, they should not be overly concerned when students voice objections or counter with complaints of "what if. . . ." In the event of an actual crisis, students look to the teacher and expect the teacher to take charge.

Few students have any concept of the chaos a shooting or bombing can produce, and although they may bluster about what they will do should an act of violence occur, most will be understandably terrified and thankful that an adult can assume control.

EMERGENCY PROCEDURES TO BE FOLLOWED IN THE EVENT OF A SCHOOL CRISIS ON A MASSIVE BASIS. Students first need a detailed and thorough explanation of all emergency procedures—what they are, how they will operate, and why they are important.

Once all plans are presented, regular and frequent practice sessions should be scheduled to address each crisis and each threat. If the students are to be prepared, they must practice every plan that has been written for crisis response.

AUTHORS' NOTE: Schools that decide to stage an enactment of some violence, a shooting or a bombing, for example, need to proceed with caution. They might even wish to poll parents and students about using such props as fake blood, hostages, victims, and the like.

If any voice even minor objections, they should be notified well in advance of the mock drill. Unless the event is well planned and scrupulously thought out, the school could find itself in the middle of a public relations nightmare and accused of traumatizing students.

Students, as well as staff, need to practice the different scenarios, particularly those in which they would be forced to flee from the school by the quickest and safest route because of an act of violence. Procedures should be reviewed immediately before the drill, and students should be reminded that the objective is to reconvene in another location away from the campus. They must not wander about. This exercise is serious.

Most schools recognize there is a direct but inverse proportion between the number of years students have been in school and the seriousness they give to fire drills. Nor was it so long ago when spring time attracted more harmless bomb threats than robins. But students must understand times are different; such drills must be taken seriously.

USE OF THE STUDENT HOTLINE FOR REPORTING POTENTIAL CRISIS INFORMATION. Students need to know how to use a hotline (if one is available to them or their district) and should know the number.

They should also have the procedures explained to them: that their calls are anonymous, that they can call back to see how the school responded, and that they can call back to provide any additional information.

Certainly, students should be encouraged to report any crime or potential crime or act of violence to their school counselor or an administrator first, but when some students are afraid of retaliation or even feel they will not be believed, the hotline can make the school aware of certain problems it might not have known about otherwise.

Parent Awareness

Parents must not be excluded from the security awareness loop. They can be of tremendous assistance to the school security task force if they are brought in early and advised as to what the school is attempting to do to make the entire campus safe and more secure through a security program.

They can also be a prime motivator by encouraging their child to participate. Conversely, parents can become suspicious and distrustful when school officials fail to inform them about the school's security plans. Security awareness briefings for parents should include the following.

THE NEED FOR THE SCHOOL SECURITY PROGRAM. More than likely, one or several members of the task force who may be designated to make the first presentation to the parents may certainly wish to touch on the national trends of school violence.

Their main focus, however, should be on any local problems or threats the school feels it must be prepared to defend itself against.

Local law enforcement can also help by explaining and detailing any crime conditions that surround the school and have the potential to carry over into the school.

AN EXPLANATION OF THE MISSION AND THE GOALS OF THE PROGRAM. Just as with the staff and students, parents also should know the purpose for the program and what it plans to accomplish.

A REVIEW OF THE VARIOUS SECURITY PROCEDURES AND TECHNICAL APPLICATIONS THAT ARE TO BE ADOPTED. Including the parents and making them familiar with each aspect of the program before certain features are implemented can go a long way to avoid countless problems. When parents learn of the program solely through their child, interpretations can, and will, vary widely.

No doubt some students will refuse to cooperate with certain security procedures. Waiting until they are facing a disciplinary action to introduce the system to the parent is unquestionably bad timing. It may unnecessarily challenge the discipline, the school, and even the security program. In turn, the parents may feel the school has failed to exhibit a sense of fair play.

From the outset parents should be involved in the school's security program as it develops. They can then encourage their child to cooperate. Many problems can be avoided when schools deal forthrightly with parents.

Identification badges are an example. The school that is just starting a badge program may just as well expect a handful of students to object. But when parents realize identification badges also list certain health information about their child, which in the event of an accident or even a sudden illness could be invaluable, they can become the motivator and insist the child wear the badge, rather than the school.

The task force should make certain parents are thoroughly informed of this quick, efficient life-saving potential well before students are required to begin wearing identification badges.

From the standpoint of such vital information, most parents become far more concerned about their child's safety and decidedly less sympathetic to such objections as "an identification badge interferes with my individual freedom" or "a badge labels me."

The same approach holds true for security cameras. Many parents are already familiar with security cameras from their own workplace. They understand theft and threats.

The school can hope their experience with security has been positive, but the task force should not make such assumptions. Instead, it should proceed by explaining the school's program and the "how's" and "why's" it will evolve.

A REVIEW OF THE PROGRESS TIMETABLE THAT OUTLINES WHEN ELEMENTS OF THE SECURITY PROGRAM WILL BE IMPLEMENTED AND AN EXPLANATION OF HOW PARENTS CAN CONTRIBUTE. Parents need to realize the school is working toward a full security program. They need to know just what the school has determined it needs, how much money is involved, and why certain features of the program take priority over others.

Although the task force does not want parents to feel as though they are only being informed so they will contribute or take on some fund-raising activities, parents certainly must be told that protecting their children costs money, and security is not something many districts fund, nor can the school's budget cover much extra.

Many parents are often surprised when they learn their child's school has had so little security to date. Although they may visit their child's school frequently, many parents, even those who have elaborate security arrangements in their own workplace, often fail to notice their children are totally vulnerable to both outside and internal threats. Once they are made aware of the problems, they are often more than willing to help the school financially and significantly fast-forward the timetable.

THE NEED TO PROMPTLY REPORT TO SCHOOL OFFICIALS ANY INFORMATION THEY MAY LEARN FROM THEIR CHILD ABOUT ANY CRIME OR POTENTIAL VIOLENCE THAT MAY AFFECT THE SCHOOL. Most likely more tragedies have been averted than have transpired because a student or parent intervened and informed the school that a mass shooting or bombing was being planned.

Students are often reluctant, and understandably so, to report another student who has a gun in his or her locker or who is showing around plans of the building and talking bombs, or who is threatening to shoot another student or a teacher.

Such scare tactics may be nothing more than teenage boastings, adolescent sounds of being tough. On the other hand, they may indeed be quite real.

Certainly, the school encourages students to report such concerns, but parents should also impress on their children that although the threats may be nothing more than idle talk, they could be real. Waiting to find out could cost many lives.

"SELLING" SCHOOL SECURITY

Philosophically, few, if any, deny the value of a school security program, especially in light of the current trend of violence and other forms of victimization that have become increasingly common in the halls and within the classrooms of our schools.

Few will argue with the position that schools need a proactive, well-planned security program that focuses on suppressing crime and preserving life.

That being the case, why then is the topic of security in our schools met with such skepticism, even hard-core resistance?

Perhaps, since the first tax dollar was earmarked to fund education, the public has voiced its various and always varied opinions about just how schools should be run.

Schools themselves, ever focused on the freedom to think, to speak, and to encourage those same ideas within their students, have envisioned themselves as open, free societies.

Security has been perceived as having too many restrictions. It suggests a repressive environment.

Boards of education disagree about it. Students and parents refuse to tolerate it. And schools themselves believe it is counterproductive to education.

Ironically, however, it is often the very ones who will fall under the protective umbrella of a system of safeguards who are also too busy espousing preconceived negative notions to even consider any contrary opinions.

This, in short, is the exact challenge the school security task force must anticipate and be prepared to counter. The task force may find itself facing some hurdles, but it will encounter none any higher or more daunting than those within its own ranks.

It must become a master of sales, ready to convince even the most resistant staff and students, through a logical, commonsense awareness presentation that a security program within this school is not only necessary but also worthwhile.

The selling points for the school security program should:

1. Convey the need for security to be implemented at this time. Later isn't better than sooner, at least when the issue is school security. Getting the full program in place will take some time.

   Teachers and staff need to know their school is working toward a goal of comprehensive security, but the complete program cannot, nor should it, be implemented overnight. However, concerns and needs have been prioritized. The most crucial head the list and will be attended to immediately.

2. Stress the need for everyone to become involved and provide the necessary information about how each staff member can contribute. Staff members and teachers can be involved anywhere from direct participation, such as volunteering for positions of responsibility during mock drills, to simply being vigilant to violations of policy and procedures, such as noticing students who are not wearing their identification badges and then alerting the administration.

3. The task force, however, needs to remember to play fair with its colleagues. While it is certainly attempting to keep staff and students safe, it needs to outline the new security program and list the staff responsibilities each phase will require before the program actually begins. Such professional consideration goes a long way toward enlisting cooperation.

4. Affirm the fact that the school's security arrangements are not designed to abridge anyone's rights nor are they intended to create a "police state" atmosphere on campus.

5. Describe in detail the various procedural and technical security measures that are to be incorporated.

6. Stress that deterrence and prevention of crime and violence are the objectives of the program rather than just detection and apprehension.

7. Affirm that the program is not targeted toward any particular student group or association.

8. Create the idea that security awareness is an ongoing process of the security program.

9. Emphasize that the security program is not meant in any way to be punitive action taken by school officials but is strictly to serve as a system of defenses designed to protect lives and property by suppressing crime and violence.

10. Highlight that security measures and controls are not meant to be any more restrictive than is necessary for the proper level of protection the school needs.

AWARENESS PROGRAM ENHANCEMENTS

POSTERS. Posters placed in areas highly visible to students, such as in the cafeteria and commons, can communicate antiviolence, crime prevention, and security messages. They can serve as constant reminders that it is everyone's responsibility to keep the school free of crime and violence. Placards that feature McGruff, the Crime Dog, popularized over the years by the National Crime Prevention Council, are a classic example of this means of awareness.

BUMPER STICKERS. Bumper stickers are always a popular way to convey messages. These colorful, decorative creations can depict a particular crime prevention message along with the school's logo.

They may be an effective way to communicate various school security/crime-fighting messages to students, staff, and parents, as well as an excellent means to raise funds for the security program.

NEWSLETTERS, BULLETINS, AND CRIME ALERTS. The school newsletter is another effective way to transmit certain security program updates and crime alerts. It can contain periodic, timely blurbs to keep staff, students, and parents up-to-date about changing crime problems and upgrades to the security program.

STUDENT PROMISE/PLEDGE. Another excellent tool that reaches individual students is the student pledge. Making a personal affirmation to protect the school and support its safeguards helps students understand they are their brothers' and sisters' keepers. They have an obligation to be responsible citizens on the school campus as well as in the larger world.

Contents of the pledge should include statements that ask each student to:

- Make a personal commitment to support the school's safety and security program
- Refrain from participating in any acts of crime or violence against the school, the staff, or other students
- Exercise personal restraint and control their interactions with staff and other students
- Promptly report any crimes or possible acts of violence they learn about to the appropriate staff person
- Report any information about a possible crime or potential violence against the school and agree that anyone who does will not be ostracized, ridiculed, or labeled as a tattle-tale
- Show proper respect to all other students and refrain from bullying, harassing, ridiculing, or in any way hurting the feelings of others
- Show the proper respect to all teachers and other staff members at all times

- Show the proper respect for the property of others and refrain from damaging or vandalizing school property
- Promptly report any suspicious activities or anyone, whom they may not know, who acts suspiciously around the school
- Practice good citizenship at the school and at its activities at all times

An added enhancement is to have faculty, staff, and administrators also sign similar pledges so that students see school security involves everyone and is not just a one-sided proposition.

As a gesture of good faith, the task force could ask students to take the lead in a special secure schools project and, along with input from teachers and even parents, develop their pledge as they believe it should read.

STUDENT GROUPS

For the school's protection program to work effectively, it must involve students, not just as passive, sometimes reluctant observers who have been briefed or who have endured some form of orientation, but as active participants who can furnish useful, meaningful input about the school's safeguards and problems they believe should be addressed.

Most action groups now include teen representatives within communities and within schools. Students sit on planning boards and on councils. After all, they are the ones most directly affected by decisions about schools. Students who believe in a program can have a far greater impact on their peers than can most adults. If the school is to maintain an effective school security program, their help is invaluable.

Students may want to form their own in-house group or club, which can meet during or after the school day, or they may prefer to join a national organization. One such association, with chapters in many schools, is SAVE, Students Against Violence Everywhere (**www.saveusa.org**) whose purpose is to encourage students to interact and explore solutions to the problems and effects of violence.

Whether a school decides to start its own club or prefers to establish a chapter of a nationwide organization such as SAVE, the point is to get students involved and thinking about their school's safety and protection.

SIGNS

Signage is always a valuable aid in the overall scheme of the school's security preparation. Primarily, signs provide warnings to onlookers who may be contemplating some uncooperative or illegal act and instructions to control certain activities of those who are arriving or moving about the site.

Signs can also serve as an awareness factor, a reminder that conveys such information as, "You are entering a safe and secure school zone," or "Premises are protected by video surveillance cameras."

CHEERS AT SPORTING EVENTS AND SCHOOL FUNCTIONS

A novel idea some schools might try is to encourage their cheerleaders to develop a cheer or chant with a message that promotes an awareness of security, a zero tolerance to crime, or a stop violence now message.

STUDENT CONTESTS

Contests in the form of poster designs, essays, etc. with the theme of crime prevention and antiviolence can keep security foremost in everyone's mind. Awards can also be presented each month, each semester, and/or each year to the students who make the most valuable contribution to school's security program.

QUESTIONNAIRES FOR STAFF, STUDENTS, AND PARENTS

Answers to questionnaires from those who will be under the school's umbrella of protection are an excellent source of feedback for the task force and can provide a wealth of valuable data about any ongoing problems or trouble that may be just developing. They can also serve as a basis for fine tuning the security program and especially tailoring it to the respective school.

Not only can the answers to the questions enlighten the task force and provide early warning indications about potential threats, but properly drafted questions can also alert the respondents to certain danger points or issues that signal pending harm. So warned, everyone can be more attentive to these particular areas.

Answers from parent questionnaires can often provide additional insight about the school's safety, especially when they are compared with those from the students. Students may be expressing certain concerns about security at home but are either afraid or have not had the opportunity to inform school officials.

When responses from parents underscore certain specific concerns that students have also expressed, the task force can be alerted to an existing security problem that may have been overlooked or one that is in the making.

Chapter 7

USING PROTECTION PERSONNEL

AS A RESPONSE to increasing violence, many schools have begun to use protection personnel as a part of their total security program. These individuals may be law enforcement officers, uniformed security personnel, or a combination of both.

Security guards in the bank, at the mall, and at the airport provide us with a comforting presence. We feel assured that no one will steal our money, our wallet, or our safe trip as long as an armed guard watches over us. Introducing security persons into the school, however, is quite another matter.

Security personnel in a school present some unique considerations for administrators that private companies, businesses, and even public facilities do not necessarily face.

Foremost perhaps is the image. Although the public expects its merchandise and its money to be protected, even demands security guards in certain public and private facilities, those same individuals who are also parents, students, and even educators often believe that police officers or security officers do not belong in a school as part of its security program.

They may agree that hardware, security cameras, badge identification, and metal detectors are necessary protection, but they draw the line at uniformed guards.

There is also the image problem. School districts and principals worry that guards in a school will confirm everyone's suspicions. Schools are indeed unsafe, maybe even under siege.

Others feel that just the presence of protection hardware in a school is enough of an adjustment. Security personnel will jeopardize the free and open spirit of education.

They also argue that uniformed protection represents an attitude from the administration that says to the students, "We don't trust you." Opponents are convinced that students will resent such "big brother" authority.

TYPES OF SCHOOL PROTECTION PERSONNEL

In the past, teachers and administrators could effectively keep their own school safe. They watched their students and informally "policed" their own building until drugs, gangs, and rampage shootings overwhelmed and resisted even their best intervention strategies. Now, for many schools, uniformed protection personnel have become more than a consideration. It has become a reality. Formal school protection personnel largely falls into three categories:

The School Resource Officer

During the 1990s, when American Law enforcement began to move toward community-oriented policing, local police agencies assigned one of their sworn law enforcement officers to junior highs, middle schools, and high schools within the community.

The school resource officer (SRO) was created, and the role has become twofold: to provide a police presence, but also to interact and to provide a positive image. A more "officer-friendly" figure is the SRO's primary role.

SROs usually have lunch with students, learn their names, listen, talk with them on a one-to-one basis, even help them with some problems. Students have an opportunity to learn about the true role and duties of the police and to see beyond the hard, insensitive stereotype that is often used to characterize the police.

School resource officers usually serve within their own "bailiwicks," or jurisdictions, and have full police powers within the school. Aside from their presence and their social interactions, they may also conduct classes on such topics as substance abuse, violence, and even why students should not join a gang.

Resident Police Officer

Some schools provide a house or mobile home that is located on school property for a law enforcement officer. The idea is that the presence of an officer who actually lives on the premises will discourage burglars, vandals, and groups of rowdy partyers.

As one component of the school's total protection, this arrangement can have its advantages. However, it should not constitute the school's entire plan. It leaves far too much security to chance.

The school is not the officer's duty station, nor does the officer necessarily patrol the area. The officer's time at the site is comparable to the hours any working person spends at home. Even during the officer's off-duty hours, he or she must attend to the personal business of daily living. Shopping, errands, emergencies, even vacations, or any number of tasks may take the officer away from the site.

Because schools are often victimized at night, over a weekend, or during a holiday, they may believe that the on-site officer can provide adequate protection during these periods. Certainly, a law enforcement presence may discourage some criminals or pranksters.

However, serious thieves, or anyone, even a casual observer for that matter, can chart the officer's presence if by no other means than whether the officer's vehicle is present or absent. Nor will it take long for anyone who is interested to learn the officer's work schedule and personal routine.

Off-Duty Police Officers

The third form of protection personnel that may be selected for the campus is off-duty law enforcement officers. Just as with the school resource officer, these individuals are sworn police officers. However, their mission is somewhat different.

Their involvement with school security is more from the standpoint of extra employment. Although this additional source of personal income for the officers does not mean they are any less committed to protecting the school, it does indicate that this role is not their primary assignment within their law enforcement agency.

These officers are recognized, valid law enforcement members. However, the task force should still thoroughly scrutinize those who will work in the school. Even among police officers, some are more suited than others to work with young people.

Security Personnel

Some schools may prefer to use security personnel rather than police officers. Others may simply have no choice, particularly in smaller communities. In areas where the police department is small, a school resource officer may simply be unavailable. The agency may already be understaffed and unable to spare several officers or even one to a school.

Then there is the image factor. Some schools may not want the harder presence that a gun, a baton, handcuffs, and other police gear convey.

Before the task force rules out the police or the SRO, however, it needs to be aware of certain aspects concerning the use of security guards. First and foremost is that security guards are not police officers. They possess no powers of arrest and search and seizure, which are characteristics of the police officer's role.

Security officers primarily provide a visible symbol of authority by their uniform. They also furnish an extra vigilant set of eyes and ears and can hopefully detect and deter a problem before it reaches harmful proportions.

Uniformed private security personnel are classified into two particular groups. The first is *proprietary* or in-house. These security forces are employed by the school or the school system. They are, in fact, school employees who receive a salary and benefits just as all other school employees.

The benefit with proprietary employees is that security officers are members of the system and can be arbitrarily selected to serve in that capacity. However, there are numerous disadvantages.

For instance, any security officer who proves to be unsuitable to work in schools may be difficult to terminate because of certain job protection measures. Benefits, such as health care, overtime, and vacation pay, which usually accompany any basic employment package, can make an in-house security staff expensive to maintain. Prospective guards must be tested and cleared through extensive background checks. Those who are hired must be trained and furnished with uniforms and equipment.

The second form of security personnel that can be used in schools is the *contract* security force. Under this arrangement, the school or school system enters into a contract with a private security service, which offers uniformed guards for hire.

There are several advantages to the contract service. First is financial. All expenses of the interviewing and hiring process are borne by the independent contractor. Second, school officials can simply call the security company if a problem or a question arises about the assigned officer's performance.

The company, not the school, can quickly and easily replace that officer. If a situation does occur that necessitates additional security personnel, the school can contact the contractor and request additional officers.

If the task force is considering using security personnel, it should review both forms of security and keep the following information in mind as it determines which method best fits its school's needs.

Backgrounds and Suitability

Heading the task force's list of responsibilities for hiring security personnel must be a suitable and extensive background investigation of all prospective officers. Checks must be national and local and should begin with a nationwide criminal history review, which is currently referred to as a

"Triple-I" check.

Far too often, employers believe that examining an individual's local background will reveal a criminal history in another state. Not only is this assumption erroneous, but, in a school, it can be tragic.

Criminals can be particularly transient and are quite aware that there is currently no nationwide system that tracks their crimes. Child molesters and sexual predators can and often do obtain employment in daycare centers, childrens' community organizations, and even schools.

It is the task force's responsibility, and their's particularly, to see that the security firm investigates any prospective officers who will come into the school. The task force must not assume that the agency routinely runs such extensive checks on all its employees.

The security firm should also be directed to investigate the driving and the credit history of each officer who will work in the school. A driving record can reveal past problems with drugs, alcohol, and driving under the influence. A credit bureau report may show certain financial or business problems that can indicate a troubled or unstable individual.

Again, even if the agency does not generally run these checks, the task force must see that it is done primarily so that the school will know, in advance, the type, caliber, and character of those individuals who will work with students. The task force will also have the time to eliminate anyone with a questionable or undesirable background.

The agency must agree to permit the task force to see officers' records and confirm that prospective officers are acceptable before they are selected to work in the school.

The agency should also be directed to interview, test the prospective officers for drugs, and assess their personal attitudes and personalities. Certain temperaments and personal habits make some individuals unable, as well as unsuitable, to work with children and young people.

APPEARANCE AND ATTIRE

The appearance of protection personnel, whether the officers are private security or public law enforcement, will determine just how they are to be perceived and received by staff and students and ultimately how well they can relate to those they will serve and protect.

It is not a coincidence, in most cases, that police uniforms and security officers' uniforms look very similar. Security companies that began their operations decades ago purposely capitalized on the law enforcement appearance as a way to convey that an establishment was protected by a presence who could and would deter and stop crime. The appearance was also because many security guards were retired police officers who were used to such uniforms.

Modern-day police uniforms are functional. Each officer wears a gun belt that holds the sidearm holster, a baton, handcuffs, and a variety of other necessary gear. The attire is standard and largely inflexible because of the dictates of their job.

However, some schools may feel that the standard police look, whether it is worn by a sworn officer or a security officer, is simply too harsh for a school atmosphere. The task force may want to look at an alternative dress code for its security personnel, one that is formal and professional but also softer.

Many security officers often dress in a conservative blazer, slacks, shirt, and a tie that is selected by the company. The breast pocket on the coat may bear the security company's emblem and the individual officer's identification badge. A carrier for a radio and any other required equipment can be attached to the officer's belt.

Some schools, where the staff or students may be uneasy around a firearm, may even prefer that police officers who work security duties at the school adopt this attire. That way the blazer can conveniently conceal the firearm, which would otherwise be openly displayed.

TRAINING AND ORIENTATION

After background checks, training and orienting all protection personnel is the next most crucial step. Schools have their own unique atmosphere. Some are tighter with stricter discipline for violating the rules. Others are more flexible, more informal, even lax about certain violations and punishments.

All personnel must receive a basic orientation that prepares them for their duties, particularly in the case of security officers who are provided by a private contractor. Minimum training for an officer should include the following.

- Orientation to the security function
- Duties of a security officer
- Report writing and notetaking
- First aid/CPR (Cardiopulmonary resuscitation)
- Patrolling
- Emergency procedures
- Use of force/defensive tactics
- Bomb threats
- Fire-response procedures

- School-related crimes and security threats
- Law enforcement liaison
- Public relations
- Crime scene protection
- Preliminary investigation
- Uniform and equipment use
- Appearance and uniform requirements
- Interviewing
- Security procedures
- Communications procedures

Once the task force feels confident that all security personnel have had basic instruction in the various aspects of security functions, it should provide follow-up training in specific duties and functions that are relevant to the school setting, including the following.

- Confrontation management
- Operation of security equipment, i.e., metal detectors, CCTV cameras, access control
- Shooting and bombing incidents
- Problem identification and indicators
- Handling recovered firearms
- Locker inspection procedures
- Student and staff interactions
- Hostage situations
- Emergency communications procedures

In the case of proprietary security officers, the school or school system should offer training or arrange for it to be provided.

If the school plans to use security services from an outside company, then the task force should stipulate that the officers must receive sufficient training that is suitable for the job.

ARMED PROTECTION PERSONNEL

It is the position of the authors that firearms have no place in any school. Even those that security personnel may carry can present too many ancillary problems. However, this decision must ultimately be left in the hands of the school system, its administrators, and the political structure.

With proprietary and contract security services, the issue is not a problem. The school simply does not permit security personnel to carry firearms. With law enforcement, the situation may be quite different.

Most agencies require all sworn personnel to be armed when they are working in any enforcement capacity. Even though officers may be employed by the school in an off-duty status, the agency's rules and regulations will still, most likely, supercede the school's wishes. In that case, the school must decide whether it will make an exception or an allowance about its policy of firearms on the campus.

Chapter 8

THE HIGH COST OF LOW SECURITY

SCHOOLS HAVE BECOME the newest frontier for lawsuits. Allegations from parents, students, even communities often make headlines when they charge that rules and regulations within schools are unfair or that security programs, especially with their accompanying policies and procedures, are too restrictive. Others allege just the opposite—that the school's security is inadequate.

For a number of years, inadequate security has been a growing area for legal actions from injured and affected plaintiffs. Attorneys have found the issues of a *lack of security* or *improper security* to a viable basis to compensate a victim for damages.

One of the early, most famous cases of security-related liability was *Garailli v. Howard Johnson's Motor Lodges, Inc.,* more popularly known as the "Connie Francis Case."

The issue was that the Howard Johnson's, where Ms. Francis was staying, had inadequate security. Faulty doorlocks had permitted an assailant to enter the entertainer's room and assault her. Ms. Francis won her suit and received a substantial reward.

Since this case, many other lawsuits involving some aspect of protection, or the lack of it, have been filed in courts all across the country. Not only does it appear the trend will continue, but that it will grow, particularly because people and organizations, who should have known, should have been prepared, are consistently unwilling to recognize the duty they have toward those who work, play, or just visit their facility.

Continuing to ignore how important it is to protect people and places that are under someone else's control promises a future of potential, ongoing security-related litigation.

Authors' note: The authors are not attorneys, nor do they practice law. However, because much that transpires today has legal ramifications, the following information is provided as food for thought regarding the topic of security. It is highly recommended that in all cases involving legal questions about security issues, schools consult their school board's attorney or other appropriate legal counsel.

Schools have also become the newest frontiers for violent crime primarily because they have been regarded as "soft targets." Although most of our nation never suspected that such tragic episodes could occur within our classrooms and on our campuses, perpetrators are quick to spot such conditions when they can destroy others. Obviously no bomb wielding, gun-toting adolescent has burst into a police department or military installation and assaulted them.

Violent teens have turned to the source of their hatred, or at least where they believe it lies–the school and its people. Perhaps more than anyone, frustrated, angry, depressed adolescents know the school is unprotected and vulnerable to virtually any form of violence, particularly the element of surprise. With nothing in place to stop them, short of police intervention, which usually requires a certain response time, a disturbed gunman can strike with relative ease to inflict maximum harm.

It may take years for America to see the conclusion to the tragedies in Littleton, Colorado, Paducah, Kentucky, Pearl, Mississippi, and the lesser known, less publicized acts of school violence. Until that time, schools must understand their own potential for lawsuits. Charges of inadequate or nonexistent security can not only cost a school system large sums of money but can also destroy the careers of long-standing, highly regarded educators.

It is, therefore, imperative that school administrators clearly understand that the potential for such liability can exist within their own school.

However, they can lessen such legal repercussions. Currently, avoiding security-related liability is far from a clear-cut path, at least so far, because many "gray areas" have yet to be defined by the courts. Even in the few cases that have established a standard in one particular state, the decision may not apply in another state, because lower court decisions often vary from state to state, as do decisions between the levels of judicial systems, such as from state court to federal court.

Until certain precedents are established that determine and define just what constitutes adequate security, schools have few guidelines.

Court decisions are based on the conduct, the conditions, and the activities of the litigants. In security cases, reasonable actions and preparations by the organization and by those in charge are reviewed. If the court determines that those who have been harmed, as a result of a particular event, were denied a suitable level of protection, the defendant can be held liable. If, however, adequate arrangements were in place, the defendant is apt to be viewed more favorably, even though a tragic event did occur.

For a school administrator or anyone in the management role who is responsible for an organization, security-related liability takes on a variety of consequences. For the organization that is found liable and is judged negligent because its lack of security cost others their lives or subjected them to injury, the foremost problem is undoubtedly the injury or loss of life that precipitated the lawsuit. Morally, it is a heavy judgment.

Professionally, it can ruin its people and damage the organization. Schools are not buildings. They are people. They are principals, teachers, counselors, custodians, cooks, nurses, and many others—people who can only do their job with children, and do it well, if they have the public's trust. Once a reputation is tarnished, whether it is the image of a single individual or that of the entire faculty and staff, the school stands to lose the public's confidence. It sacrifices its credibility. Parents and the community doubt, maybe even totally discount, its message of "trust us because we have your childrens' best interests at heart."

Last, such judgments can be extremely expensive. The slightest injury can translate into a significant judgment that results in possible punitive and compensatory damages levied against the school, the system, and those in decision-making roles who should have known better, who should have ordered protection, but, for whatever reason, did not.

School administrators would do well to heed the lessons private industry has learned about loss and inadequate security.

ISSUES FOR CONCERN

Although legal precedents do not yet provide the necessary guidance for a liability-free security program, officials should consider certain concepts as their school develops its security program. The following three factors, which may play a crucial role in a case should it ever go to court, will determine whether the school exhibited responsibility by providing adequate protection for its people.

The first legal issue for concern is *foreseeability*. This is the prior conditions or circumstances that permitted threats and vulnerabilities to manifest themselves to the extent that a person or persons should have realized a security problem existed and then should have implemented the necessary actions that would have corrected this difficulty before it was allowed to create harm.

Simply put, there were known hazards or events that should have been recognized as threats by those who had the decision-making authority to change the situation and make it safer.

Although foreseeability can arise from one incident, it is generally based on a pattern of activity where there has been obvious or demonstrated victimization and where the lack of attention to this series of crimes has permitted the threat to persist and to worsen.

For instance, a student or a staff member who is attacked could allege the foreseeability issue, if, in the past, perpetrators had entered the school unchecked and even wandered freely, but administrators did nothing substantial to stop the intruders. On the basis of past criminal activities, those in charge should have realized the danger and acted to prevent unauthorized individuals from coming into the school.

Foreseeability can also involve the total atmosphere of the school, one where administrators permitted a virtual plethora of crimes, such as thefts, assaults, and the like, to continue but did nothing to reduce the incidents. Under this charge, administrators' motivations, the reasons why they failed to act, could also be targeted.

In the aftermath of a tragedy, no school administration wants to acknowledge that it failed to remedy a dangerous situation, both correctly and permanently, because it lacked the knowledge or because it felt a security program was too restrictive.

Nor does it want to admit the most damaging of all—that implementing a security program that might have challenged the local school board, or that parents might have resisted, or that students might have protested was simply too much trouble.

In other words, the administration had been apathetic. Or because of possible criticism, it chose to ignore the safety and well-being of its staff and students.

Foreseeability, however, given the nationwide alarm and current atmosphere of school violence, may extend beyond the localized conditions of a particular school. Schools have witnessed the problems. They have seen the injuries and the deaths, and they should realize they must implement good protection to counter the various threats that can target their staff, their students, and their premises.

Common sense dictates that past events of school shootings, bombings, and other violence should have put schools on notice, and those that have no protective measures in place must do so, and do so immediately. Seeing what has happened, there is virtually no excuse for schools to do otherwise.

Another issue in school liability is *negligence*. This is the action that a reasonable, prudent person would or would not do in a similar situation. In terms of school security, negligence is a charge that administrators failed to take the appropriate actions that would have effectively eliminated a threat that could have eventually caused harm.

Negligence targets the inaction or wrong action of those in responsible positions. It charges that those who should have paid attention to threats either failed in that responsibility, or they should have taken appropriate steps to correct a problem that was developing or was already a clear and present danger, but did not.

The legal question with negligence is first, "What was the threat?" and second, "What was done about it?" If the answer to the second is nothing, then the issue becomes, "Why was nothing done?" Given that school officials knew about this obvious danger, "What was their reason for no action?"

The third legal issue that concerned administrators should understand is *good faith*. Although schools cannot anticipate or even implement a security program that addresses every specific, minute threat that may arise, they can and must, on the basis of all they knew before the event, exercise good faith, primarily by doing everything possible to see the school is a safe place.

Good faith demonstrates fair play and an intent to try to do everything reasonable to provide a suitable atmosphere of protection for the school environment. It shows that officials made every effort and sincerely attempted to protect their school and were not remiss in their responsibility.

Good faith should also clearly indicate that the school's security was based on a commitment to discover any possible threats to the facility and its people and determine what measures would properly protect them. It must also show that school officials sought to have the necessary security applications in place and that the security program was not just some token arrangement that amounted to little more than a collection of uncoordinated, inefficient measures.

Such a program may give the appearance of good security, but under judicial scrutiny, it may be quickly revealed that it was little more than a sham and actually had little effect.

Although these questions are just a few of the issues a school could face, officials who can show a serious effort to achieve adequate school safeguards may avoid the harsh reality of financial judgments and legal fees should a lawsuit arise and a case go to court.

PITFALLS AND TRIPWIRES

The security program must perform numerous functions if it is to effectively protect the school, but when certain conditions change, so must the school's security. However, there are some constants and some pitfalls and tripwires that school administrators must observe if they hope to avoid legal repercussions. These include the following.

FAILURE TO IMPLEMENT A COMPREHENSIVE SECURITY PROGRAM. All too often administrators fall victim to apparent quick-fix solutions. Although popular measures such as metal detectors and "hotlines" may pass for security, they may, in reality, be little more than an ill-conceived panacea.

Genuine security requires thought and in-depth planning. If the program is to be fully developed and comprehensive, it must bring its people, its procedures, and its technology together and keep the total unit running smoothly. The school can only reach this level of protection if it first begins with a thorough security survey.

Once the school determines just what threats and vulnerabilities it actually faces, then it can adopt the necessary measures to protect itself. Calling a single measure, or even several, a security program, for reasons that are often no better than "something is better than nothing" is a hazardous approach. Gaps may result. If people are exposed to danger, the school could face a legal disaster.

FAILURE TO KEEP STAFF PERSONNEL AWARE OF SCHOOL SAFETY AND SECURITY RESPONSIBILITIES. Many states have enacted laws that place certain responsibilities for a safe school atmosphere not only on schools boards and administrators but directly on local teachers and staff. Administrators must realize it is their direct responsibility to keep teachers and staff informed.

In turn, teachers and staff must make it clear to their administrators that they must be continually updated and made fully aware of any such legal mandates, many of which, because of continuing lawsuits, may change frequently. All persons, who have been cited by law by virtue of their position, must remain fully informed at all times of their responsibilities to safeguard students.

FAILURE TO DOCUMENT ALL SECURITY POLICY AND PROCEDURES IN WRITTEN FORMAT. Not only is it important to have security procedures in place, but they must also be thoroughly and clearly explained in written form. Having specific methods recorded and spelled out as to how problems should be handled provides additional structure for the security program. It lessens the chances that procedures will be circumvented, misunderstood, or altered without authorized change.

Written procedures also provide school attorneys with tangible evidence that can be presented to the court. Such documentation will reinforce the school's position that it did have a viable protection program in place and that the program was established on the proper principles for adequate safety as evidenced by its depth and its detail.

FAILURE TO INFORM ALL PERSONS CONCERNED ABOUT THE PARTICULARS OF THE SECURITY PROGRAM. All staff and students must be fully advised about the various aspects of the security program, first, because of the obvious–informed individuals are more cooperative individuals. Second, when everyone knows the parameters of the program, they will be less likely to disobey security procedures and less resentful when they are held accountable for any violations.

Students and staff appreciate their school when it is concerned about their safety. When they understand, in advance, what they must do to comply, as well as why, most are more than willing to cooperate.

Forcing new security arrangements, even on the ones who will directly benefit from it, builds resentment. The resistance may eventually weaken the overall program. However, by taking the time and effort to inform staff and students, the school is in effect saying it has a genuine interest in their safety and, in turn, is asking for their direct involvement by making them stakeholders in their own protection.

By the same token, imposing disciplinary actions on individuals who have not been adequately informed can cause misunderstandings, even flagrant violations. Such attitudes can eventually destroy the program to say nothing of the legal repercussions that may result for the school and its decision makers.

RECKLESS USE OF "HOTLINE" INFORMATION. Hotlines have been heralded as a major solution to warn the school about a pending act of violence. No doubt, their use has merit, but schools must also recognize that the information that the callers provide can be easily, even unknowingly abused. Kids play pranks. It's natural, expected as the rain. But when they are offered a number, a way to phone in information and still remain anonymous, the temptation to play a joke on another student may be too good an opportunity to pass up.

School officials must implement a system that carefully screens the information they receive. Then they should proceed cautiously if they decide to use this information to confront a student who has been named or accused of contemplating or planning some act of violence against the school.

At all costs, schools do not want to find themselves undertaking a witch-hunt, whether perceived or real. Administrators must be proactive. They must always attempt to deter violence in their school, but they must also use such information carefully, as only part of their investigation.

What if the information has been a trick, just a "harmless prank?" Accusing a student of planning or plotting some act of violence solely on the basis of hotline information will, at the least, lessen the administrator's credibility. It may also be interpreted as violating the student's legal rights. More than likely, the student and the parents may not be so understanding, and could, in fact, hold the school liable for false accusations, for numerous other charges, and even for psychological damages.

FAILURE TO IMPLEMENT TIMELY SECURITY PROGRAM UPGRADES. Because threats and crime problems change, school officials must be vigilant, or they may see what was once a strong security program develop serious breaches and expose the campus to crime and violence.

FAILURE TO RECEIVE APPROVAL FROM THE SUPERINTENDENT'S OFFICE REGARDING A SCHOOL'S SECURITY PROGRAMS. Once the school determines what particular security arrangements it needs, the task force should have its entire program reviewed and approved by the superintendent or his or her representatives. Upper management levels must be informed about the programs their schools are implementing.

Once higher level officials are fully aware of what is in place at the school, approving or modifying the arrangements becomes their responsibility. This step makes it their call about whether security is either too restrictive or too lax, a position they should embrace, because ultimately it would be the district that would be held liable for any lawsuits about security.

Second, the school is assured that its security plan is appropriate, neither discriminatory nor inconsistent with the overall security practices that have been approved for all schools within that jurisdiction.

SEARCHES OF STUDENTS—BOOK BAGS, LOCKERS, PERSONAL VEHICLES, ETC. Do schools have the authority to search students and their property? The issue is sensitive and has been a long-standing legal question. Court rulings have given schools the authority, taken it away, only to return it again. Different school jurisdictions around the country also have their own interpretations. No doubt, the subject will be one that will continue to change.

Drugs, then guns, in the schools made the controversy even more heated. The issue now is often a question of the individual's rights, and "Are such searches an infringement?" As schools witness more episodes of violence, teachers and staff are told to scrutinize students more carefully. Pay close attention to their attitudes, their book bags, their clothing. Try to detect problems and head them off before someone is hurt.

Such heightened awareness combined with metal detectors, searches by police or drug dogs, and cameras, to name only a few areas, has created issues that only the courts can eventually resolve.

For now and for the school officials who must deal with the situation, the best approach for them is to adopt search and seizure practices that apply both fairly and evenly to all students, carefully and thoroughly advise all staff and students about these intrusive procedures, and establish and demonstrate an atmosphere of "fair play."

However, even fair play does not lessen an administrator's duty to change the school's policy and procedures as legalities change. More and more students are challenging the schools. In what appears almost a daily litany, they cite the Fourth Amendment to the Constitution, demanding everything from exemptions, to exclusive protection, to new definitions of their rights.

To avoid or minimize the possibility that the school may violate a student's rights, administrators must remain alert and in contact with the school board's attorney about any such changes.

Any policies and procedures that are affected must be updated immediately. Even in the course of maintaining a safe atmosphere, schools cannot trample a student's rights.

LACK OF INTERVENTION PROCEDURES DESIGNED TO DETECT AND RESPOND TO THE WARNING SIGNALS FOR SCHOOL VIOLENCE. By law, schools must have warning bells for fire drills and evacuation procedures. Yet few have any measures in place to detect, intervene, or evacuate in the event of a crisis other than a fire.

Teachers who have successfully dissuaded a student with a gun from shooting himself or his classmates, testify it was their crisis intervention training that saved them and their students from harm. Without it, they have said, they would not have known what to say or what to do.

But, despite their assurance that the training no doubt saved countless lives, few faculty and staffs have had such instruction. Likewise with emergency evacuations. By law, all schools have a standard fire bell or warning system but using that same bell or code for another scenario could invite tragedy. During the 1998 school shooting incident at Pearl, Mississippi, the fire bell was pulled for the very purpose of evacuating students from the building and sending them directly into the shooters' gunsights.

If the school has reason to suspect a shooter is within the building, or if the school has been alerted to a bomb threat, sounding the traditional fire bell may send fleeing staff and students directly into harm's way. Schools should develop a signaling system code for emergency evacuations other than just for fire.

One type of crisis alert should warn everyone within the building to lock their doors from the outside, to shelter-in-place, and to remain in the building until instructed to do otherwise.

Schools must also designate a safe facility, away from the school building. If staff and students must run beyond the school grounds because of a shooting or a bomb, they need a designated shelter where they can reassemble.

Everyone must be familiar with the location of this off-campus site and the procedures that would automatically begin to restore order, determine who is present, and try to account for those who may still be within the school building.

FAILURE OF THE SCHOOL SYSTEM TO ALLOCATE THE NECESSARY PROFESSIONAL DEVELOPMENT TRAINING TO TEACHERS, COUNSELORS, AND ALL AFFECTED STAFF THAT PERTAINS TO THEIR ROLE IN THE SECURITY PROGRAM AND TO CRISIS INTERVENTION. The most crucial part of any security program is its early warning system. At that point, containing or avoiding harm is still possible. Who is in a better position to detect such a problem within a school than those on the front line, the teachers and counselors.

Yet these professionals, the ones in the trenches know, although it may seem incomprehensible to the general public, they are often the most overlooked and the least informed.

Seminars, conferences, and workshops about school violence and security issues routinely address administrators and public officials, but far too often, the information flow stops there. Not only are teachers and staffs excluded from many initial presentations, they are also often denied vital in-service training that could help them cope with a crime or take charge during a sudden act of violence. Such instruction is far too often a low priority item within their school system.

When a teacher is trained in confrontation management and knows how to cope with an armed student who bursts into a classroom and threatens to shoot, such knowledge could make a life-and-death difference. It could be the exact tactics that persuade the gunman to turn over his weapon. On the other hand, no training or inadequate instruction could be the very catalyst that provokes him into carrying out his plan.

An essential part of any security program must include training and frequent updates in crisis intervention, emergency procedures, and confrontation management for all teachers and staff.

LIABILITY FATALISM

Many organizations in the private sector continue to regard an adequate security program as an enigma, especially when it comes to liability. Certainly there are few precedents to dictate exactly what should be done, and considering the current atmosphere that encourages attorneys and plaintiffs to sue organizations for even the slightest, most ridiculous complaints, fatalism, although it may be understandable, is more like a game of Russian roulette. The issue for school security readiness should be based not only on *if* a tragedy should happen, but *when*.

However, many are aware they cannot foresee every possibility for violence and remain convinced that no matter what they do, they will still be held accountable. Such schools worsen an already bad situation by doing nothing.

Others calculate their odds. Beyond locks and lighting, they wait. If an incident does happen and the expected lawsuit occurs, they will have a court ruling to define just what security they need. The result of such logic has been unfortunate but predictable—courts are faulting businesses for negligence, for failing to address security matters properly, and awarding victims of crime and violence in the workplace substantial monetary sums.

In light of the current trend of school violence, administrators cannot afford to take such a wait-and-see approach. The potential for tragedy is simply too great. Schools must undertake a viable security program for their campus as if many lives depend on it. They do.

Chapter 9

MAINTAINING THE
SCHOOL SECURITY PROGRAM

T HERE IS A SAYING in security: "Security is like humility. Just when you think you have it, you don't!" Truer words were never spoken about the processes and applications of security.

All too often an organization will decide it wants a formal security program to protect its assets. It goes through all the necessary motions: it conducts a survey to determine the threats and vulnerabilities it confronts, it determines just what protection applications it needs to counter these problems, it commits to the expense of purchasing equipment or other security services to make the program a reality, and it usually holds some sort of formal kickoff to announce the security program is here and here to stay.

Ironically, it is at this point that a healthy and effective program can fail. Organizations often believe once they arrive at this point, they have achieved their desired level of protection. They have accomplished all that is necessary to do. Actually, nothing could be further from the truth.

Maintaining the school's security program is one of the coordinator's most important functions. The school has neither the time nor the expense to go through all the motions to establish a program and then implement it, only to ignore or minimize the maintenance that will ultimately jeopardize a once-effective program.

It must not assume the program will simply continue to function, unaided, at optimum levels. Even the best equipment can malfunction, the most comprehensive procedures can become outdated or unworkable, and the most informed people can become complacent. In addition, because many ongoing activities within the school will, no doubt, be associated with security, maintenance must be an integral part of the school's overall system of safeguards.

Often the term maintenance is used to identify equipment failure and/or repair, but, in the context of this chapter, maintenance will not refer solely to equipment, equipment repairs, or replacement but rather to all areas within the entire security program that require special attention.

The security maintenance process is somewhat analogous to the concept

132

of the spinning plates. Consider the familiar stage routine. The performer gets a series of plates spinning, one at a time, each atop an upright stick. Before long, one after the other begins to slow in its rotation. Periodically, the entertainer touches one plate, then another, giving them all another spin to keep them true and aloft.

Similarly, those who are responsible for program maintenance must periodically check each component of the program and administer some necessary momentum here or perhaps a slight adjustment there.

To get the maintenance component started in its protection program, the school should assign this responsibility to an individual who will supervise these timely activities. This person should have the authority to oversee and direct the many functions that are necessary and should report directly to the school's security coordinator.

For a security program to be effective, it must also be comprehensive. Not only must every phase or component of the program work independently, but each must also function correctly and easily in tandem with the other parts of the program. Periodically, the individual in charge of maintenance should review the program to see it is running smoothly. The following four criteria should be considered.

- Is this particular security component functioning as it was originally intended?
- Does this particular component continue to function properly in conjunction with the various other security components? Do all of them together continue to provide sufficient in-depth protection?
- Does this particular security component need upgrading because new threats or conditions have weakened its original capability to provide adequate protection?
- Has the maintenance review uncovered new or developing areas of threats or vulnerabilities that need to be addressed?

Essentially, each of the preceding four points apply to all aspects of the school's comprehensive security program, which has been previously summarized by the three P's of protection: the people component, the physical security measures, and the procedures element.

The maintenance person would also be responsible for seeing the following tasks were completed:

1. Review the security awareness training program to insure that its message is current and it adequately acquaints and refreshes students, faculty, and staff regarding:
    - The mission of the school's security program. Does it need to be adjusted or changed?
    - The structure and functions of the security program.
    - A detailed justification and rationalization of those security mea-

sures that seem to intrude on or restrict peoples' movements and
activities while on the campus.

- An explanation of the role, the involvement, and the responsibilities that students, staff, and faculty have in the school's protection activities.
- An in-service training program for any security personnel used on campus, to update their functions, role, interactions with students and staff, and to apprise them of any new threats that have developed along with any other related information about the school's protection.

2. Complete inspection of all physical security, technical, and hardware applications, which include, but are not limited to:
   - Locking devices
   - Closed-circuit television cameras and components
   - Access control equipment
   - Lighting
   - Metal detectors
   - Signage
   - Communications systems
   - Fencing, barriers, doors, and windows
   - Landscaping and the placement of shrubbery, etc.
   - Emergency equipment

3. Review all procedures that are used to protect the school and include:
   - Entry and movement controls
   - Parking controls
   - School property marking and identification system
   - Key control procedures
   - Badge identification procedures
   - Security officer procedures
   - Locker inspection procedures
   - Police and other emergency services recall procedures
   - Drug dogs and their use
   - Emergency/crisis response procedures
   - Employee screening
   - Security reporting procedures
   - Confrontation management procedures
   - School "hotline" procedures

If maintenance is to be effective, it must be conducted regularly, and the results should be completely documented. The findings for each component should be reviewed carefully and fully noted so they can serve as a basis for making future decisions about improvements or necessary upgrades.

This reporting phase also helps the school remain disciplined about maintaining its system of regular checks which are designed to keep the program effective and efficient.

Part 2

WHEN RAMPAGE VIOLENCE STRIKES: INTERCEPTION AND RESPONSE

U ntil now, *Essential Strategies for School Security* has discussed a broad array of security measures and has applied their formulas to the school setting. Many of these applications and procedures are standard use in business, industry, and government. Others are innovations that have been designed with the unique characteristics of a school in mind. The overall goal has been to prevent and deter the various forms of crime and violence that might threaten a school, its students, and its staff.

The reality is, few things in life are absolutely foolproof. Likewise with security. Were it otherwise, crime would not be a problem. It would be a fossil relegated to the past.

But for every effort to devise better locks, alarms, or electronic surveillance equipment, somewhere, someone is nearly as quickly figuring out a counter-effort that will circumvent it. In turn, security professionals redesign and restructure. Law enforcement regroups. And so the cycle continues.

The school security program must be structured with this absolute truth in mind. Even with the best technology, the most detailed procedures, and the most active vigilance, there is always the possibility that a person or persons determined to cause a tragedy can slip through the most secure defenses.

However, simply because the possibility exists that the system may be circumvented, school officials must not be deterred from moving forward with all due speed. They must wholeheartedly implement the necessary security arrangements for their school.

But if the school cannot absolutely guarantee that it can stop violence, and it cannot, then its security program must anticipate such possibilities and provide contingencies. It must incorporate certain special considerations.

Primary among these is awareness training for staff and students. Once violence erupts, teachers, counselors, and all staff must know just which responses are appropriate and how to minimize harm.

A classic example is the public's current perception of emergency services, particularly "911." Most people believe that if they have a problem,

137

they can simply dial "911" and the police will immediately materialize at their door. What most victims fail to realize is that there is a critical response time.

For the school under siege, this interval is crucial. Whether the violence will be controlled or at least minimized, or whether it will escalate into a full-blown tragedy depends directly on what school personnel should do and should not do during this period.

If students burst into a classroom and brandish firearms, do the teacher and the other students know what to do to prevent the situation from worsening? Do they know what not to do? Has the teacher been trained in techniques for talking the gunmen out of committing any further violence or for defusing the episode?

If a rampage shooting is underway at the school and the local police and special weapons and tactics (SWAT) team arrive, are they thoroughly familiar with the school layout, its security features, and other vital factors?

If a shooting results in an extended siege that forces teachers and students to shelter-in-place away from harm but also removed from emergency medical help, can they administer life-saving first aid? Have first aid kits been placed in strategic locations? Are they accessible?

If a bomb is discovered, have staff members been trained about the proper procedures for responding and evacuating the building?

These scenarios are but a few of the many considerations that a school security program must acknowledge, understand, and anticipate. Physical measures and procedures can deter a crisis, but a thorough program is one that recognizes that even the most extensive preparations can sometimes fail.

With that in mind, the school can prepare to respond to an episode of violence, even rampage violence, and emerge with minimal consequences, perhaps even no injuries or harm.

Chapter 10

THE ROLE OF LAW ENFORCEMENT

W HEN VIOLENCE STRIKES, the police respond and immediately assume the responsibility for resolving the crisis and restoring order. To do so, they must sometimes use certain specialized services.

School officials who understand what law enforcement will do and know how to assist the police can avoid being frustrated and confused during a crisis. Not only does such knowledge eliminate any guesswork during the emergency, but it also prepares the school, well in advance, to work with the police, especially during an episode of rampage violence.

America relies on law enforcement to contain disorder, but it is sometimes confused and often critical of the police, particularly during acts of rampage shootings and bombings. Much misunderstanding is due to movies and television dramas about the police. Generally, the bad guy is found, arrested, and prosecuted all within a given time frame. Such fiction, even sensationalism, may appeal to viewers, but it often gives a distorted picture of what the police and their mission are all about and, in the event of an actual shooting or bombing, can actually complicate the crisis.

Armed suspects, explosive devices, hostage negotiations, and criminal violations of the law require the police force to be the lead agency. Although other community services may also be involved, depending on the situation, such as the fire department and emergency medical personnel, most likely, it is the police who will be in charge.

Officials at the school and on the board level should meet with various law enforcement agencies, the fire department, and emergency medical people well before the school completes its security program and work out details that specify exactly what each agency would like to see in place if a violent situation occurs.

POLICE RESPONSE TIME

A crucial piece of information for school officials to know is how long it will take each agency to respond. When tensions are running high and danger looms, victims and bystanders alike expect the police to be on the scene immediately.

Unfortunately, a zero response time is not possible although a downtown school can usually expect a quicker response than a school that is located in a rural area. Obviously the greater the distance the longer it will take emergency services to arrive on the scene. Add inclement weather, even winter snow and ice, and the time factor increases even more.

Although most police agencies are prepared to respond to a variety of emergencies, they are not psychic. They simply cannot predict when an crisis is about to strike, hence the need for "911."

Schools also need to realize that responding units will require travel time, that cruisers may get detained at a railroad crossing by a train, that the beat car may be tied up on another call for service, and that another unit, farther away, must be dispatched. The responding unit itself may even be involved in a traffic accident. Any number of unforeseen contingencies can slow the police response.

Teachers and staff who are on the scene must be able to make positive decisions and take the appropriate and necessary actions until help arrives. They must know how to contain the crisis and certainly avoid jeopardizing any more lives, but they must also understand that their endeavors must remain within the goals and objectives of law enforcement.

FUNCTIONS

Once police are on the scene of a school crisis, they will manage the various emergency personnel and response units. First, however, their mission will be to preserve life. They must not only deal with school personnel and students, but bystanders, the media, their own officers who are involved, and the perpetrators. When the police are notified that the school needs emergency assistance, they will begin the following procedures:

DETERMINE THE CIRCUMSTANCES AND ASSESS THE SITUATION. In an ideal call for service, the "911" dispatcher obtains all of the necessary information so that responding officers can assess the scene correctly. Realistically, this seldom happens.

Often the police and emergency response units lose vital time because callers are frantic. Their panic is understandable, but they deliver only fragments of information to the "911" dispatcher. Oftentimes, they only know that some type of violence is happening, but they do not know what, where, who is involved, or any of the other essential facts.

The task force needs to address this part of its emergency response plan during the awareness briefings that will be held at the beginning of the school year. Guidelines should be placed at every phone in the building, and the entire staff, especially those individuals who are responsible for answering phones or who have immediate access to a telephone, should be thoroughly briefed. Even if they are panicked or know only a few details, they can still follow the written guidelines.

For instance, if there has been a shooting and the gunmen are still inside the building or are barricaded in some room, the caller must communicate that information. The police will attempt to discern the shooters' location so that they do not arrive at a particular place on campus that is within the shooters' line of sight. Information that should be given to "911" to help the police includes:

- What has happened so far?
- Have gunshots been heard?
- Have explosions been seen or heard?
- Who and/or how many persons are committing the violence?
- What do the perpetrators look like? Include age, description of their clothing, and any other details that will distinguish them from any hostages they may have.
- Where are the perpetrators or what was their last known location?
- When did the incident begin?
- Any other pertinent details?

Awareness training for the staff should stress that the caller needs to stay on the telephone with the dispatcher as long as possible or until the "911" operator says to hang up.

Training for staff and students must also address the issue of cellular telephones. Many students, and at some schools, most, carry a cell phone. Although direct access to a phone might seem to be a decided advantage during a crisis, too many calls can jam the "911" circuits and prevent dispatchers from contacting emergency units.

On the other hand, the school certainly does not want to run the risk that no one will make a call, especially if those who are involved believe no one else knows what is happening.

Victims may have no way to verify if someone else knows about their crisis and has already called for help. The task force should establish guidelines about who will make calls to "911" and how. These procedures should then be carefully and clearly communicated to staff and students.

CONTAIN THE SITUATION. Once the police arrive on the scene and determine that the emergency involves a rampage act, their first action will be to intercept the perpetrators and take them into custody if at all possible.

At that point, medical units will be brought in to treat the injured, and the police can conduct the necessary follow-up investigation of gathering evidence and questioning witnesses.

If, however, the shooters are controlling certain areas or classrooms and are holding students or teachers hostage, the resolution may be difficult and take time. At that point, the situation is considered a high-risk incident and will remain so until all perpetrators are in custody and law enforcement announces that conditions are safe.

Law enforcement's first step at that time will be to establish a *perimeter*. This enclosure will surround the school or the immediate area of the incident. It will contain the situation, protect the crime scene, and prevent anyone who is not directly involved from entering the immediate area.

If the suspects are apprehended quickly, police may set up only one perimeter. It will preserve the crime scene and keep it from being contaminated, hold back relatives, the media, and a curious public.

However, if the perpetrators are still inside the school and refuse to surrender or are holding hostages, the police will establish two secured boundaries, an outer and an inner perimeter. The *outer perimeter* will surround the school and the entire area and restrict everyone, except essential persons, from entering. This boundary is primarily to prevent the gunmen from shooting someone on the outside and is usually placed according to the perpetrators' line of sight. Anything or anyone that could be a target is considered within the line of sight.

The *inner perimeter* is the closest distance that the police and emergency response teams can get to the immediate high-risk area without putting themselves in jeopardy from the suspects' gunfire. Police, fire personnel, and paramedics will work inside this isolated layer, which is between the two perimeters, and remain there until the scene is secured and victims can be treated.

Hostage negotiations will most likely take place from here, as will any preparations to deploy the SWAT team if it is needed (see Figure 10).

PROVIDE TACTICAL SUPPORT. If the on-scene commander for the police concludes that a high-risk situation exists, then he or she will call for tactical support units. Tactical support usually takes the form of hostage negotiators, bomb disposal technicians, and SWAT team officers.

Negotiators will first try to make contact with the perpetrators and attempt to have some or all of the hostages released. Suspects will be asked to state their demands. Hopefully, they can be persuaded to surrender, but the process can take hours. It can even take days. Regardless of how long it takes to resolve the crisis, the police will not "hurry up and get the incident over." Law enforcement's every effort is to preserve life, even the perpetrators'.

Bomb technicians play a valuable role when explosive devices are found at the scene or just suspected. However, "bomb-techs" must often wait until the entire area has been secured and everyone has been removed before

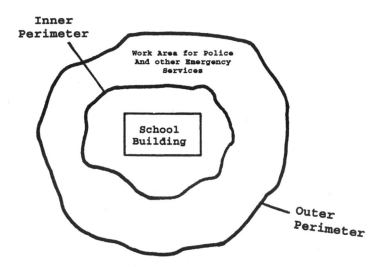

Figure 10. High-Risk Crisis Scene Perimeters

they can properly search the school and, if any bombs are discovered, render it safe.

A SWAT team has become such a recognized police unit for dealing with high-risk situations that the initials have become a household word. However, as much as movies sensationalize, even glamorize, SWAT teams, the news media often portrays them as ruthless "storm-troopers." Both extremes have created many misconceptions. SWAT teams oftentimes draw undue criticism, largely because the public fails to understand their nature and their mission.

When a law enforcement agency becomes involved in a high-risk encounter, such as one involving hostages, its regular police patrol units make every attempt to resolve the situation peacefully. However, after all other attempts fail, then it activates its SWAT team, if it has one. Many police departments, especially smaller ones, do not have their own unit but can request one from a neighboring agency through a mutual aid arrangement.

Part of the public's misconception about SWAT is based on its formidable appearance. The army-styled kevlar helmet, body armor, leg holster, and military-type rifle such as the M-16 suggest an infantry rifle squad rather than American law enforcement.

However, SWAT teams are not domestic commando units. They do not charge blindly into a hostile situation. They are not in combat, nor is their mission a military operation. Such action is foolish. It forces hostage takers to suddenly make life-and-death decisions. They will, almost certainly, vent their rage and frustration on their hostages.

SWAT operations have also come under various criticism during rampage shootings. Rather than being too aggressive, SWAT teams have been faulted because they did not suddenly converge on the scene, swarm into the building, and in a hail of superior firepower, take out the suspects and rescue the hostages.

The total and final objective in any high-risk situation is to resolve the crisis without any loss or further loss of life. SWAT teams are not makeshift operations of hastily assembled police officers. They are carefully selected, highly trained, efficient units whose first function is to gather intelligence about the adversaries.

Answers to questions such as who are the suspects, what type and quantity of weapons do they have, exactly where are they inside the school? will help the SWAT team develop a plan. Making a blind assault on a school may just provoke the shooters and quickly turn what began as a hostage situation into a total tragedy.

CONDUCT HOSTAGE NEGOTIATIONS. Armed gunmen may suddenly find themselves trapped when police units arrive. They seize students and staff, not necessarily because hostages were part of their plan, but because they suddenly have no other way to escape. A police negotiator must convince the hostage takers otherwise.

The first step toward a peaceful resolution is to establish *rapport* with the suspects. During this phase, negotiators try to establish a line of communication and some dialogue while they simultaneously slow the situation. The idea is to buy time and to ease some of the tension. If the assailants can be calmed, they may think more rationally. Police can then learn what the suspects' demands may be and negotiate for the hostages' release.

COORDINATE MEDIA RELATIONS. Most police organizations today have specially trained personnel who remain on the scene of a crisis to handle the press. These individuals know what, when, and how certain information should be released. They are also versed about which facts or details should not be broadcast.

Often in a protracted siege, releasing too much information at the wrong time may actually work to the perpetrators' advantage. Most school districts have their own media relations spokesperson; however, schools, unlike police, usually have little to no experience with a rampage shooting or a hostage situation. Not only can such inexperience aid the perpetrators, it can also endanger the hostages and create even further liability for the school. A public relations spokesperson for the school should work with and defer all information to the police.

PROTECT THE CRIME SCENE. Law enforcement's responsibility for a school shooting or bombing does not end when the suspects are arrested. The crime scene must be processed for evidence that will be crucial to any subsequent criminal prosecutions.

Police will cordon off the affected area and may shut down the entire campus. School officials may be asked to provide plastic cones, wooden horses, and other barriers that will deny access.

ARREST THE PERPETRATORS AND PREPARE THE CRIMINAL CASE. Once the siege is over and the suspects have been taken into custody, police investigators must gather evidence from the crime scene and obtain statements from victims and witnesses.

School officials will be asked to keep those persons who have pertinent information at the scene or move them to another designated location so that they can be debriefed by the police.

Chapter 11

SHOOTING AND BOMBING INCIDENTS

RAMPAGE VIOLENCE usually involves handguns and explosive devices. These two weapons remain the most popular, primarily because they are readily available and simple to operate.

Gun ownership is a hotly debated issue, partly because guns have held such a long and large presence in American culture. However, many adolescents, as well as adults, generally accept firearms to be an essential part of our society. Many parents are gun owners. Some are hunters and take their children along at an early age and teach them to shoot.

Movies often glamorize firearms of all types. Most every action episode is a layman's guide to weaponry although firearms are generally quite simple to operate. Minimal training and a little common sense can transform even the most fearful novice into a formidable shooter. For the individual who is so inclined, using a gun can easily and quickly become second nature—the evening news shows us just how easily and how quickly.

People of all ages, not just our youth, are saturated with violence. We are no longer shocked nor even surprised when minimal, even inconsequential, occurrences are resolved by the maximum consequences of a gun. Rather than enlightening us, our familiarity with guns has desensitized us.

Bombs are another popular "street" weapon that have been used in many cases of rampage violence. As with guns, the scope of their destruction has become too familiar. Even the most casual television viewer knows the various types of bombs and that a concoction of ingredients found in most garages or at least as close as the local hardware store can and has killed and maimed scores of innocent people of all ages.

Readily available books and manuals provide the novice with precise details for making a bomb. Even the Internet has been blamed as a plentiful source of information.

Schools today must be prepared to address all of the potential problems that students or anyone else creates when they bring a gun or a bomb into the school. The school must have a reliable defense.

First, it must have a comprehensive security program, which the preceding chapters of this text have presented in detail. However, the school still must take into account that even with all of its many protection arrangements, a gun or bomb might still make its way onto the premises. School officials must be prepared to deal with such a possibility with specific measures.

BULLET AND SHRAPNEL CHARACTERISTICS

When a gun is fired, tremendous amounts of explosive pressure are released that drive the bullet down the barrel and toward its intended target. Bullets, however, do not always follow a straight path. They may strike hard objects as they fly through the air producing a ricochet. Simply attempting to "get out of the way" may be an inadequate response in such a life-threatening circumstance.

When a bullet strikes an object or surface, it can do one of three things:
1. It can hit the object and stop. It will remain either inside the target or on its outer surface.
2. It can penetrate the object, punch through, and continue on its flight to strike another object.
3. It can hit the surface of a hard object and, depending on its angle of strike, glance off, then continue its flight with a slightly altered trajectory.

In each case, it is important for people to hide behind some shield or barrier that will protect them. However, in instances two and three, the danger is still not over. With the third characteristic, a bullet that strikes a hard surface can take on a new flight pattern and further endanger anyone within the proximity.

If a bullet strikes a hard surface such as a masonry floor or ceiling, or perhaps a locker-lined hallway, it can ricochet at an odd angle. Most people assume that a bullet works like a billiard ball. The ball hits the bumper and bounces off at the same angle of the strike.

However, a high-speed nose cone-shaped bullet is quite different, particularly if it hits a solid wall or another surface that resists penetration. If the bullet strikes at an angle of less than forty-five degrees, it tends to ricochet at a lesser angle and travel just a few inches away from and parallel to this surface until it finally comes to a stop. In shooting parlance this characteristic is known as a "rabbit round" (see Figure 11).

Because schools are built for durability, floors are usually tile, tables and benches in cafeterias are hard plastic and steel, lockers are steel, and walls are cinder block. All such surfaces will deflect a bullet and create a "rabbit round."

Few individuals beyond firearms experts, police officers, and the like are aware of "rabbit rounds," but the knowledge can be a vital survival tip. The

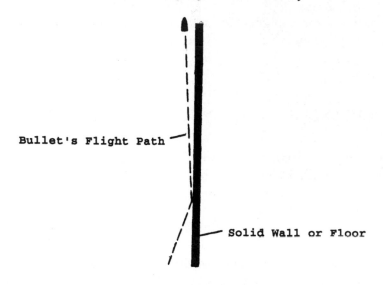

Bullet's Flight Path

Solid Wall or Floor

Figure 11. The "Rabbit Round" Bullet Flight Path

natural inclination for anyone caught in a shooting is to get down. Most think that lying flat is more preferable. Such a belief come become a dangerous misconception.

People who are stretched out on a hard surface, surrounded by more hard surfaces, are a possible target for "rabbit rounds." They may be almost as vulnerable as if they were standing up.

Although crouching or kneeling might be more advisable, people caught in such a situation should keep their head and chest area off the floor. However, the best position is often situational and is a judgment call that persons facing the danger must make for themselves.

Simply because the numbers of students in a classroom or in the building are greater than the numbers of teachers, more students may be in danger in the event of a rampage shooting. However, educators often object to instructing students about every specific of guns and bullets. "Rabbit rounds" is one such topic.

Educators, parents, and the public often believe that young people do not need to hear "one more thing" about guns. Some may feel that if adults recognize the growing role weapons play in our society, they may inadvertently encourage more violent behavior. Others may say such information is too graphic. It will frighten students more than it will help them, especially if such a tragedy never happens in their school.

Parents and educators instruct young people on the likelihood of many dangers: smoking, drunk driving, AIDS, drug abuse, and suicide to name a few. The philosophy is that teens cannot have too much information to save their lives.

The adolescent world has changed. Guns have become as much a part of growing up as all the other perils that threaten our youth. Although information about guns and specific survival tips such as how to avoid "rabbit rounds" should be handled as judiciously as is the instruction about all the other dangers our youth face, the knowledge could save a teacher's or a student's life.

HANDLING FIREARMS

In the event that a firearm is discovered on school property or in the possession of a student, it must be taken into the care, custody, and control of school officials until it can be turned over to local police. Handling a firearm requires that certain safety measures be observed at all times.

First, the weapon must be rendered safe before it is moved to or stored in a secure place. Recovered weapons can accidentally and easily discharge, usually because the weapon is poorly manufactured or the handler is inexperienced. Oftentimes, it is a combination of both.

Sometimes it may be that the circumstances of the recovery are difficult, such as a student who has a gun in his pocket and the hammer is cocked. If the weapon is a "Saturday night special" variety or is made from a cheap pot-metal grade steel, it may still discharge even if all the necessary precautions are taken.

Having just any teacher or anyone else who is personally unfamiliar with the proper procedures for handling a gun confiscate it can be highly dangerous.

Many faculty members will not feel comfortable handling any type of firearm. Some may even have an overwhelming fear of guns and want nothing to do with them.

Certain teachers or staff who are familiar with firearms, however, or feel comfortable learning, should be trained to recover weapons. Their training should include the following.

- How to retrieve the weapon safely once it is discovered
- How to unload the weapon safely in a location that is away from others
- How to clear a weapon safely that is jammed or cocked
- How to handle and deal with each category of firearms such as revolvers, semiautomatic pistols, shotguns,and rifles
- How to properly store and safeguard the recovered weapon until law enforcement can be contacted and retrieve it

Police firearms specialists or range officers who periodically conduct police firearms qualifications within most law enforcement agencies can train school personnel to handle guns safely. Schools can also contact local chapters of reputable firearms associations such as the National Rifle Association (NRA) for advice about such programs.

Schools might also ask to receive training in automatic firearms, which is becoming increasingly popular, if the instructors have this expertise and these "machine-guns" are available.

Schools should also consult their respective board of education for approval and make certain that whoever provides the instruction is a trained professional. Refresher training should be scheduled, at least, on a annual basis or sooner if time and circumstances permit.

BOMB THREATS AND SEARCH PROCEDURES

Schools have long been plagued with bomb threats. Usually the scares have been phoned in and the results have been nothing more than pranks. They have been a way to get out of class, to disrupt the school day, or to otherwise stir up a little excitement.

However, bombs have become a far more significant threat in the past few years. Schools should not become desensitized and offer a lackadaisical or even no response. In all cases bomb threats must be taken seriously, and all necessary response procedures should be followed.

Although guns and bombs are both serious threats, certain characteristics of bombs make them more difficult to detect and to handle than guns. Bombs, unlike guns, can be brought into the schools and hidden for future use. They can also take any form or size, unlike a gun, which can be readily identified by a standard shape.

Bombs may also be assembled from many different components. They may be chemical, mechanical, electrical, or a compilation of electronic components. They may also be made from defective or highly unstable parts or elements, which adds to the danger.

Whatever the device, no one, regardless of what they may know about chemicals, mechanics, or electronics, should attempt to disarm the device or handle it in any way.

In the event that a bomb threat is received by phone, the individual receiving the call should obtain as much information from the caller as possible. The receiver should attempt to:

    1. Keep the caller on the line as long as possible. The receiver should signal a coworker (by a prearranged silent or hand signal or a written note) to contact the telephone operator by dialing "0" on an alter-

nate phone line. The coworker should identify himself or herself, describe what is transpiring, and request an *in-progress trace* of the line that is carrying the threat. The operator can isolate the line for future identification and investigation purposes.

AUTHORS' NOTE: Some areas have a type of trace facility. When the caller hangs up, the receiving party can dial a certain code and learn the caller's number.

Unfortunately, this service does not always provide a number if the caller is outside the dialing area. The school should not depend on this feature. Obviously, a wise use of school money is to purchase the caller ID service that is used in many homes.

2. Document the telephone number, time, and date the call was received.
3. Write down the caller's exact words.
4. Note any background noises.
5. Note any characteristics of the caller's voice, such as an accent or a speech impediment.
6. Determine whether the caller's voice sounds familiar.

Even if the caller refuses to answer some or any of the following questions, the receiver should still ask:

1. What time is the bomb set to explode?
2. Where is the bomb placed?
3. What does the bomb look like?
4. Did the caller place the bomb or did someone else place it?
5. What kind of bomb is it?
6. What will cause the bomb to explode?
7. What is the caller's name?
8. Why was the bomb placed?
9. Is there more than one bomb?

Once the school receives a bomb threat, officials should contact the police immediately. All staff and students should follow established procedures and quickly evacuate the building and wait for the police in an area that is a safe distance away from the evacuated building.

AUTHORS' NOTE: Most schools have a designated location for students to gather during a fire drill, such as on an athletic field. If this area is relatively close to the school building, officials should determine another area to use during a bomb threat, because explosions can propel debris for considerable distances and cover a large area.

As in any other emergency, the staff will be responsible for evacuating students from the building. However, unlike a shooting or even a fire, where the threat is visible, a bomb may be hidden. Even if it is in plain sight, it may still be unrecognizable. It can be concealed in a backpack, a box, planted in a closet, a trash can, a desk, or even hidden in an acoustical tile ceiling. Schools contain nearly an infinite number of places to hide a bomb.

The task force, therefore, needs to keep the following information in mind as it establishes certain guidelines for bomb threats.

1. Everyone, including administrators, must turn off all cellular phones, walkie-talkies, or any other radio frequency-emitting devices immediately. If the school uses a wireless radio frequency intercom, it must certainly develop another way to communicate a warning about a bomb threat.

2. Teachers should quickly scan their classrooms for any unusual or suspicious looking package or object as they leave the room.

3. No one must touch any light switches. They could trigger an electrical bomb. Leave all lights just as they are. Certainly, the police bomb squad will need to see the room and its contents as it conducts a room-by-room search, but bombers sometimes use a secondary device that is specifically intended to maim and kill responding police officers.

   As the police investigate the first explosion, a second bomb is ticking. It has been set to allow investigators sufficient time to enter the building. Then, with them inside, it detonates. If the teacher turns the lights off, then police turn the lights back on, the switch could be connected to a secondary device.

   Bombers can ease their conscience if they feel they were not really responsible. After all, they may reason, someone else detonated the device. In turn, the bombers can become more difficult to apprehend when they believe that the victims themselves were to blame for detonating the bomb.

4. Since students will follow the teacher, they should also be instructed to leave all electrical equipment and switches just as they are.

5. All doors should remain open. Doors that are closed and locked on the outside become time-consuming obstacles for the bomb squad.

6. Most schools have cafeterias. Some have common areas, where large numbers of students gather. The task force should consider ways to alert students in these areas and in other inside places where numbers of people gather.

   Because such areas are usually noisy and communications from an intercom are often drowned out, the task force might consider installing a large message board like a scoreboard, which could be activated from the main office. Flashing lights or loud sounds are far better attention-getters than verbal warnings.

   However, staff and students must remember the caution about individual rooms and to never use the standard light switch to flash a warning.

7. Staff and students should be instructed to touch nothing once the alert is sounded. A bomb could be hidden in a backpack, a bag, a box, a purse, and placed in a hallway, a doorway, or a main exit. Regardless of the container's size, students must not pick up, kick, step on, or make contact with any object as they exit the building. Even letter-bombs and small package bombs cause extensive injuries and death.

In the past, some schools have used an informal procedure in which a group of teachers return to the building to make a cursory check. For obvious reasons, this procedure is unwise and can be extremely dangerous.

Personnel can best help by evacuating everyone safely from the building and then, if they noticed a suspicious item, convey a description of it along with the room number to school officials and the police.

The school should train all personnel to recognize a suspicious package. Certain signs can indicate that a parcel that has been received through the mail might contain an explosive device. Potential indicators can include the following.

- Rigid or lopsided envelope
- Protruding wires or tin foil
- Oily stains or discoloration on the outside of the package
- Excessive binding material such as tape, string, or other securing materials
- Too much postage
- Misspelled common words
- No return address
- Special markings such as "Personal," "Confidential," etc.
- Excessive weight for the size of the shipping container or package
- Address that lists the addressee only by title and not by name, (even the title may be incorrect)

SURVIVAL STRATEGIES

Victims who survive a bombing or a shooting must think in the midst of panic, fear, and oftentimes a mass stampede. However, they can heighten the probability they will survive by being prepared and aware of certain considerations.

1. Acknowledge that a shooting or a bombing could happen here. Schools that discount such a possibility leave staff and students totally unprepared if the unthinkable really does happen.
2. Locate vending machines or other large pieces of equipment, which may be in a cafeteria or commons area, where people can use them

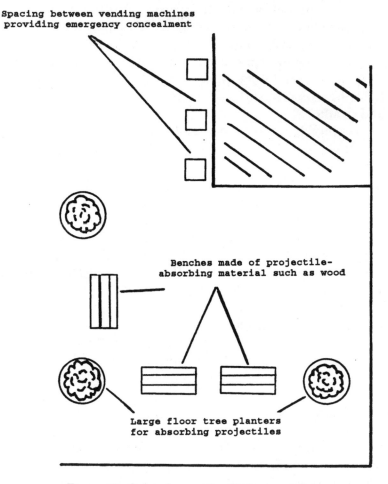

Figure 12. Safety Layout for Gathering Areas

as a shield in the event of a shooting. Space them far enough apart so that individuals can run between them and hide (see Figure 12).

3. Prohibit the use of cell phones by panic-stricken students or others who can jam communication lines at the emergency services center. The result will delay the response from police, fire, and medical personnel.

4. Place large decorative floor planters made of projectile-absorbing material such as wood in cafeterias, commons areas, or any places, both inside and outside, where numbers of students congregate. Fill them with dirt or gravel, which will stop a bullet or bomb fragments.

5. Hold first-aid awareness briefings for students and staff.

6. Hold emergency sessions for students. They must understand that in the event of an emergency, they must wait for the teacher to check the hallways. They could stampede out the door and charge directly into the gunsight of a waiting shooter.
7. Lock the classroom door immediately if gunfire is heard. AUTHORS' NOTE: The task force should check with the local board of education and local fire officials to make certain this procedure does not conflict with certain fire or safety regulations.
8. Instruct students to use their book bags as a shield. If the bags are permitted within the classrooms, they can be held in front of the body to absorb bullets and bomb fragments, or at least minimize some injuries, depending on their contents.

Schools are far from identical. Although their function and their purpose may be the same, they differ in building design and size, student population, and geographical location, to name only a few variables. Like a small community, each school has a complex structure that shapes its own particular personality. Each is unique.

As such, each must develop its own individualized security program. One school cannot and should not attempt to copy another school's protection design. What works successfully in one school may be a dismal failure in another school just a few miles away.

Chapter 12

CONFRONTATION MANAGEMENT
AND THE HOSTAGE SITUATION

ANY VIOLENT EXPERIENCE is terrifying. Rampage violence is especially so. The definition says it all. *Rampage violence* is the sudden, spontaneous use of force intended to rampantly impart mass killing, injury, and destruction on unsuspecting, innocent victims and their locations.

Even as frightening as rampage violence is, it still may not end immediately with an uncontrolled frenzy of shooting or detonating explosives.

Rampage violence can also be a gunman who bursts into a classroom or commons area and threatens to shoot other students or staff. In just minutes, the threats can escalate into a protracted standoff that may last for hours or even days.

Classrooms are often vulnerable, especially in contemporary schools where sprawling designs often distance buildings or wings far from the main office and leave them isolated. The teacher or staff member may be alone or may have a class full of students when armed gunmen burst into the room. Within seconds, one or many individuals become hostages, and their lives turn into bargaining chips.

Erratic captors may demand any number of things, but primarily they want to stall the police and stave off arrest. Ultimately, their main intent will be to escape. Their insurance markers will be their hostages.

Police are immediately and somewhat at the mercy of the captors. They must walk the fine line of negotiation, constantly appeasing the often violent hostage takers, on the one hand, while simultaneously, and frequently to the frustration of both captives and bystanders, slowing the perilous atmosphere, on the other.

At this point, police can best protect the hostages by calming the captors, who, given enough time, will wear down from their own stress and fatigue.

Any encounter where people are held against their will until the demands of a captor are met can present many difficulties before the crisis is resolved. However, when the hostage takers are adolescent, the scenario can be even be more complicated.

Adult hostage takers usually have demands. They want something that

156

negotiators can use as a bargaining chip. They want to keep the money from the bank they have just robbed. They want to leave the country on a jet, or they know prisoners whom they want released. Most importantly, they also want to survive this situation.

Juveniles waving guns are more than likely operating from fewer life experiences than adult hostage takers. Teen assailants may not plan to take hostages until police sirens or a face-to-face confrontation suddenly makes them realize they are cornered.

Unlike their adult counterparts, they may have few to no specific demands beyond a desperate need to assert themselves, take control of their surroundings, or call attention their frustrations. They may be ill equipped to deal with such life-and-death decisions. Largely unable to see much beyond this moment, adolescent gunmen can, in a moment of hopelessness, suddenly vent their rage on their captives or themselves.

The single and most paramount concern in such a situation is that the hostages survive. Improving their odds may depend as much on their own actions as on the police and other emergency personnel. Negotiators can do only so much for the captives during the standoff.

If, however, the hostages themselves understand and follow some critical dos and don'ts, they can hopefully minimize any irrational acts from their captors and, in turn, improve their own chances to survive or avoid further harm.

Because teachers or staff may also be taken hostage, they must be oriented to certain critical techniques that may help everyone survive. They will become the unofficial, but nonetheless designated, leaders in such a scenario and will be expected to assume whatever control is possible from within.

Teachers must be trained in *confrontation management,* which is the skills and awareness necessary to cope with a hostile individual who is bent on violence and the ability to defuse a potentially deadly situation and resolve it peacefully.

Student hostages, parents, the public, and perhaps even the hostage takers themselves will look to any educators particularly for guidance, for some measure of control, and for stability. A successful resolution may very well depend on a teacher's knowledge and preparation for such an emergency.

THE HOSTAGE SITUATION

Life-threatening situations can overwhelm victims and cause them to react in unusual ways. Such is the phenomenon known as the "Stockholm Syndrome." The behavior was first identified in 1973, when robbers in the city of Stockholm botched a bank robbery, then seized a group of hostages. During the six-day standoff, several hostages actively resisted rescue attempts.

When the siege finally ended, some of the hostages refused to testify against their captors and even went so far as to raise money for their captors' legal defense. One hostage eventually became engaged to one of her captors.

Hostages may even help commit crimes or aid the perpetrators in their siege against the police. Experts believe this syndrome results when the fear of death is coupled with the trauma and frustration of being helpless. Cut off from support and at the mercy of their captors, certain hostages can experience a psychological isolation of effect. At that point, they no longer view their captors as criminals nor their actions as crimes.

The Preparation

At best it is difficult to completely and accurately prepare an individual to cope with a face-to-face confrontation. Even with the best preparation and training, teachers cannot simply follow a blueprint of cause and effect. Much of their response will be based on "gut feelings" and a "play-it-by-ear" approach.

They must, however, be under no illusions or misconceptions. Armed gunmen, determined to go on a shooting spree, are extremely dangerous whether they have already fired shots or not.

Survival Tips

Movies and media accounts of hostage situations often give the impression that all interactions during these crises are between the police and the hostage takers. There is, however, a third party. The hostages themselves, those who are the reason for the standoff, need not consider themselves totally helpless.

Hostages can assist the negotiators and contribute directly to their own survival by their conduct, their interactions with their captors, and by following the following survival tips.

STAY CALM. Within the classroom, teachers are masters at minimizing, even suppressing, their own emotions. They are daily, hourly, required to appear calm, controlled, and capable of taking charge. Nowhere will these qualities be so tested, and ultimately judged, as huddled inside a classroom.

When twenty to thirty terrified, excited, and confused adolescents are taken hostage along with a staff person or teacher, by a threatening, erratic gunman, the educator becomes the recognized leader and must assume whatever control is possible under the circumstances. The teacher should:

- Instruct students to be quiet.
- Tell them to cease moving about and sit down if space permits. Stopping all movement and unnecessary noise can help calm the captors.
- Avoid any physical actions that are sudden or abrupt. The captors may feel threatened and respond with violence.
- Speak slowly and quietly yet confidently.
- Reassure the captors that she or he in charge of the students.
- Listen attentively to the captors. Often they have taken hostages to gain an audience. Whether they are right or wrong, they are convinced that no one is listening to them. Acknowledge their feelings without agreeing to their actions.
- Listen to their reasons and ask for their suggestions. Do not automatically reject their demands.
- Be patient. Work time to your and the negotiator's advantage. Impatience will only irritate the captors and make them edgy or more irrational.
- Project concern. Avoid hostility, coldness, a "strictly-by-the-rules" approach, or a general attitude that gives them a feeling of the runaround.
- Attempt to limit their unreasonable behavior by being cooperative.
- Reassure them that you and the students will be cooperative and attempt to establish some ground rules.
- Use delaying tactics to give them time to calm down. Offer them a place to sit, a drink of water, whatever might make them feel a little better.

RECOGNIZE THAT YOU AND YOUR STUDENTS ARE HOSTAGES. Whether the hostages are students, teachers, or staff members, everyone must recognize that this is a dangerous situation. Even hostages who know the perpetrators must not be fooled. Past familiarity is absolutely no guarantee that gunmen will have any special regard for their captives.

As matter of fact, it may be the relationship particularly, whether it is real or assumed, that has driven the captors to take these specific hostages. Anger and desperation, accompanied by a weapon, produce a precarious and highly dangerous situation.

There may be times though when the captors are quite decent and civil. On the other hand, there may be just as many episodes, especially as negotiations get tense or conditions become uncomfortable, when the captors become quite brutal or violent.

DO NOT ANTAGONIZE THE CAPTORS. Without a doubt, the captors will be the ones most on edge throughout this confrontation. Hostages who create additional problems and provoke their captors can be injured or killed. The teacher should:

- Be the one to deal with the gunmen
- See that student hostages remain obedient
- See that student hostages follow their captors' instructions
- Stop students from arguing with each other
- Stop any students from challenging, threatening, or daring the captors

THINK SENSIBLY. If hostages make sudden moves or attempt to overpower the suspects and they fail, captors may retaliate against one or several hostages. Teachers should:

- Point out to the captors that they have choices
- Not be a hero, nor permit students to do so
- Not make promises or false statements they may be unable to keep
- Not take the captors' sides nor agree with their distortions

APPEAL TO THE CAPTORS TO RELEASE ANY WOUNDED, SICK, AND/OR HANDICAPPED PERSONS. Although the assailants may not be concerned with anyone who was injured or shot during the takeover, it is critical for the teacher to point out to the captors that victims must have immediate medical help. The teacher should:

- Gain the captors' cooperation by appealing to their basic human decency
- First attempt to get the wounded treated or released
- Next ask to get the sick or handicapped released, in that order
- Remind the captors that treating hostages humanely can be a point in their favor when this situation is over

REMAIN ALERT. The teacher should:

- Listen to the captors' instructions.
- Respond promptly. An incorrect or slow response can provoke the captors into harming one or several hostages.
- Watch for signs that the situation is deteriorating. If the police are forced to send in the SWAT team, hostages will need to react immediately, get down on the floor, take cover, and stay out of the line of fire. When the episode is concluded, police will conduct a follow-up investigation. Hostages will need to give statements, which is a third reason they should listen and carefully observe everything around them. Hostages will also be called to testify if the case eventually goes to trial.

MONITOR VERBAL INTERACTIONS. Except for a very businesslike, matter-of-fact approach, students should refrain from communicating or conversing with their captors.

- If students are asked a direct question, they should respond.

- Students should not attempt to chat with their captors.
- Students and the teacher should not be condescending, sarcastic, or contemptuous even if the suspect is a juvenile or is well known to them.
- Students and the teacher should not reprimand, talk down, humiliate, or attempt to instill guilt in their captors.

DO NOT GIVE UNNECESSARY ASSISTANCE. Fearful hostages may believe that if they do certain things, their captors will be so pleased or appeased that they will not harm them. The teacher should not:

- Attempt to read the hostage taker's mind.
- Try to guess what the captors may want or need.
- Offer unsolicited advice or assistance, even if it might seem to ease the tension. Such efforts may actually hamper the police's efforts, particularly if the captors misinterpret such "help." The teacher's and the students' safety could be jeopardized if the captors respond with violence, and such actions could encourage some students to develop the "Stockholm Syndrome."
- Try to make the situation seem less serious than it is.

DO NOT STARE AT THE CAPTORS OR MAKE EYE CONTACT WITH THEM. Hostage takers resent being challenged, especially by their hostages. They usually have their hands full just dealing with the police and attempting to figure an escape plan from their current predicament. Hostages who make lengthy eye contact with their captors risk irritating or provoking them.

PAY ATTENTION TO BODY LANGUAGE. Hostage takers are in a highly agitated state; some may even be suicidal. They may interpret certain actions as threats and react without thinking. Advice for the teacher is to:

- Keep your distance.
- Do not invade the captors' personal space. Try to keep 3 to 6 feet between you and them.
- Do not project a challenge with such postures as standing directly in front of the captors, crossing your arms, or putting your hands on your hips.
- Avoid making physical contact with your captors.
- Do not point your finger at them.
- Maintain a relaxed, yet attentive posture.
- Stand at an angle and turn slightly toward your captor rather than full face.
- Move slowly.

FOLLOW THE CAPTORS' INSTRUCTIONS. There is no truer slogan applicable to a hostage situation than "those who have the weapons make the rules." Hostages must realize their very survival depends on their willingness to comply when their captors issue a command. They:

- Should respond to the precise letter of the directive
- Should not be creative or clever
- Should not be stubborn or sluggish or they can quickly endanger their own life as well as everyone else

TURN OFF ALL CELLULAR TELEPHONES. In many schools today, a large number of students and teachers often have a cell phone in their possession. The school should have a fundamental, no exception rule: at the very first indication of a potentially violent situation, every cell phone in the entire school, even those that administrators may be using, must be turned off immediately.

Because some bombers like to construct explosives that can be detonated with a remote-control unit, one of these devices could be present during a school siege. Equally possible is that a bomb could be inadvertently detonated by the same radio frequencies that carry cell phone transmissions.

Warnings about cell phones hold doubly true for any hostages who are taken. It should go without saying that captors will become angry if any of their hostages attempt to communicate with their own cell phone.

However, an even greater danger for the hostages, which they and school officials may not know, is that the captors may also have planted bombs within the school or in the area where the hostages are being held. A hostage taker could have wired his own body and be a walking time bomb himself.

HAVE CONFIDENCE IN THE POLICE. Hostages will teeter on an emotional see-saw. They will see their very life hang in the balance yet realize they are largely helpless to save themselves. They may fear their captors or be angry at them, but they may also doubt those on the outside.

Hostages can feel frustrated, but because there is often no way for them to receive news, updates, or reassurances from the outside, they may believe that nothing, the right thing, or enough is being done. Hostages should:

- Be patient, even if such advice seems difficult to follow. Anyone who becomes trapped should be assured that the police are doing absolutely everything they can to resolve the crisis peacefully and safely. Police will mount a full-scale rescue effort. All the tricks-of-the-trade, every talent, every technique, and every available form of technology will be mobilized toward a successful rescue, for everyone, including the hostage takers.
- Be aware of any chemical agents the police may use against the hostage takers. Victims should cover their eyes and breathe through a piece of cloth or clothing such as a shirt to absorb chemical irritants.
- Have faith in the police.
- Try to avoid becoming frustrated with negotiators.
- Try to avoid doubts that negotiators are doing all they can.
- Do what they can from the inside.

- Do not lose hope and act irrationally.

Hostages have everything to lose and absolutely nothing to gain if they anger their already volatile captors. Plus, unbeknown to them, their actions may actually work against the police's efforts.

In a hostage situation in which little is certain, victims have one guarantee. From the moment they are seized until the crisis ends, the police will not stop working for their safe release.

Chapter 13

MOCK DRILLS

ONE OF THE MANY LESSONS students first learn in school is that fire drills are important. Even first graders are taught to recognize the warning signal, evacuate the building at the nearest safe exit, and reassemble in a designated area.

Schools, which have practiced these drills for decades, realize that when they anticipate an emergency and the response procedures are routine, lives can be saved. Even injuries can be minimized if not altogether prevented. Schools need to be just as familiar with emergency procedures, which would be necessary if the school experienced an episode of rampage violence.

However, procedures that apply to an evacuation for a fire do not necessarily apply to a scenario of violence. Staff and students may need to evacuate. On the other hand, they may need to remain in the building, depending on the threat.

To familiarize everyone with the numerous types of threats and emergencies and how best to respond, the task force should schedule no fewer than two *mock drills,* more if time permits. The first one should be a *controlled walk-through.* The second, and subsequent ones, should be *scatter drills.*

SHELTER-IN-PLACE

Before the task force begins to plan its mock drills, it may wish to consider an additional hardware advantage. If the school has a CCTV system or is considering implementing one and has monitors in most classrooms, it may wish to consider linking the monitors into a schoolwide video network. Costs could be minimal for those schools that already have an in-house television station and currently broadcast to each room.

If a code yellow or code red signal sounds, the camera images can be channeled to the classroom monitors. Staff and students can then see into the hallways and determine whether they can evacuate the building safely or whether they should lock their doors and shelter-in place.

PREPARATION FOR THE DRILLS

As with the entire protection program, the task force should work from a reverse timeline. The most effective method to ensure that the drills will be held in a timely fashion is first to set dates for each.

The task force should decide on these dates well ahead into the school year, record them on a master calendar, then communicate them to all staff members who will also need their own briefings and advanced preparation to direct the students. Once the dates are firm, the task force should work backwards and determine dates for each awareness activity that will lead up to the final mock drill.

AUTHORS' NOTE: The task force may also wish to reserve the day after the controlled evacuation drill just in case of rain, and the drill must be postponed. However, because of the numerous other agencies involved, the task force should make every effort to see that the drill continues as scheduled. Otherwise, all those involved must be notified as soon as possible that the drill has been postponed.

OFF-CAMPUS RENDEZVOUS SITE

One of the primary differences between a fire drill and a drill for an episode of school violence is the crucial factor of safe distance. During such a crisis, students and staff will need to move away from the school, not just to an adjacent athletic field or parking lot where students often wait during a fire drill but well away from the school and especially out of a shooter's line of sight.

Students and staff will require a facility away from the school where they may gather, particularly in inclement weather, where they may be sheltered, and where the staff can account for all students, each other, and other adult personnel.

In selecting an off-campus site, the task force should look for one that:

- Is within a reasonable walking distance
- Is out of the line of sight or safely away from the school and an explosion that might occur
- Can be isolated or cordoned off to keep everyone away from the students and staff except law enforcement and designated school officials
- Is large enough to hold all the students and staff
- Has restroom facilities
- Has a parking lot or adequate off-street space to accommodate emergency vehicles that may need to treat any injured or wounded or trans-

port them to the hospital
- If possible, has a computer system and more than one main phone line
- Has additional rooms that can be used as temporary headquarters for the staff, for school officials, and for on-site police officers to meet with any witnesses to the violence

A excellent choice for an off-campus site is a public building or a church. Not only can a church provide all the necessary facilities, but the minister can also begin helping those who have been traumatized by the violence. Some areas also have ministerial associations whose members from many different faiths and denominations are on call as grief counselors during such a tragedy.

Once a site has been identified, several members of the task force should visit, explain their purpose, and request assistance. Churches are always most cooperative, but the task force should make certain that a church, or whatever facility extends its services, is open and accessible during the school day.

Some schools may be located in an area where they are fortunate enough to have several choices. However, the size of the student body will often determine which facility can more easily accommodate such a large group. The task force should choose only one site. It should not select a primary and an alternative site, even reserving one as backup. In the event of an actual tragedy, students can become easily disoriented and scatter to both sites. Staff and students who are fragmented between two locations will compound everyone's problems.

Accountability will be more difficult as law enforcement and emergency response personnel attempt to deal with two situations rather than one. Staff must identify which students, staff, and other school personnel are at which facility, who has been accounted for at first one place then another, and who has not been located at either area. All staff, school officials, and law enforcement will be divided between the two sites and can lose valuable time, as well as possibly jam phone lines between the two sites.

Once the facility agrees to house the students, the task force should identify a contact person. All parties should, at this time, agree on the dates for the mock drills. Busy schedules for both groups might necessitate juggling some dates, but if the task force plans several months ahead, well in advance of the drills, everyone should be able to agree.

If the task force has also scheduled the following day as a backup in case of rain, this meeting is the time to make certain that procedures are clearly and carefully established about how the drill will be postponed. The group might also wish to agree on a time for a last-minute cancellation. If no one has received word by this certain time, then the drill is a go.

COOPERATION WITH LAW ENFORCEMENT

Most likely the task force has been working with law enforcement to develop the school security program. The liaison officer may wish to visit the off-campus site along with task force members and make certain that the location is acceptable.

Schools that must choose an off-campus site that is limited in either space, phone lines, accessibility, or any number of other conditions should work closely with law enforcement well ahead of the mock drill, and certainly well in advance of any tragedy, to determine the best ways to deal with these shortcomings. A school does not want to conclude that its evacuation plan is flawed or incomplete in the middle of panic and confusion. During the mock drills, law enforcement will need to:

- Direct traffic to make certain staff and students are safe as they walk to the off-campus site
- Monitor the school and keep all vehicular traffic away from the scene and out of the parking lot until the drill is concluded
- Direct and control all emergency response units on the scene

EMERGENCY RESPONSE UNITS AND TRANSPORTATION

It is hoped that the off-campus site will have adequate parking space. During an actual emergency, paramedics can pull into the parking lot, where they can safely administer first-aid to victims or load them into emergency vehicles for transport to a hospital.

Just as with law enforcement, emergency response personnel should be contacted by the task force well ahead of the actual mock drills. They will need to know how many individuals must be transported and how mobile each person is. Emergency personnel will also assess the layout of the building and determine which exits are accessible based on those who must be transported.

AUTHORS' NOTE: During an actual emergency, all accessible exits or those that were used during mock drills may be blocked off or under siege. However, because emergency personnel and law enforcement participated in the mock drills and know the layout of the building, both agencies can confer and decide to either use a different route to transport these individuals or have them shelter-in-place, depending on the type and extent of the crisis.

Many schools house various groups of children, such as those in special education, daycare, or even nurseries. The task force must make arrangements for these children to be moved to safety. Paramedics may not be the best choice here, since their units can usually only accommodate two individuals at a time, and they may also be needed to transport those who are injured or wounded.

Paramedic units can refer the task force to an alternative agency if the school system itself does not have vehicles that it can summon quickly to transport handicapped students. These students may need to be moved in special rolling chairs similar to wheelchairs but that can be lifted and managed more easily.

In some cities that offer public transportation for handicapped riders, specially equipped vans or buses may be the designated response units.

Young children and babies can be carried and transported by most any vehicle. However, the problem is not moving each child easily but moving several children quickly, particularly if they outnumber workers. This same ratio problem may also be true in special education rooms. Several children may be essentially mobile but their conditions such as frequent seizures or unsteady gaits may require two adults to assist one child.

Certain staff members may also have mobility problems or even physical conditions such as heart problems that will prevent them from walking during the mock drill. They too must also be accommodated and their needs anticipated and managed.

During a tragedy, the school must not depend on student mothers to transport their own child. Assailants, bullets, or bombs may shut down certain hallways. It is the task force's responsibility to anticipate how to move these children and to clearly communicate this plan to those parents whose children are in daycare or special education areas.

One plan for moving children, injured students, or even disabled staff is to consider designating several specific staff members who drive vans to park their vehicles in certain areas. These vehicles could be stationed in these spots for the mock drills and even routinely parked in those spots during the entire school year so that they could be quickly pressed into service in case of a crisis.

If the school has health or medical personnel, all, or at least one representative, should be involved at this stage. They will certainly be familiar with the health conditions of special students and children and can work with the emergency medical personnel.

The task force should meet with the teachers who are in charge of these groups and discuss how the plans for the mock drills will affect these children. Parents must also be contacted. They can be informed by phone, but to make certain that they clearly understand how their child will be transported and by whom, a brief letter should follow-up any telephone calls.

AUTHORS' NOTE: As the school begins to prepare for these mock drills, the task force should deal realistically with everyone, including students. Obviously, during a real crisis, many of the arrangements that went smoothly during the mock drill may not be as infallible.

However, the more problems the task force anticipates and handles, the more likely that casualties, perhaps even injuries, can be avoided in an actual violent situation.

REVERSE TIMELINE FOR THE FIRST MOCK DRILL

The first drill should be strictly a controlled evacuation walk through. It is an orderly instructional drill to show students and staff where they are going, how to get there, and what they are to do once they reach the off-campus site.

Approximately Four Weeks Before the Drill

The task force should:
1. Decide what time of the day the drill will be held. Consider traffic patterns within the area and try to avoid those hours when traffic is heaviest. For maximum cooperation, the suggestion is that drills not be scheduled during the lunch hour, first thing in the morning, or last thing in the afternoon. Disrupting lunch will be a hardship on the cafeteria staff. Plus, hungry students tend to be uncooperative students.
   This same advice applies to early mornings and late afternoons. Some students may plan to arrive late or leave early to skip the drill.
2. Communicate plans for the mock evacuation drill to the school board attorney because accidents or injuries are always possible.
3. Ask the principal to inform the superintendent or whoever should be told at central office unless the mock drill procedures have already been communicated. Unfavorable press or public relations can completely destroy a school's efforts to keep staff and students safe, regardless of how well intended those efforts are.
4. Inform the parents about the date and time. The task force should communicate this information in several different forms and at several different times. The first time parents learn about the drill should not be through the evening news, or worse, on the radio and think it is a genuine disaster. Parents should also be encouraged to avoid scheduling a doctor or dentist appointment for their child on this day at this time.

5. Decide which route to the off-campus site is the safest.
6. Walk to the off-campus site and back. Time the round trip.
7. Add approximately fifteen to thirty minutes, depending on the numbers of students and how long they will need to spend on site. The task force should now have a fairly accurate estimate for an altered schedule. Tell staff and all personnel, including cooks, custodians, and part-time staff, early on just how long the first drill will take.
8. Decide what arrangement students should use to reassemble once they arrive at the off-campus site. One suggestion is to use whatever method the school uses to check the daily attendance for the entire building. If the school uses the homeroom method, students should assemble at the site by homerooms. The idea here is to quickly and efficiently account for every student, every teacher, and every staff person who was present before the evacuation.
9. Meet with any school health or medical personnel to see if they have a medical bag or emergency supplies they can transport to the off-campus site. If the bag is heavy, perhaps supplies can be divided or redistributed so that the container can be carried along the route. It must not be transported on ahead to the off-campus site.

   In an actual emergency, injured or wounded students might start on the route but be unable to reach the site. Others could be hurt as they flee. Adults could also experience cardiac problems along the way. Until emergency response units arrive on the scene or backtrack along the route, medical assistance must be administered by school personnel.

Approximately Three Weeks Before the Drill

1. Locate a bullhorn or a portable public address system.
2. Meet with staff and tell them the distance they will be walking and whether the terrain is rough or hilly. Ask for names of those who will need transportation.
3. Organize roles that list every student by homeroom or by whatever method the staff will use to check attendance and take them to the off-campus site. Because the drill may occur at a time when students and teachers alike are not in their homeroom or the setting where daily attendance is normally taken, lists need to be on the scene and ready to be distributed to teachers.

Accountability at the off-campus site, especially in a real emergency, is crucial. It is at this point that the school must account for everyone in the school, including: students, staff members, support personnel, volunteers, and even visitors. If any are missing on the basis of this assessment, the police will begin to determine whether those individuals are still inside the building and what their status is.

Schools may vary in their methods of checking daily attendance, but essentially the procedures fall into two broad categories: *traditional paper checks* or *computerized systems*.

TRADITIONAL PAPER CHECKS. One suggestion is for the task force to have signs made from a durable card stock. These should be easily visible from a distance, at least a size of $8^{1}/_{2} \times 11$, and each should identify a specific homeroom section or grouping, whichever method will be used to organize students at the off-campus site. They can be held up so that arriving students can find their group. The task force might want to have these signs laminated so that they can be reused.

An easy method for taking attendance here is to glue or staple a brown clasped envelope on the back of each sign. Place several copies of the roles for that group in the envelope along with a pencil or a pen.

The task force should then meet with attendance clerks and discuss the information these staff members must bring to the scene. Data should include a copy of the daily absence sheet or whatever written form the school uses to post those students who are absent and a complete list of all staff members, including cooks, custodians, support personnel, visitors, substitutes, and volunteers.

The school should have a list on file for every adult and every student in the building. A large student body will involve a great many records. Because they may be heavy, they should be transported to the off-campus site and left in a secured location.

Periodically, a designated individual should visit the site and update any information.

The attendance clerk or one designated individual should be responsible for checking the lists of teachers and staff, volunteers, and visitors. If the school is using paper roles, this person should be the one who also collects all paper roles from the teachers.

This individual along with the administrator and any task force members who are on the scene then need to determine why certain individuals are missing.

COMPUTERIZED ROLL TAKING. Some schools have dispensed with paper lists for daily attendance and check role through computer programs. Those schools should assess their system and determine just what method they can use to account for every student. Depending on their system, they may consider placing a CD ROM of their computer program at the off-campus site.

If the off-campus site can provide a computer system, the task force must determine whether the systems are compatible. Can this backup system run the school's program? If not, the task force can delegate several individuals to bring laptop computers to the scene. Placing this responsibility on several people avoids relying on just one person who may be absent that day, injured in the crisis, or even taken hostage.

Perhaps the school's attendance program can be accessed from the off-campus site. If so, the information should be protected with a special password that only certain key persons know.

In schools where staff and students buy their lunch, check out library books, and access numerous other in-house services with their bar-coded identification badges, the task force can set up several card readers at the off-campus site. Students can simply swipe their cards through the readers as they arrive.

Identification badges with life-safety information on the back may literally save a person's life during a real crisis. Paramedics who have been briefed about the badges can check the reverse side for the victim's blood type, any drug allergies, or any serious medical problems, as well as other information.

Identification badges can also be encoded with a special microdot that contains the individual's entire medical history. Many hospitals can quickly assess the information so that they can begin immediate emergency treatment.

AUTHORS' NOTE: The task force must certainly coordinate this procedure with all area hospitals. It must also check with the school board's attorney. Laws in some states may prevent such information from being used because of the right to privacy.

Regardless of the system the school uses, however state-of-the-art or paper-and-pencil traditional, it must be available at the off-campus site. There, it must be organized, it must be demonstrated to the staff and students during the controlled evacuation mock drill, and above all, it must be accurate.

Approximately Two Weeks Before the Drill

The task force should:
1. Remind the parents once more. Depending on the means the school uses to inform parents of important information, the task force must see that parents, the community, and school officials are completely and thoroughly informed about the drill.
2. Begin to brief students about the drill.
3. Tell students the date and the time. Do not try to surprise them at this point. Many will become confused and could panic.
4. Be truthful. Without becoming overly graphic, explain why this type of drill is necessary.

5. Be creative with student orientation. Adolescents often resent something new, and when students brief other students, the results can be far more successful than if the adults were responsible.

   If the school has a morning television show, students can present minipresentations, much like public service spots on commercial television.

6. Detail the route. Some students will be unfamiliar with the off-campus site. Have a film group, media class, or the school newspaper group walk the route and make their own edited version to show to the student body.

One way for students to participate in the actual drill and also lend valuable assistance is for the task force to request help from certain groups. Uniformed units, such as junior ROTC or even student council members in monogrammed tee shirts, can assume posts along the route to help direct students, keep the walkers out of residents' yards and off the grass, and also fall in behind the last students to sweep the route of any litter that has been dropped. Any videos can feature these students as they walk the route.

One Week Before or Week of the Mock Drill

The task force should:

1. Prepare a one-page flier that announces the drill, the date, the time, and specifies approximately how long the exercise will take. Include the name of a contact person at the school who can answer any further questions and distribute these fliers throughout the community. If the school is located within a residential area, the community must be told in advance that students will be participating in a mock drill and that the police will be directing traffic.

   A courteous gesture is to tell property owners that students will stay off their lawns, will pick up any trash they leave, and that cars may wish to avoid the area during this time. These announcements can be hand-carried by a group of students to every house or business that is along the route or will be affected.

2. Deliver signs, roles, or computer software to the off-campus site and store everything together in a durable container. Place it in a secure location and inform those who are to be stationed at the off-campus site where the container is located. They will need to have the information ready when students arrive.

3. Check to see that emergency cards for all school personnel are present, if the school is using a paper system. Signs, roles, and cards should all be stored together.

4. Determine who will be in charge at the off-campus site and who will

remain behind until the building is cleared. If the school has more than one administrator, one should be at each location.

For this first drill and to minimize the initial confusion, these authors suggest that students who will distribute signs, the administrator who will direct the off-site scene, and at least one or two task force members, depending on the size of the group, drive to the scene in as few vehicles as possible and wait for the first students to arrive.

5. Advise students to wear comfortable walking shoes. If, on the day of the drill, they feel they need a jacket, they should have it with them. If the school has a policy about no coats in the classroom, the task force needs to decide how to handle this rule. Just as with a fire drill, students should not go to their lockers before they evacuate the building.

6. Advise students that they are not permitted to carry any food or drink away from the school because they may litter with wrappers and bottles.

7. Advise students that all backpacks, all books, and all belongings, except for purses, must be left in the school.

8. Instruct students to hurry but not run to the off-campus site.

9. Instruct them to find their group immediately by looking for a sign if this is the procedure the school will use. Explain to them that attendance will be taken and why, in the event of a crisis, this procedure would be so vital.

10. Explain to them how they will be grouped, by homeroom, etc. or whatever procedure the school plans to use.

11. Tell them that once they locate their group, to sit down immediately. If students are to swipe their identification badges through card readers, the task force needs to determine an organized, efficient, but rapid system. The drill can quickly turn chaotic at this point unless this procedure is precisely organized.

    If all the students and the staff cannot fit into the off-campus facility, but the parking lot or grounds are sufficiently large, have students gather in those areas for a roll check. Each group needs to sit in its assigned area at every drill. On paved lots that have been stripped for parking, each group of students can be assigned to a numbered space.

12. Sound the warning for an evacuation in case students have not heard it before. *Do not* use the fire system alert. Different crises require different responses and must have different warnings.

13. Advise students to leave the building by the nearest safe exit.

14. Remind everyone that when they hear the warning, they must turn off all cellular phones immediately.

15. Schedule a brief staff meeting for all personnel. Distribute copies of the procedures. Review each item and ask the staff for input. Has the task force forgotten anything?
16. Assign those staff members who asked for transport to a vehicle.
17. Check with law enforcement, emergency response personnel, and the contact person at the off-campus site to see if everything is ready.
18. Contact the media. Superintendents or central offices often have a list of television and newspaper reporters who cover the education beat. Schools should not ignore or ban the press. Refusing to notify or work with the press can suggest that the school has something to hide.

    The task force might ask reporters not to interfere with evacuation efforts and to shoot any photos or live footage from a reasonable distance. Reporters will have an opportunity to interview students and staff at a press conference after the drill. The task force might ask for a group of students or call for volunteers to talk with the press along with an administrator and a member of the task force when the drill is concluded.

    A mock drill is not dramatic or particularly high profile. Actually there is not really much to see, but it clearly communicates that the school recognizes violence is possible and is preparing its staff and students in the event a tragedy does occur.
19. Check the student body for anyone on crutches, etc. the day before the drill. They may need to be transported in a designated staff van. Tell them where they should report and who will transport them.
20. Follow-up with wheelchair students. Can they navigate the route on their own or do they need assistance? Depending on their needs, they may need to be transported by emergency medical personnel or several of their friends may be able to assist them along the route.

The task force should avoid basing too much of the emergency plan on designated volunteers. Such help during a crisis is often spontaneous and heroic, but, at that point, students or staff who had previously agreed to assist a particular student or even a group may be victims themselves. They could be a hostage, trapped, or cut off by an explosion or a fire. They could even be severely injured.

Day of the Drill

The task force should:
1. Remind students about each part of the drill. (See the complete list under the previous heading: "One Week Before or Week of the Drill.")

2. Remind everyone that except for emergency response vehicles, which will be transporting disabled students or children and a certain number of previously designated staff vans which will transport any injured or disabled individuals, everyone will walk the route.
3. Repeat all the instructions that have been given "During the Week of the Drill" about cell phones, the walk, backpacks, procedures for taking attendance, etc.

Procedures for the Drill

The task force should:
1. Excuse all staff and students who will be at the off-campus site or along the route approximately one-half hour before the drill time so they can get in place.
2. Position one or two task force members in various sites throughout the school such as where emergency medical personnel will transport disabled students, where workers will transport babies at a child-care center, and where staff will load disabled staff and students for transport.
3. See that the health nurse and any school medical personnel divide their responsibilities between the staff and students along the route and any individuals within the school who may need assistance.
   Schools that have only one health nurse may prefer that this individual attends to any injuries or problems along the route because emergency medical personnel will be in the school.
   The task force needs to assess the evacuation and look for any weak procedures or any unanticipated problems in evacuating the building. Task force members who are already at the off-campus site will evaluate that aspect of the emergency plan.
4. Introduce students to their off-campus site host and acquaint students with restroom facilities, etc.
5. Ask uniformed groups, who swept the route as they fell-in behind the last students, to return to their posts along the route.
6. Check with law enforcement to make certain no problems arose and that the route is clear for the students to return.
7. Announce *"All Clear"* with the bullhorn or public address system when attendance is completed and activities are concluded.
8. Return to the school.
9. Have an interview session at the school for the press to talk with a group of students, a member of the task force, and an administrator.

Mock Evacuation Scatter Drill

The *scatter drill* is not a great deal different from the controlled evacuation drill. The scatter drill, which is similar to a fire drill, signals students to clear the building quickly and safely. It may be a surprise, at least to the students.

Because of the various agencies involved and even the courtesy of notifying residents, the task force may wish to wait until about the third or fourth mock evacuation drill before they choose a day for a scatter drill. At this point, a scatter drill may be one that surprises the staff and students because everyone, including all agencies, should be familiar with their role by this time.

A surprise scatter drill will permit the task force to assess how quickly law enforcement and emergency medical personnel respond, how efficiently all procedures work when the element of surprise is added, and what parts of the program need to be revised.

Schools can vary their drills and further evaluate their procedures by changing certain elements. For instance, they can block off a major exit so that staff and students must change their escape route. Because the drill has so many variables, one or several can be slightly altered to present new challenges and let the task force see just what works and why or what should be changed.

REALISTIC MOCK DRILLS

Some schools have experimented with certain elements to make their mock drills appear more realistic. They have used props such as fake blood, drama club members posing as victims and assailants, even the local SWAT team pointing real guns that have been loaded with blanks. The results have varied.

A few learned that even when students were carefully told their drill would attempt to simulate a real rampage shooting, some students panicked. Other students professed genuine trauma.

In one instance, the result was a firestorm of criticism for the school. Despite the fact that many parents and students rose to commend the administration for being concerned and trying to prepare the school, some vocal parents, the media, and even the school board recoiled in outrage.

The message was clear. Although those who are not in the school may fear an episode of rampage violence, although they may acknowledge that many children routinely watch movies and television programs that are far more graphic than a mock drill, and although they may agree that even the media regularly reflects back our senseless mayhem, they nonetheless insist that educators will somehow continue to hold danger at arms length.

But primarily they believe that because the prospect of rampage violence is just too disturbing, it simply will not happen here.

Chapter 14

WORKING WITH THE MEDIA

EDUCATION IS SCRUTINIZED and criticized from the president of the United States to the neighbor next door. Educators hear themselves chastised, called morally irresponsible, and oftentimes held legally liable for an offense no more threatening than attempting to enforce their school's rules.

Even on relatively minor educational issues, schools are often dismayed at the unrelenting coverage they receive in the media.

Yet, this intensity immediately pales when an episode of rampage violence strikes. However, schools do not have to see their reputation destroyed. They can do much to determine just how they are portrayed if they should undergo such a crisis.

Previous chapters in this text have emphasized that a principle of effective security is to acknowledge violence can strike, even with the best protection, and that the school that is properly prepared can certainly minimize injury if not completely avoid it.

The same holds true for dealing with the media during a crisis of violence. The task force must prepare a comprehensive plan that will make it as ready to handle the media as it is to protect itself. Even if the school's protection is already unquestionably strong, the strength or the weakness of this component can very well determine just how the public judges the school's entire security program.

Obviously, a compelling media presence cannot disguise protection that is weak or ineffective. However, relying on a weak plan to deal with the media or, worse yet, no plan can irreparably damage the school's relationship with its community and may even ultimately determine just how well or how poorly the school survives the crisis.

In the past, schools have not normally considered themselves to be public relations specialists. They feel their job is to deal with children. They do so with honesty and integrity and rely on their efforts to speak loudly of their sincerity.

However, the task force must recognize that the school will be judged during an episode of rampage violence. The school will be perceived by its appearance in the media. Negative images can haunt even the most security-conscious facility long after the crisis ends.

For years to come, the mere mention of a school's name can conjure images of deaths and injuries. Extended litigation, exorbitant lawsuits, and the tarnished reputations of long-standing educators will simply confirm public opinion: that the school was irresponsible, unprepared, and, worst of all, unconcerned because the injuries and deaths were preventable.

To avoid such judgments, schools should initiate contact with the media and establish communication before a crisis ever occurs.

WORKING WITH THE MEDIA DURING MOCK DRILLS

The task force does not need to court the media but merely recognize that in this information-driven age reporters are simply doing their job. The nation demands immediate coverage of every news event, and violence in a school is a powerful draw.

An ideal time to introduce the media to the various areas of security that the school is developing is during the school's mock evacuation drills.

AUTHORS' NOTE: In Chapter 13 the task force was advised not to ignore or exclude the media but to invite them to film the event from a reasonable distance. It was also recommended that the task force schedule an interview session after the drill so that reporters could talk with students and staff.

At this time, a member of the task force can invite reporters to meet the task force and to tour the school and see the various phases of the protection program that are in place and working.

If the task force is struggling to get programs and hardware funded, it should be honest. Say what procedures are currently implemented and what is planned. Show them that the school is making a sincere, maybe even a Herculean, effort. It is doing as much as it can and struggling to stretch the limited resources it has.

PREPARING TO WORK WITH THE MEDIA
BEFORE AN EPISODE OF RAMPAGE VIOLENCE

As the task force develops its in-house security program, it should also develop a plan for working with the media during an episode of rampage violence. Attempting to establish the following procedures during a crisis will be far too late.

The task force needs to determine who will be the spokesperson for the school. The absolute critical value of this position cannot be emphasized enough.

Historically, principals or local school administrators have stepped to the forefront during a school crisis and spoken to the media. Neither approach may be in the school's best interest.

A principal may be the one who is organizing and essentially implementing her or his school's security program, especially if the school is small. On the other hand, the principal of a large school may have delegated much of the responsibility and development to the task force and be unable to speak about the nuts-and-bolts operations; likewise, with a superintendent or an administrator from the district or central office.

The school's best choice most likely will be a member of the task force. At all costs, the school wants to establish clearly and early in the crisis that it has a program in place that will minimize harm, that staff and students have been oriented and received training for just this type of emergency, and that the school has procedures in place to restore order.

The best staff person to convey this information and this image of a prepared, responsible school is someone who can speak knowledgeably about the security program.

District or central office officials, by virtue of their job, may supervise several or even many schools. They may not know each one thoroughly or, at least, well enough to answer the many questions they may be asked.

Certainly in such a crisis, even the most prepared school may experience some unforeseen difficulties and be uncertain how to handle them. No one can ever be 100% prepared for the unexpected.

However, spokespeople who appear to be largely uninformed about many of the school's procedures or preparations or who seem surprised by questions can do irreparable harm, even if the school was prepared and does have the necessary, appropriate answers.

Local officials can also inadvertently convey the impression that the school has been incompetent. It has failed to protect its students and staff so now high-level administrators must step in and take charge. No supervisor who is distanced from a school, either by title or miles, knows the heart and attitudes of the school better than the school's own people.

Ideally, the task force should select one or even several of its own members who are articulate, low key, and confident under pressure. Several members can relieve each other, particularly if part of the crisis involves a hostage situation that may take hours, even days, to resolve. Having more than one spokesperson also allows for the possibility that one of the designated individuals is absent that day, has been injured, or even is a hostage.

Those who are selected must have excellent communication skills. They should:

- Project a patience with questions that may be repetitious, occasionally challenging, and sometimes obvious.
- Be able to remind reporters without offending them that some victims and assailants alike may be juveniles and, as such, certain information is confidential.
- Be able to explain certain points without becoming angry or defensive.
- Be quick thinkers. Certain questions may ask for responses they cannot give because of confidentiality, because the crisis is ongoing such as a hostage situation, or because the information is unknown at this time.
- Be honest with what they can reveal. Explain why they cannot answer a question, but avoid "No Comment." It suggests the school is keeping secrets, that it really does not know something it should, or that the situation is different, even worse, than it appears.
- Project a professional but pleasant demeanor, at least as much as is appropriate in the situation. Spokespeople who appear aloof, condescending, or cold can witness their school's demise, as well as their own reputation. Their retorts will be replayed on local and national television newscasts for what may seem like centuries.
- Be far-sighted and realize that footage of what they say or refused to say may be used as evidence for further litigation or in a court trial.

It is not enough to be right. The school, by virtue of its spokespeople, must look right. Their voice and their presence will both go far to project an image of believability and communicate that the school did have a good readiness posture in place, took the necessary precautions, and now has procedures in place that will restore order.

MEET WITH LAW ENFORCEMENT AND COORDINATE HOW PRESS RELEASES WILL BE HANDLED

With the advent of community-oriented policing, many police departments began appointing a public information officer. If the school's local law enforcement agency has such a position, that individual will be responsible for press releases from the police.

The task force should meet with this officer during the time it works with the police department to coordinate an emergency response plan. It should also consult with this officer about the school's first controlled evacuation mock drill and include her or him in the procedure if possible.

Schools should remember that an episode of school violence is not only a school issue. It is also a crime and, as such, certain decisions must be guided by law enforcement.

However, that does not mean the school should relinquish all responsibility to the police for dealing with the media. Parents, relatives of students and staff, and friends, as well as the entire community, will expect to see and hear from the school. They will see that the police are involved, but they will need reassurance from the school.

Although the school must be in control, it should not be, or appear to be, controlled by the police.

ESTABLISH A MEDIA CENTER

As the school selects on off-campus site to rendezvous after an evacuation, it should also establish an area at the site where police and school spokespersons can brief the media.

Unless access is especially limited at the off-campus site because of dead-end streets, narrow roads, limited parking space, or the small size of the facility, the site will be the best choice for a media center because school officials and law enforcement will already be present. As the task force decides on a location for the media center, it should:

- Establish a location either at the off-campus site or close by to facilitate communication. Spokespeople should not travel between sites. The atmosphere will be confusing enough without spokespeople having to either drive or tie up phone lines to receive new developments.
- Determine where at the off-campus site the media center will be located. If the facility is large enough, briefings can be held inside. If it is too small, select a section of the grounds or a parking area that does not impede law enforcement or emergency response vehicles.
- Allot enough space to keep the press away from all students and staff. Those who have witnessed fatalities or woundings may be traumatized and need to talk with counselors. They are also witnesses to a crime. The police will need to interview them, not to build a criminal case, at this point, but to gather intelligence about the perpetrators. If the situation is ongoing, police will need information about the assailants, their weapons, their locations, and about any victims who may still be inside the school and their conditions.
- Consider where mobile news vans can park. An episode of school violence is immediately a national, often an international, story. Expect and anticipate a massive response, especially if the scenario is ongoing such as with a hostage situation.

DURING AN EPISODE OF VIOLENCE

If such an event does occur and the school must use its disaster evacuation plan, students and staff will flee to the off-campus site for shelter.

Prior planning should have identified the spokespeople for the school and for law enforcement and selected rooms or areas where law enforcement will interview witnesses, where school officials will meet, where students and staff will be accounted for, and where the media center will be located.

More than likely, the press will have heard about the episode over their police scanners and will converge on the off-campus site nearly as quickly as law enforcement and emergency response units.

At this point, members of the task force should direct reporters to the media center and tell them that a spokesperson from the school and one from law enforcement will hold a briefing shortly. They should state a time so that a sense of order and organization will be established immediately.

Naturally, a barrage of questions will be directed at the task force members. However, they should not make any statements at this point.

At the designated time, the school spokesperson, along with the law enforcement spokesperson, should meet with the press and:

1. Be ready to respond confidently and quickly. Do not wait for rumors to get a head start. Even a well-prepared school that tries to play catch-up will appear unorganized. Ultimately, that appearance could be translated into the legal term of negligence.

2. Keep the press away from students and staff. Some students and even some adults may be hysterical. Because their observations of the scene may have been brief, they may be repeating incorrect information from another person or confusing names, types of weapons, extent of wounds and injuries, or any number of vital facts.

3. Work from a jointly prepared statement. School and law enforcement spokespeople need to agree, before they issue any information, just what and how much can be released at this point.

4. Acknowledge the obvious: there has been an episode of violence. If the siege is continuing, live coverage will show emergency medical personnel standing by, law enforcement securing the scene, even SWAT teams deploying to the building.

   However, even if some witnesses have reported that students or staff members were killed, spokespeople do not need to use the word "fatalities." Wait until the police confirm the information. Spokespeople can simply say there have been injuries, which is apparent if paramedics have transported individuals from the scene. Until the police can confirm the identities of the victims and can notify their relatives, the school must not verify or deny this information.

Families must never learn about the death of their loved one from a reporter.

5. Consult with the police before releasing the names of students and staff who are fatalities or are injured. The fact that students are juveniles adds the element of confidentiality to an already sensitive issue. Reporters will certainly know that the wounded have been transported to a hospital and can quickly determine which one. The media will attempt to interview medical personnel at the emergency department.

   Whether victims' families wish to speak with the media and release what they know at that time is their decision. Revealing a victim's name and medical condition is certainly within the relatives' rights. It also ensures that the school and law enforcement have not violated confidentially laws or communicated incorrect information.

6. Do not speculate or theorize about the perpetrators' motives or mental states. If any litigation or a court trial results, lawyers may include clips from television coverage and newspaper articles.

   The school does not want to hear its own ill-advised or even damaging words repeated back and used as evidence to prove it was negligent, unprepared, unaware, or even unconcerned about such a known threat. Leave such analyses to lawyers and mental health specialists.

7. Do not flatly deny something that is unknown at this time. The information could be true. Then again, it could be one of the infinitesimal numbers of rumors that will take flight far ahead of the facts.

8. Plan to update the media at scheduled intervals. Tell them that these briefings will be held every hour, every several hours, as information becomes available, or a combination of both, whichever is workable.

9. Work closely with law enforcement about releasing updates. If the situation is ongoing, the assailants may very likely be watching or listening to news reports of the crisis. Conveying sensitive information could interfere with any negotiations and jeopardize efforts to free the hostages.

10. Do not say "No Comment." Even if the school or law enforcement should not comment about a particular issue at this time, the phrase can generate bad press for several reasons. First, the phrase suggests a lack of common courtesy and a curt retort to what might be a logical question or one that viewers are asking. Second, the phrase can suggest that the school and law enforcement are conspiring to hide something.

    A better approach is for spokespeople to simply say, "We don't have that information at this time. Events are still unfolding."

If reporters ask for the names of the fatalities or hostages, spokes-people can gracefully decline and soften their refusal, perhaps even appeal to the emotions of reporters and viewers alike with a response such as, "We can't release that information at this point, not until all the families have been notified. I'm sure you would understand if one of these students or staff members was your family."

11. State the information that is currently available and can be released, then call for questions. During this phase, the spokespeople may wish to establish some ground rules.

    For instance, they may say that they can only answer questions about certain points, because perpetrators are still inside the building and the police are currently assessing the situation.

12. Defer to law enforcement if the school spokesperson is uncertain whether to answer the question. Law enforcement can also, in turn, defer certain questions. The school spokesperson will have more knowledge about certain school issues or even about security arrangements.

    For instance, a reporter may say that she or he has learned that the security cameras were turned off or were malfunctioning. The spokesperson, who is either a member of the task force or is thoroughly familiar with the security program, needs to quickly and clearly dispel any such rumor by stating that she or he is in a position to know and can categorically say that the video system was operating and fully functional.

Most certainly, the media will want to know whether the school was prepared. Reporters who were present during the mock evacuation drills will know that the school had a program in place and should be able to speak more knowledgeably and, perhaps, more favorably about the school's protection efforts.

Chapter 15

SCHOOL READINESS CHECKUP

ONCE RAMPAGE VIOLENCE strikes, it is too late for a school to wish it had implemented an effective security program. What could have been done or what should have been done are tragic excuses for what was not done. Only advanced planning can prepare a school, its staff, and its students for an episode of violence.

Such preparation begins by understanding that even a well-established, comprehensive security program can break down. Various components can fail and permit an incident to occur. Technology can be defeated, and procedures can be circumvented by those who wish to cause death and destruction.

The task force must recognize that for every system of protection there is a potential for failure. At that point, it can then plan a security formula that will be sufficient to meet the threat of school violence.

As with the entire protection program, planning must be comprehensive. It must address the various possibilities that might arise as an episode of rampage violence progresses through its various stages. Each stage of the event, the *before,* the *during,* and the *after,* requires graduated preparations, and each should address the spectrum of possible occurrences.

THE BEFORE

The "before" phase essentially prepares the school for all other arrangements. The safeguards to have in place before a tragedy strikes include the following.

ATTITUDES AND PREDISPOSITIONS. School officials have a sensible attitude about the potential for school violence and recognize it could occur on their campus. This attitude has been translated into the necessary protection arrangements that, in turn, have been implemented to safeguard the school, the staff, and the students.

SCHOOL SECURITY PROGRAM. The school has implemented a comprehensive security program that is based on a thorough analysis of the school and its premises. The analysis has considered, among other factors, the building and facilities, the campus culture, school activities, numbers of staff and students, area crime, past incidents of violent crime in the school, and any other information that reveals threats or the potential for threats to the school.

The program is comprehensive in its approach to protection because it uses a combination of human, technical, and procedural elements to provide well-rounded coverage. Officials have been careful in their security planning to ensure that the school's protection arrangements do not lean too heavily on one or two applications such as cameras or metal detectors.

TASK FORCE. A school security task force has been established to ensure that the protection arrangements for the school are in place and are maintained at proper levels. The task force is responsible for an ongoing inspection of the school's changing conditions and its activities. Any changes may require the security arrangements to be periodically upgraded.

AWARENESS TRAINING. Staff and students have received proper training and orientation about the school's security program. Training has also included conflict resolution and management, hostage encounters, bomb threats, and other presentations to prepare everyone for rampage violence.

CRISIS RESPONSE DRILLS. Staff and students have practiced mock drills and other rehearsals for a hands-on understanding of what could occur during an episode of school violence and what their role would be. A pre-arranged rendezvous location that is well away from the danger zone has been designated as a makeshift refuge for staff and students.

After a mass exodus from the school, this location would shelter staff and students and allow the school to carefully account for everyone who was in the school building before the evacuation.

ACCOUNTABILITY SYSTEM. An orderly system has been devised that will quickly and accurately account for all students and staff once they reach the emergency rendezvous location. The system will identify anyone who is missing so that the school or the police can promptly follow up and confirm their whereabouts.

THE HANDICAPPED. Special arrangements have been instituted to safely remove handicapped students and staff from the school in the event of a sudden evacuation.

SURVEYS. A formal survey has been conducted with staff and students that asked them about school security, campus crime, security threats they know about or feel endanger their own personal safety, and any other information the school can use to enhance its security.

HOTLINE. A dedicated telephone line has been established that permits students or others who know about a threat to the school to communicate their knowledge. Their call is received by a designated contact, and the information is promptly and properly passed along to school authorities for their disposition.

POLICE INVOLVEMENT. School officials have had meetings with leaders from local law enforcement to discuss the various aspects of the school's security arrangements. The police have been invited to tour the campus and become thoroughly familiar with the different security applications that the school has adopted. Team leaders for the police department's SWAT team have also reviewed the entire campus layout and have been given black outline floor plans of the entire building.

FIRST AID. All staff and students have been given the necessary first-aid briefing, so they can render help to those who are injured until emergency medical personnel arrive. First-aid kits have been strategically placed around the school to use in the event of an emergency.

SIGNAL SYSTEM. The school has devised and implemented a signal system (chimes, bells, etc.) to alert teachers and staff that a possible threat (bomb, armed suspect, etc.) exists somewhere within the facility. Staff members have been trained to recognize such signals and to regard them as serious. Once personnel receive the signal, they know to initiate an immediate and appropriate response.

COMMUNICATIONS. School officials have installed a system that permits teachers to communicate with the front office or other necessary locations and summon assistance if they have an emergency in their classroom or elsewhere on campus. The communication system is a hardwired variety or another means. It does not use radio waves to broadcast information because radio waves could inadvertently trigger an explosive device that has been planted within the school.

CCTV CAMERAS. The school's CCTV camera system is located in an area where school officials can disable it in the event that they must evacuate that section of the building. Any perpetrators of rampage violence would then be prevented from seizing those offices and using the cameras to watch all police response operations.

THE DURING

Even the best security is not totally foolproof. Something can slip through the defenses and create a life-threatening situation. An angry student may devise a way to smuggle a gun or bomb into the school, or a parent, frustrated with a custody case, may burst into the classroom to make a "statement."

However, even if a shooting or an explosion does result, all is not lost, nor is the situation hopeless. Quick-thinking staff members can initiate certain actions that can minimize further harm. To intercept an event of rampage violence, the school should be prepared with the following responses.

"911" NOTIFICATION. Certain staff members have been designated to notify "911" for emergency services assistance. These individuals have been selected and specially trained to deal with this aspect of the crisis so that vital information will not be overlooked in the midst of a panic.

HOSTAGE TRAINING. Staff and students have received training about a hostage situation and know how they should respond if they become a hostage. Teachers are acquainted with the negotiation strategies that they may use if they have an opportunity to develop rapport with the captors.

BOMB THREATS. School personnel are acquainted with the necessary procedures that will prevent them from inadvertently detonating a bomb if they discover one. Staff members know to leave lights or other electrical devices as they are, to make a quick scan of their work areas or classrooms for any suspicious packages or containers that could contain a bomb, and to advise the police if they find something.

CELLULAR TELEPHONES. Staff and students have been cautioned about the use of cell phones, which can trigger an explosive device. They also know that a flood of calls to "911" can jam the emergency communications network and delay or even prevent a response.

LOCKING DOORS. To prevent armed gunmen from gaining access to a classroom or another location where people are gathered, teachers have been briefed to lock their doors. The perpetrators would be denied entrance or at least have their movements limited. Local fire department authorities have approved this procedure and confirm it does not violate any fire codes.

QUICK PEEK. Teachers have been trained to take a quick peek into the hallways if they hear gunfire and make certain the area is safe before they send students out of the room for an emergency evacuation.

CONFLICT RESOLUTION. Teachers and staff are acquainted with "talking" tactics, which, in the event of a face-on dialogue, can calm and dissuade an armed assailant from committing further violence.

THE AFTERMATH

The period after an incident of rampage violence can result in chaos and confusion, especially for a staff that is unprepared.

Immediately after the incident and after the perpetrators have been taken into custody or they and their threats have been nullified, the school must respond with its people and procedures.

A worst-case scenario may have resulted in fatalities, serious wounds and injuries, mass destruction to the facilities, or any number of other related emergencies. Staffs and students, who were unprepared and who never accepted the possibility that such violence could happen in their school, can continue to worsen their conditions.

RENDERING FIRST AID. Staff and students may need to administer first aid to victims. Even with the assistance of emergency medical services personnel, the sheer number of injured may be so overwhelming that others must give first aid to save lives. All individuals within the building should receive emergency medical training that identifies the types of injuries victims could suffer and the immediate treatments they should receive.

CRIME SCENE. Once an act of rampage violence occurs, the school essentially becomes a crime scene. Conditions that the perpetrators created become evidence. The police will process the area to prosecute those who are responsible. Staff and students can best assist by avoiding the area and remembering they must not touch, move, or in any way alter the situation.

PRESS RELATIONS. Rampage shootings and school violence are news. Regardless of how school officials feel about seeing their own students and staff who are victims on national television, the public expects to be informed, and television stations and newspapers will jockey to get the information first.

School officials should anticipate this eventuality and have designated personnel who can deal with the press. School leaders should meet with the press information officers of local law enforcement well before a tragedy strikes and coordinate how a release will be made, when, and who will make it. Most likely, school officials will be interviewed on camera.

However, there may be certain information that the police and the prosecuting attorney's office may not want released, because it could jeopardize subsequent court actions. Generally, the local police or the prosecutor can greatly assist the school's media relations person with what is appropriate to release after such an incident.

ASSISTING EMERGENCY SERVICES. Staff members may be required to assist police, fire, and emergency medical personnel on the scene of school violence and should be briefed about the particular types of support they may be asked to give.

They may also need to assist public utility agencies to shut off gas and electricity. Several staff members should know where the control units are located and how to operate them in case maintenance workers have been injured.

POST-TRAUMA COUNSELING. Emotional trauma will be one of the primary results of an episode of rampage violence. Staff and students most likely will experience a psychological shock from what they have witnessed and will require special and immediate attention. The school should prepare for such a possibility and assemble a team of counselors, religious leaders, and specialists.

ADDITIONAL CONSIDERATIONS

The previous checklist provides a review for the task force to assess its school's readiness should rampage violence strike. However, each school is different. Each will have different needs, special situations, or exceptional threat problems that may require it to further fine tune its preparations to be fully prepared.

Chapter 16

PRAEMONITUS PRAEMUNITUS

"FOREWARNED IS FOREARMED." One episode of rampage violence is too many. To date, there have been many, more than a sufficient number to alert school officials that they must put measures in place that will protect their staffs and students. Yet, many continue with inadequate programs. Even more alarming are the numbers that, aside from locks on the doors, continue to ignore security completely.

If you have reached this point in *Essential Strategies for School Security,* you have learned about the numerous strategies that will strengthen a school's defenses. You have seen that a comprehensive program must use technology and procedures. Most importantly, it must involve the human element. Staff and students must become stakeholders in their school's protection, which is ultimately their own protection.

In the national media, the topic of school security has oftentimes generated more hysteria than a reasonable, sensible approach. Schools, in turn, have scrambled for a quick fix. Many have resorted to the popular defenses such as metal detectors or surveillance cameras. But will the technology protect them? It's a question few dare to ask.

Through its broad overview, *Essential Strategies for School Security* has repeatedly emphasized that relying on a single measure or a limited application, regardless of how popular the protection product or idea may be, is neither reasonable nor sound security. Without a solid understanding of what the school needs, the technology can at best be a waste of money. At the worst, it can permit the school to believe it is secure yet leave it nearly as vulnerable as if it had no protection at all.

The key to effective school security lies in implementing protection measures that are necessary–those that address the actual threats and those that are potential. From the common everyday criminal activities such as theft and drugs to the more lethal potential of rampage violence, each campus must assess its own atmosphere and implement measures that are specifically designed to meet its own needs.

Technical innovations, in and of themselves, will not provide a lasting atmosphere of protection. Nor will procedural measures alone, regardless of how recommended they are.

The secret to effective security is really no secret at all. Effective security rests squarely on the shoulders of those who benefit. Only their ongoing determination and the commitment from those in authority can produce a school security program that protects, and will continue to protect, its students and its staff.

Appendix A

SCHOOL SECURITY SURVEY

(Example Format–Please feel free to copy and use as needed.)

School: _____

Address: _____

_____

Phone: _____

Date of security survey: _____

Name of school official responsible for the security survey:

_____

Survey team members: _____

_____

Names of school security task force: _____

_____

_____

Person responsible for the school's security program:

_____

Name of security consultant (if used): _____

_____

Name of police crime prevention specialist (if used):

_____

Name of any other security (outsource) assistance?

_____

What crime problems has the school experienced in the last three years?

_____

_____

_____

What types of violence have occurred on campus in the last three years? (nature of? police involvement? specific details? etc.)

_____

_____

_____

Are any particular security concerns expressed by the students, the parents, the faculty or other staff members?

_____

_____

Hours of operation (from opening to closing) for the school facility for each day of the week:

_____

_____

Yes   No

___   ___   Does the school currently have any form of security program?

___ ___ Has the school had to implement any emergency security measures in recent times? If yes, what?

_____

Does the school have an open or a closed campus?

___ open ___ closed

___ ___ If it has an open campus, are there any plans to close it?

AREA STUDY

___ ___ 1. Do any crime problems from the neighborhood threaten the school?

2. If yes, what are these threats? _____

_____

___ ___ 3. Does the school receive good community emergency services support? (police, fire, emergency medical)

EMERGENCY PLANNING

1. Does the school have emergency plans for:

___ ___ Fire?

___ ___ Bombing incident?

___ ___ Bomb threat/bomb discovery?

___ ___ Medical emergency?

___ ___ Shooting incident?

___ ___ Violent disorder?

___ ___ Accident?

___ ___ 2. Are the school's emergency plans in written form?

___ ___ 3. Have students, faculty, and staff members been briefed on emergency plans?

4. Who is responsible for emergency planning?

_____

___ ___ 5. Does the school practice mock drills to prepare for emergencies?

___ ___ 6. Are emergency first-aid kits placed at strategic locations throughout the school?

CLOSED-CIRCUIT TELEVISION SURVEILLANCE SYSTEM (CCTV)

___ ___ 1. Does the school currently have a CCTV system in use?

___ ___ 2. If yes, is it functioning properly?

3. Make a tour of the campus and determine which locations are places for known or potential problems:

_____ Regular campus congregation points?

_____ Locations where fights or disorders occur?

_____ Parking areas where thefts or vandalism to vehicles can occur?

_____ Remote sections of the grounds that are not in easy view from regular people traffic?

_____ Locations where suspected drug activities may be occurring?

_____ Interior building locations where teachers or students perceive there is of a threat or problems?

_____ The four sides of the school's buildings that provide coverage to entrances and exits?

_____ The school's commons areas?

_____ The main office?

_____ The teachers' lounge?

_____ Other vulnerable locations that could be subject to theft or other crime victimization and the school security task force deems that CCTV coverage is necessary?

SECURITY PERSONNEL

___ ___ 1. Are security personnel currently in use on campus?

___ ___ 2. If yes, have they undergone a thorough orientation as to working with young people and working in a school environment?

___ ___ 3. Do security officers wear the traditional security uniform or has the school adopted a "softer" look of a blazer, slacks, and the suitable security marking located on the left breast pocket?

___ ___ 4. Are security personnel needed to patrol school grounds or building facilities for more comprehensive security?

___ ___ 5. Are off-duty police officers needed for the school instead of unarmed security personnel?

6. At what locations and times do security personnel need to be posted about campus?

_____

COMMUNICATIONS

___ ___ 1. Does the school have sufficient intercoms with two-way capability for communicating between the classrooms and the main office in the event or a crisis or other emergency?

2. What upgrades are needed to improve the system of communications throughout the school?

_____

___ ___ 3. Does the school have a special system to create a subtle alert in the event of some act of violence or other hostility that puts the staff on alert without overtly alerting the perpetrators?

___ ___ 4. Are secured telephones situated throughout the facility that are only accessible to teachers or staff and can be used in the event of an emergency.

___ ___ 5. If yes, are the telephones in sufficient numbers and strategic places?

6. Where are additional phones needed? _____

_____

___ ___ 7. Has the school created or updated a special telephone directory of emergency telephone numbers that is accessible to teachers and staff?

___ ___ 8. Does the school have sufficient numbers of walkie-talkies for emergency communications?

___ ___ 9. If yes, are they in proper working order?

___ ___ 10. Are there sufficient numbers of bullhorns for emergency communications?

LOCKING DEVICES

___ ___ 1. Have all locking devices, e.g. door locks, padlocks, combination locks, which are used throughout the school facilities been inspected to see they are functioning properly?

2. What locks have been found missing or malfunctioning?

_____

3. What locations need locks that have not used a locking device before?

_____

4. Who is responsible for maintaining locks and for installing new ones if needed?

_____

5. Who conducts a regular schedule of checks and inspections on all locks that are used on the school's premises?

_____

___ ___ 6. Is there an established reporting system for personnel to report broken locks so prompt repairs can be made?

___ ___ 7. Does the bolt or throw to each door lock extend at least one inch into the door jam?

KEY CONTROL

___ ___ 1. Does the school have a formal key control system that manages and tracks all keys that are issued and are in use throughout the premises?

2. Who is responsible for the key control system for the school?

_____

___ ___ 3. Are all keys that are issued signed for by the recipient?

4. If yes, who maintains the log of assigned keys?

_____

___ ___ 5. Are keys retrieved from departing personnel?

___ ___ 6. Is there a system for promptly reporting lost keys and determining whether the lock needs to be replaced to ensure the integrity of the key control system?

___ ___ 7. Are all school keys stamped on the bow of the key "Do Not Duplicate?"

___ ___ 8. Are master keys in use at the school?

9. If yes, which personnel have possession of these keys?

_____

___ ___ 10. Are grand master keys in use at the school?

11. If yes, which personnel have possession of these keys?

_____

12. How often are locks changed? _____

_____

___ ___ 13. Are all spare keys kept secured at all times?

14. Where are the spare keys kept?

_____

___ ___ 15. Are students ever issued keys to school facilities?

16. If yes, what is the basis or criteria for issuing keys and is the standard valid? _____

_____

SECURITY SIGNAGE

1. Are signs posted about the school's premises that advise:

___ ___ The campus is protected by a security program.

___ ___ All loiterers, unauthorized persons, and those who commit crimes will be vigorously prosecuted.

___ ___ The campus is under surveillance by a closed-circuit television system.

___ ___ All visitors are routed to the proper parking area.

___ ___ All visitors are instructed where to report to register and receive a visitor's pass.

___ ___ All persons are directed to the different specified parking areas.

2. Where is additional signage needed to enhance security?

_____

___ ___ 3. Are signs visible for easy observation at night?

BADGE IDENTIFICATION

___ ___ 1. Does the school have a system of badge identification?

___ ___ 2. Are the badges worn on outer garments to easily and quickly determine who is a student, staff member, visitor, or other authorized person?

___ ___ 3. Is each badge constructed of tamperproof, laminated material to maintain the integrity of the system?

___ ___ 4. Does each badge (excluding visitors' badges) have a picture with accompanying data about the bearer?

___ ___ 5. To enhance the badge's value, does it contain life-safety information about the bearer, such as blood type, emergency medical data, parent/guardian to contact in the event of an emergency, allergies to medications, family physician, other pertinent data?

6. Who is responsible for issuing the badge identification?

_____

___ ___ 7. Are students and staff charged a replacement fee for lost badges?

___ ___ 8. Are there challenging procedures for all persons found not wearing a badge?

___ ___ 9. Are there disciplinary measures imposed on those who fail to wear their school identification badge?

10. What upgrades are needed in the current badge system?

_____

___ ___ 11. Are all badges retrieved from departing personnel and students?

___ ___ 12. Is there a reporting system for documenting all lost badges?

PROPERTY IDENTIFICATION

___ ___ 1. Does the school use a system of marking equipment and other property that belongs to it?

2. What type of system is used?

____ Self-adhesive label

____ Inscribed/etched marking or number

___ ___ 3. In addition to the standard labeling method is there a system of inscribing a hidden serial number on each item?

___ ___ 4. Does the school maintain a record of serial numbers and hidden numbers that are recorded on each piece of equipment or property?

5. Who is responsible for marking/labeling of all school property?

_____

___ ___ 6. Are there written procedures regarding school property and identification?

INVENTORY CONTROLS

___ ___ 1. Does the school use a system of inventory control for all property and equipment that belongs to the school?

___ ___ 2. Does the school document, log, and maintain the records of all serial numbers on all school equipment and property?

___ ___ 3. Are lost, damaged, or stolen items documented as such?

___ ___ 4. Does the school investigate its lost, damaged, or stolen property?

___ ___ 5. Does the school report stolen property to the police?

___ ___ 6. Are there written procedures for inventory controls?

7. Who is responsible for inventory controls for school property?

_____

___ ___ 8. Is all school property maintained in a secure facility or kept in storage when not in use?

LIGHTING

___ ___ 1. Are all areas of the campus sufficiently illuminated for good visibility at night?

___ ___ 2. Are all entrances to school buildings sufficiently illuminated?

___ ___ 3. Is there sufficient interior lighting for easy observation by police patrols?

___ ___ 4. Are repairs made to the lighting system, and are lighting outages replaced promptly?

___ ___ 5. Is the lighting system inspected regularly to ensure that it is functioning property?

6. Who is responsible for maintaining the lighting system?

_____

___ ___ 7. Are all controls and switches for the lighting system protected from tampering?

___ ___ 8. Are there any locations on the school's premises that need lighting or need the lighting upgraded?

9. If yes, where?

_____

___ ___ 10. Are there nighttime, environmental, or regular weather conditions, e.g. fog, smog, that affect the lighting and reduce its effectiveness?

11. If yes, what are these conditions, and what remedies are needed to overcome these problems?

_____

___ ___ 12. Does the school use timers to turn off lighting in areas that are not in use after certain hours? (The timers conserve energy but do not compromise the security of the facilities.)

ALARM SYSTEMS

1. What types of alarm systems does the school use?

___ ___ Fire alarm?

___ ___ Intrusions detection (burglar) alarm?

___ ___ Panic alarm?

___ ___ Other?

___ ___ 2. Is each building within the school complex alarmed?

___ ___ 3. Are all alarm systems in proper working order?

4. How often are the alarm systems tested?

_____

5. Who is responsible for maintaining the alarm systems?

_____

___ ___ 6. Are the alarm systems monitored by the appropriate community emergency services, e.g. police, fire, paramedics, so that the necessary service would respond in the event of an emergency?

___ ___ 7. Is this function tested regularly?

MONEY

___ ___ 1. Are cash sums (petty cash, coinage from vending machines, etc.) maintained on the school premises?

___ ___ 2. Is all money secured at all times?

3. Who is in charge of money kept at the school?

_____

4. How often is money audited?

_____

5. How often is money deposited at the bank?

___ ___ 6. Have there been any losses or shortages in the past accounting of school funds?

7. If yes, what was the problem and was it corrected satisfactorily?

PARKING CONTROLS

___ ___ 1. Is the school's parking area separated into specific parking locations for students', staff, and visitors' vehicles?

___ ___ 2. Is the parking area patrolled by police or security officers?

___ ___ 3. Is the school's parking facility under surveillance by closed-circuit television cameras?

___ ___ 4. Does the school issue parking stickers or placards for vehicles that denote the owner's status and authorized presence on campus, e.g. student, staff, visitor, etc.?

___ ___ 5. Are all parking areas sufficiently lighted for good night visibility?

VISITOR CONTROLS

___ ___ 1. Are all visitors sufficiently informed by signs or other means of communication as to where they should report to register?

___ ___ 2. Do visitors have a specially designated area for parking that is visibly identified?

___ ___ 3. Are visitors issued a temporary pass or badge that is worn on outer garments and identifies them as a visitor?

___ ___ 4. Is the pass/badge that the visitor is issued retrieved when they depart, or does it self-destruct after one use and can be discarded?

—— —— 5. Are visitors escorted to their destination within the school complex?

—— —— 6. If no, are they allowed to move about freely?

SECURITY POLICY AND PROCEDURES

—— —— 1. Does the school currently have written policy and procedures for any or all of its security measures or activities?

—— —— 2. Do the school's policy and procedures comply with the security policy and procedures as outlined or mandated by the county or state school boards?

3. Who is responsible for developing, reviewing, and updating the school's security policy and procedures?

_____

—— —— 4. Do the school's policy and procedural guidelines cover all aspects of the school's security program?

5. If no, what areas need to be developed?

_____

CHEMISTRY LABORATORY

—— —— 1. Is the school's chemistry laboratory kept secure at all times when not in use?

—— —— 2. Are all chemical, glassware, and other equipment that could be used to manufacture illicit drugs accounted for and kept secure at all times?

—— —— 3. Have there been any mysterious losses or ongoing shortages from the chemistry laboratory that have not been explained?

4. If yes, what has been the problem?

_____

___ ___ 5. Has the U.S. Drug Enforcement Administration (DEA) been consulted about the presence of any chemicals that may be present in the chemistry laboratory and could be used to manufacture illicit substances?

___ ___ 6. Were any chemicals identified?

___ ___ 7. If yes, have they been properly secured?

8. Who is in charge of the chemistry laboratory?

_____

SECURITY AWARENESS TRAINING

___ ___ 1. Does the school have a security awareness and orientation training program for students and faculty?

___ ___ 2. Does it sufficiently acquaint all persons about the various aspects of the school's security program?

___ ___ 3. Does the security awareness program encourage those who are protected to support and participate in the program to ensure that it continues to be effective and efficient?

SECURITY REPORTING

___ ___ 1. Does the school document all security problems that are discovered?

___ ___ 2. Does the school have a disposition system for routing and filing security reports?

3. Who is responsible for completing reports regarding security at the school?

_____

___ ___ 4. Are students and staff fully aware that it is most important to report any security problems promptly?

___ ___ 5. Has a criteria been established so that students and staff know the type of problems they should report?

__ __ 6. Does the school have a dedicated security report form that is used for documenting security-related matters?

7. Who reviews reports for a final disposition?

_____

__ __ 8. Are copies of reports regarding theft, vandalism, or other criminal activities that affect the school forwarded to the local law enforcement agencies for a follow-up investigation?

9. Who is responsible for the school security reporting system?

_____

CAFETERIA/VENDETERIA

__ __ 1. Is the cafeteria area secured at all times when it is not in use?

__ __ 2. Are food storage units, freezers, and other locations where consumables are maintained kept under secure conditions at all times?

__ __ 3. Are regular audits conducted of the cafeteria's foodstuffs and other supplies that are used in its operation?

4. Who is in charge of the cafeteria?

_____

__ __ 5. Are all vending machines emptied of money at the close of business each day?

6. Who is in charge of handling all monies recovered from vending machines?

_____

__ __ 7. Is the money received from the vending machine business audited regularly and carefully controlled?

__ __ 8. Does the cafeteria/vendeteria have an intrusion detection alarm to detect a break-in?

BARRIERS

1. What types of barriers are used to cordon off school property?

___ ___ Chain-link fence?

___ ___ Shrubbery?

___ ___ Building surfaces?

___ ___ Natural features (body of water, wooded area, natural land features, etc.)?

___ ___ Other?

2. Does the barrier system serve a security purpose or does it just delineate school property lines?

_____

___ ___ 3. If the current barrier system does not serve a security purpose, does it need to be reconfigured to provide a more protective function?

___ ___ 4. Are there particular buildings within the school's premises that need protective fencing to provide them with additional protection?

5. If yes, which buildings?

_____

If chain-link fencing is used as a barrier:

___ ___ 6. Is the fence of at least a number 9 gauge or heavier?

___ ___ 7. Does the fence have a top rail for added stability?

___ ___ 8. Is the fencing free of vegetation growth, underbrush, etc., which cause corrosion and limit visibility through the fence?

___ ___ 9. Is the fencing fabric pinned into the ground surface at the midpoint, between the line posts, to prevent an intruder from lifting it up and crawling underneath?

___ ___ 10. If the fencing crosses over culverts or other ground depressions, have additional sections been added to prevent circumvention of the barrier?

___ ___ 11. If the fence does not have the three-strand top-rigger situated atop it, does it need such an addition?

___ ___ 12. Are there additional barriers that need to be added to the existing barrier system surrounding the school?

13. If yes, where?

RECORDS SECURITY

___ ___ 1. Are all school records maintained in secure cabinets or other protective arrangements to prevent access by unauthorized persons?

___ ___ 2. Does the school have established, written procedures for handling school records and other sensitive documents?

___ ___ 3. Are all computers that contain school records or sensitive information maintained in secured conditions?

___ ___ 4. Do computers have passwords to prevent any unauthorized access?

___ ___ 5. Does the school use a shredder machine to destroy sensitive documents that are discarded?

6. Who is responsible for the school records?

PERSONNEL SCREENING

___ ___ 1. Does the school system conduct background investigations on all personnel assigned to the school?

2. What types of check are made?

___ ___ Criminal history (nationwide triple I check)?

___ ___ Credit history?

___ ___ Professional credentials?

___ ___ Driving records?

___ ___ 3. Are drug screens conducted on all personnel?

___ ___ 4. Are all references checked on the applicant's application?

5. Who conducts the background investigations for the school system?

_____

SECURITY PROGRAM MAINTENANCE

___ ___ 1. Does the school's security program have a component that schedules checks and inspections of all its aspects and sees that it complies with proper operations?

2. What components are inspected on a regular basis:

___ ___ Security equipment for repairs, additions, and upgrades?

___ ___ Security procedures upgrades?

___ ___ Student and staff updates on necessary changes to the security program?

___ ___ Security awareness updates?

3. Who is responsible for maintaining the school's security program?

_____

___ ___ 4. Are there written guidelines that outline the procedures that should be followed when conducting security program maintenance inspections?

___ ___ 5. Are the repairs or needed upgrades to the security program's various components made promptly?

OFFICE SECURITY

___ ___ 1. Are the school's offices outfitted with intrusion detection and panic alarm systems?

___ ___ 2. Are the offices secured each day at the close of business or when unoccupied?

___ ___ 3. Are all exterior doors of sufficient strength to withstand an easy break-in?

___ ___ 4. Is each door equipped with a suitable locking mechanism to prevent easy circumvention?

___ ___ 5. Is the office monitored by a closed-circuit camera system?

___ ___ 6. Does a "clean desk policy" exist for all office personnel that outlines that each desk is to be clear of any documents and that the individual's office is to be secured when unoccupied?

___ ___ 7. Is the door to each staff person's office closed and secured when the office is not in use or is unoccupied?

___ ___ 8. Does each piece of office equipment have a property marker or label affixed to it identifying it as school property?

___ ___ 9. Do office personnel keep their personal property, e.g., purses, coats, secured at all times?

___ ___ 10. Are office computers, copy machines, and any other portable items secured in place by cables or other locking methods to prevent them from being removed easily?

___ ___ 11. Is there an office location where all mail and packages are secured when they are delivered to the school and that prevents loss until the items are picked up by the recipient?

Appendix B

WEB SITES OF SECURITY
PRODUCTS AND SERVICES

The following web sites are a representative listing of online information to provide an overview of understanding as to the various technologies applicable for a comprehensive school security program.

AUTHORS' NOTE: This listing is not an endorsement of any company or their security products or their services.

Access Control

Access Control & Security Systems Integration
www.securitysolutions.com

Access Control Technologies, Inc.
www.neurotag.com

Access Denied, Inc.
www.ultradog.com

Access Specialties, Inc.
www.access.specialties.com

Access Technology
www.alltecindustries.com

Cardkey
www.cardkey.com

Cardkey Systems, Inc.
www.cardkey.com

Checkpoint
www.checkpointacpg.com

Continental Instruments LLC
www.cicaccess.com

Detex Corporation
www.detex.com

Diebold Inc.
www.diebold.com

Essex Electronics Inc.
www.keyless.com

Federal APD Inc.
FederalAPD.com

HID Corporation
www.proxtrak.com

ILCO UNICAN Corporation–UNICAN Electronics Division
www.ilcounican.com

Keir Systems Inc.
www.kerisys.com

Libert Corporation
www.liebert.com

Locknetics Security Engineering
www.locknetics.com

Monitor Dynamics Inc.
www.mdisafenet.com

Northern Computers Inc.
www.nciaccess.com

Philips Communication & Security Systems Inc.(BURLE)
www.philipscss.com

Secura Key
www.securakey.com

Security Door Controls
www.sdcsecurity.com

Sensormatic/Software House-Access Control Division
www.swhouse.com

Simplex
www.simplexnet.com

Synergistics Inc.
www.synergisticsinc.com

Alarms

Ademco Group
www.ademco.com

DETECTION SYSTEMS
www.detectionsys.com

Badge Identification

Comprehensive Identification Products Inc.
www.compid.com

Eastman Kodak Company-Identification & Security Solutions
www.kodak.com

Eltron
www/eltron.com

FARGO
www.fargo.com

IDenticard Systems Inc.
www.identicard.com

J.A.M. Plastics, Inc.
www.badgeholder.com

Laminex (D & K Laminex Inc.)
www.laminex.com

Temtec/TEMbadge
temtec@tempbadge.com

Barriers

Anchor Fence/Master Halco
www.mhfence.com

Biometrics

Biometric Identification
www/biometricid.com

EyeDentify Inc.
www.Eyedentify.com

Identix
www.identix.com

Recognition Systems Inc.
www.recogsys.com

Bombs and Explosives

www.bombsecurity.com

Bullet Resistant Materials

Fargo Electronics Inc.
www.farge.com

Closed Circuit Television Systems

CCTV Corporation (GBC)/A Sentrol Company
www.gbc-cctv.com

Closed Circuit Television Manufacturers Association
jmcmahoneia.org

JAVELIN SYSTEMS
www.javelin.com

PELCO
www.pelco.com

Vicon Industries
www.vicon-cctv.com

Watec America Corporation
www.watec.com

Communication Systems

Aiphone Corporation
www.aiphone.com

Glass (Security Glazing)

ACE/ClearDefense Inc.
www.acecleardefense.com

Allied Security Inc.
www.alliedsecurity.com

INSULGARD CORPORATION
www.insulgard.com

Guard Personnel

Allied Security Inc.
www.alliedsecurity.com

America Protective Services Inc.
www.apsinc.com

Guardsmark Inc.
www.guardsmark.com

Pinkerton
www.pinkers.com

Stanley Smith Security Inc.
www.initialsecurity.com

Hotlines

Security Voice
www.schoolhelpline.com

The Network
www.tnwinc.com

Integrated Security Systems

Northern Computers
www.nciaccess.com

Key Control Systems

Key Trak
www.keytrak.com

Knox Company
www.knowbox.com

Morse Watchman
www.morsewatchman.com

Lighting

LightGuardian
www.lightguardian.com

Locks

Ace Lock and Security
www.acelock.com

DynaLock Corporation
www.dynalock.com

Kensington
www.kensingtonlock.com

Locknetics Security Engineering
www.locknetics.com

Sargent & Greenleaf Inc.
www.sglocks.com

Simplex
www.simplexnet.com

Winfield Locks, Inc.
www.cssmain.com

Metal Detectors

Garrett Metal Detectors Inc.–Security Division
www.garrett.com

Publications

AIMS Media
www.aims-multimedia.com

Butterworth-Heinemann
www.bh.com

Charles C. Thomas Publishers
www.ccthomas.com

Signage

Seton Name Plate Company
www.seton.com

Signs of Security
www.signsofsecurity.com

General Security Information

American Society for Industrial Security (ASIS)
www.asisonline.org

ASISNET
www.asisonline.org

AIMS Media
www.aims-cultimedia.com

International Foundation for Protection Officers
www.ifpo.com

International Security Review–DMG Business Media
www.dmg.co.uk

Intertec Publishing
www.securitysolutions.com

Security

www.securitymagazine.com

Security Publications S. A. (Pty.) Ltd.
www.secpub.co.za/sf.htm

Security Sales
www.securitysales.com

Security Sales Magazine
www.securitysales.com

Security Products
www.secprodonline.com

Security Booths

Austin Fabricating, Inc.
www.austinfab.com

Par-kut International, Inc.
www.parkut.com

Violence Prevention

Blueprints for Violence Prevention
Internet: **http://www.Colorado.EDU/cspv/blueprints/**

Children's Safety Network
Education Development Center
Maternal and Child Health Bureau
Internet: **http://www.edc.org/HHD/csn**

National Organization for Victim Assistance (NOVA)
Internet: **http://www.try-nova.org/**

U.S. Department of Education *(Safe and Drug Free Schools, Office of Special Education)*
Internet: **http://www.ed.gov**

U.S. Department of Justice *(Office of Juvenile Justice, Kids Crime Prevention)*
Internet: **http://www.usdoj.gov**

Violence Institute
Internet: **http://www.umdnj.edu/vinjweb/**

Appendix C

SECURITY ASSOCIATIONS
AND ORGANIZATIONS

The following list of security associations and organizations may serve as a valuable source of information and assistance regarding the development of a school security program.

American Association of School Administrators
1801 North Moore Street
Arlington, Virginia 22209
Phone: 703/528-0700

American Society for Industrial Security
1625 Prince Street
Alexandria, Virginia 22314
Phone: 703/519-6200

Center for the Study and Prevention of Violence
University of Colorado
Box 442, Building #10
Boulder, Colorado 80309-0442
Phone: 303/492-1032
Web site: **www.colorado.edu/CSPV**

Community Policing Consortium
1726 M Street, NW
#801
Washington, DC 20036
Phone: 202/833-3305

D.A.R.E. America
P.O. Box 2090
Los Angeles, California 90051
Phone: 800/245-DARE

International Association of Chiefs of Police
515 North Washington Street
Alexandria, Virginia 22314
Phone: 800/The IACP

National Association of Elementary School Principals
1615 Duke Street
Alexandria, Virginia 22314-3483
Phone: 703/684-3345
Web site: **www.naesp.org**

National Association of School Resource Officers
2714 SW 5th Street
Boynton Beach, Florida 33435
Phone: 516/243-1506

National Association of Secondary School Principals
1904 Association Drive
Reston, Virginia 20191
Phone: 703/860-0200

National Center for Conflict Resolution Education
110 West Main Street
Urbana, Illinois 61801
Phone: 217/384-4118

National Clearinghouse on Alcohol and Drug Information
P.O. Box 2345
Rockville, Maryland 20852
Phone: 301/468-2600

National Crime Prevention Council
1700 K Street, NW
Washington, DC 20006-3817
Phone: 202/466-62372
Web site: **www.ncpc.org**

National PTA
330 North Wabash Avenue
Suite 2100
Chicago, Illinois 60611
Phone: 312/670-6782

National School Safety Center
4165 Thousand Oaks Boulevard
Suite 290
Westlake Village, California 91362
Phone: 805/373-9977
Web site: **www.nsscl.org**

National Sheriffs Association
1450 Duke Street
Alexandria, Virginia 22314-3490
Phone: 703/836-7827

National Youth Gang Information Center
P.O. Box 12729
Tallahassee, Florida 33217
Phone: 850/385-0600

Safe and Drug-Free Schools Program
Office of Elementary and Secondary Education
U.S. Department of Education
600 Independence Avenue, NW
Washington, DC 20202-6123
Phone: 202/260-3954

Youth Crime Watch of America
9300 South Dadeland Boulevard
Suite 100
Miami, Florida 33156
Phone: 305/670-2409

Appendix D

SECURITY REFERENCE SOURCES

The following source documents and references are suggested additions to any security reference library.

Protection of Assets Manual
Volumes 1-IV
Authors: Timothy Walsh and Richard J. Healy
Publisher: The Merritt Company
Santa Monica, California

The Complete Manual of Corporate and Industrial Security
Author: Russell L. Bintliff
Publisher: Prentiss-Hall, Inc.
Englewood Cliffs, New Jersey

Encyclopedia of Security Management—Techniques and Technology
Author: John J. Fay
Publisher: Butterworth-Heinemann
Stoneham, Massachusetts

Effective Physical Security
Author: Lawrence J. Fennelly
Publisher: Butterworth-Heinemann
Stoneham, Massachusetts

Handbook of Loss Prevention and Crime Prevention
Author: Lawrence J. Fennelly
Publisher: Butterworth-Heinemann
Stoneham, Massachusetts

Security Managers Desk Reference
Authors: David A. Schactsiek and Richard S. Post
Publisher: Butterworth-Heinemann
Woburn, Massachusetts

Appendix E

STUDENT QUESTIONNAIRE

Grade level of student completing this questionnaire?

___ Freshman   ___ Sophomore   ___ Junior   ___ Senior

Yes No

___ ___ 1. Since becoming a student at this school have you been the victim of a crime while at school?

2. If yes, describe what happened. _____

_____

___ ___ 3. Were you injured as a result of the crime?

___ ___ 4. Was it necessary to make a police report because of the incident?

___ ___ 5. Was the person responsible for committing the crime arrested?

6. Was the person responsible for committing the offense:

___ ___ A fellow student?

___ ___ A person from off campus?

___ ___ 7. If you have not been the victim of a crime at school, have you witnessed a crime taking place?

If yes, what was the crime that you witnessed? Explain: _____

_____

_____

8. Have you observed other students at school with:

____ ____ Guns?

____ ____ Knives?

____ ____ A bomb or some type of explosive device(including fireworks)?

____ ____ Clubs?

____ ____ Other weapons? Describe _____

_____

____ ____ 9. Do you feel safe at this school?

____ ____ 10. What do you think could be made safer and more secure?

Explain _____

____ ____ 11. Do you believe that security needs to be increased at this school?

____ ____ 12. Would you be willing to participate in a more active security program at this school?

____ ____ 13. Would you be interested in learning about how this school can be safer and more secure?

____ ____ 14. Have you observed students using or selling drugs on this campus?

15. If yes, where? _____

_____

____ ____ 16. Do you know of secret student gangs or groups who threaten or who do use violence?

17. If yes:

What are the names of these groups? _____

Who are their leaders? _____

Who are the members? _____

___ ___ 18. Have you been the victim of a "bully" while at school?

19. If yes, what is the bully's name?

_____

___ ___ 20. If you had a student "hotline" telephone number made available to you, would you use it to report problems that may cause harm to students, faculty, and the school? (Your identify would not be known.)

21. If no, why not? _____

_____

Signed (optional) _____   Date: _____

Appendix F

FACULTY AND STAFF QUESTIONNAIRE

1. What is your position with the school's faculty or staff?

___ Teacher   ___ Counselor   ___ Administrator

___ Maintenance   ___ Other

Yes No

___ ___ 2. Since you have been at the school, have you been the victim of a crime while at the school?

3. If yes, describe what happened and when? _____

_____

___ ___ 4. Were the police called to investigate the incident?

If no, why not? _____

___ ___ 5. Were you injured as a result of this event?

___ ___ 6. Do you feel safe and secure at this school?

7. If no, why not? _____

___ ___ 8. In your position with the school system are you fully aware of any legal requirements or other state safe schools regulations imposed on you or that you are responsible for?

___ ___ 9. Would you like to be briefed as to any regulations or other legal mandates for which you are responsible regarding state safe schools acts or other security mandates?

___ ___ 10. Do you know of any school security procedures that are in place and followed at this school?

___ ___ 11. Do you feel these procedures are adequate?

12. If no, what do you feel needs to be improved? _____

_____

___ ___ 13. If an act of school violence occurs, do you know what to do?

14. If yes, what would you do? _____

_____

___ ___ 15. If a shooting incident, hostage incident, bombing incident, bomb discovery, etc. occurs, do you know any procedures to follow in such an event?

16. Explain _____

_____

___ ___ 17. If you could improve the security of this school, what would you like to see upgraded?

18. Explain _____

_____

___ ___ 19. Would you be willing to participate in a school security task force?

___ ___ 20. Have you witnessed criminal acts or some form of violence on campus?

21. Explain _____

_____

___ ___ 22. Are you aware of any secret student gangs or groups on campus that espouse violence?

23. If yes, explain _____

_____

Signed:(optional) _____   Date: _____

Appendix G

SECURITY INCIDENT REPORT

Type of Incident:

___ Assault ___ CCTV Malfunction ___ Lock missing

___ Bombing ___ Disturbance ___ Lost key

___ Bomb discovery ___ Fight ___ Shooting

___ Bomb threat ___ Gun-involved ___ Theft

___ Break-in ___ Knife-involved

___ Other type weapon involved

Other: _____

Location of incident: (Where on the school premises?) _____

_____

Date/time of incident: _____

Law enforcement agency contacted: _____

_____

Responding police officer and unit number: _____

_____

Person(s) involved: _____

_____

Witness(s): _____

_____

Person(s) injured: _____

_____

Narrative: _____

_____

_____

_____

_____

_____

_____

Person completing the report (Print name and sign)   Date/time

GLOSSARY

Access Control–The system of security procedures and technology that is used to control the entry and exit of persons and vehicles to the protected school facility. An access control system may consist of a closed-circuit television system, signage, parking lot controls, visitor registration, card access, and a variety of other security measures, used singly or in combination, to limit the movements of unauthorized persons.

Alarm System–A technical system that signals a condition such as a fire, unlawful entry, duress, or some other emergency at the school that summons human intervention to stop or correct. The basic components of an alarm system include (1) sensors that are positioned about the premises for early warning detection of a trouble condition, (2) the control unit that processes and transmits the trouble signal, and (3) the annunciator that communicates the trouble signal to the appropriate response element such as security personnel or the police. See, Fire Alarm System, Intrusion Alarm System.

American Society for Industrial Security (ASIS)–ASIS is the premiere organization in the world for security professionals. Membership in the association is open to those who have backgrounds, careers, or interest in the field of protection. This is an excellent source for information concerning the various aspects of security. For further information: American Society for Industrial Security, 1625 Prince Street, Alexandria, Virginia 22314, USA, 703/519-6200.

Annunciator–The alarm system component that signals a change in the condition of a protected school facility or area. This change communicates a signal to a lighted control panel or an audible device such as a siren that is intended to summon a human response to the situation and intercept the problem.

Assessment (Security)–An evaluation of a situation or location to determine security needs that will improve the level of protection for the school, students, and staff. See, Security Survey.

Badge Identification–The use of a tamperproof, wallet-sized identification card that contains a picture and personal data of the bearer that can be displayed on outer garments to provide ready identification of that individual and his or her authorization to be within a protected location. The identification badge can have an extra special value with the addition of vital emergency medical information that can be included on its reverse side, such as; contact person or a parent in the event of an emergency; emergency telephone numbers for home or parents'/guardians' work; family physician; allergies to medications; blood type; any other items that will enhance the badge's life safety value.

Barrier–Any natural or man-made obstacle that is designed to deny unauthorized access to the protected school facility or to delineate its property lines. Barriers may include walls, fencing, shrubbery, a body of water, a ditch, or some other natural land feature. A closed-circuit television system can present a form of psychological barrier to a potential intruder who is otherwise dissuaded.

Biometrics–The security technology that uses the identification of a person through the measurement and confirmation of that individual's physical characteristics such as voice intonation, signature analysis, fingerprint patterns, hand geometry, and retinal (eye) pattern recognition.

Bolt–See, Throw.

Breaking and Entry/Burglary–Depending on the particular state and the language of their statutes, this is the unlawful act of entering a school's premises after closing for the purposes of committing a criminal act such as a theft, vandalism, or some other illegal act.

Camera–The component of a closed-circuit television surveillance system that receives the visual images from its zone of coverage, converts it into an electronic signal, and then communicates this information to the monitoring unit. See Monitor.

Card Access System–An access control system that requires a technically configured wallet-size card that is inserted into a processing unit that activates the access unit to permit entry. This type has an enhanced protection feature against the loss of a card through the incorporation of a PIN or personal identification number that is used in conjunction with the card to gain access.

Certified Protection Professional (CPP)–A designation that is granted through examination for certification of security professionals. This distinction indicates the certified individual is thoroughly skilled in the profession of security. The CPP program is administered through the American Society for Industrial Security.

Closed-Circuit Television Surveillance System–A system of protection that incorporates television cameras and monitors to provide low-profile observation of selected areas of the school's campus and interior facilities to deter or detect security threats before they can become completed crimes.

Community-Oriented Policing–A proactive concept that has been adopted by American law enforcement in which the police and citizens work together to suppress or eliminate crime and improve the quality of life in communities across the country. It is within the community policing units of local police agencies that are usually established to assist and advise the school security task force in their efforts to improve their school's security.

Comprehensive Security–A security program that has considered all of the known and potential threats that may confront the school and implements a thorough system of countermeasures that are designed to deter or defeat such problems. See, Security Overlap, Protection-in-Depth, Three P's of Protection.

Countermeasure–Any intervening component of the school security program that is incorporated to defeat or nullify security threats.

CPTED–The initials for "Crime Prevention through Environmental Design." (Pronounced "sep-ted") See, Crime Prevention through Environmental Design.

Crime Prevention through Environmental Design–A concept of security design in which a school's campus layout and its interior locations are arranged in such a manner so as to suppress crime, and the perception of it, by creating an openness for easy observation or surveillance throughout the premises.

Crime Prevention Specialist –A specially trained law enforcement officer who advises business owners and residents concerning the improved protection of their property and themselves. This unit is usually found assigned to an agency's community-oriented policing division.

Crime Scene –The place where an incident of crime has occurred that should be cordoned off and protected until the arrival of the police.

D.A.R.E. –The acronym for "Drug Abuse Resistance Education." This is a law enforcement program that targets certain grade levels for drug abuse awareness training in the attempt to deter student involvement with drugs in their secondary school years. See, Community-Oriented Policing.

Detection –The proactive function of security that is designed to discover threats and vulnerabilities to the school's security program before they can materialize into a criminal event.

Deterrence –The proactive function of security that is designed to discourage or prevent persons from committing acts of crime or violence against the school, its students, and faculty.

Duress Alert –The discreet prearranged signaling procedure to communicate to other affected persons that a crisis or trouble condition exists that is potentially life threatening. This method of signaling is designed to alert those persons who can then activate crisis intervention measures without alerting the perpetrators who have created the threatening situation.

Entry and Movement Controls –The procedures and technical applications that are necessary to provide a system that monitors the whereabouts and activities of persons present within a protected facility.

Fail-Safe –A built-in stopgap system within the school security program that provides additional countermeasures for complete backup protection coverage should one particular measure fail or be circumvented by a perpetrator. See, Protection-in-Depth, Security Overlap.

Foreseeability –A legal concept used as a standard for liability in security-related litigation that is also known as "foreseeable risk." It is those factors that would indicate the likelihood of a threat occurrence that could cause harm or loss that an ordinary prudent person would reasonably expect to occur. The development of a school security program in response to known or potential scholastic crime and violence is a response to foreseeability. See, Liability, Negligence.

Glazing (Security) –Having to do with high-strength glass designed for security purposes and applications.

Grand Master Key –A key that will operate all locks within a key locking system. The hazard of the grand master key system is that if this key is lost, the entire lock system is compromised.

G.R.E.A.T. –The acronym for "Gang Resistance Education and Training." This is a program administered by law enforcement agencies to dissuade students from becoming involved with street gang activities. See, Community-Oriented Policing.

Hostage –A person who is held against his or her will and who may be ransomed for something the captor seeks.

Hostage Negotiator–A specially trained law enforcement officer skilled in crisis negotiations with perpetrators for the peaceful resolution of a high-risk situation in which hostages' lives are at stake.

Hostage Situation–An incident in which persons have been taken hostage against their will by perpetrators who threaten their lives in exchange for something they seek or desire.

Independent Security Consultant–A security professional who provides advice and counsel to a client on protection-related matters but does not offer or represent any security products or other commercialized security services.

Integration–1. The careful combination of the various components of the school security program so that each complements and supports the other for more complete, comprehensive protection. 2. The use of personal computers to assist in the overall monitoring of different security technical systems such as closed-circuit television units, access control systems, security officer patrols, inventory and property management, alarms, etc. See, Comprehensive Security, Protection-in-Depth, Security Overlap, Three P's of Protection.

Intrusion Alarm System–An alarm system that is designed to alert the police, security personnel, or others as to an illegal entry by an intruder into a school building or facility after it is closed or when authorized persons are not present.

Judgment Call–The extemporaneous decision making that is required when time does not permit full and careful evaluation of all of the facts because of exigent circumstances.

Key Control System–A system for maintaining the orderly tracking of all keys to the school premises. This is best if it is under the responsibility of one person who handles key issuance, replacement, and recovery from departing personnel to ensure the complete integrity of the system.

Larceny–A term for theft or the illegal and unauthorized removal of school property from the premises.

Law Enforcement Agency–The governmental agency responsible for the enforcement of the law and that will respond to crimes and violence occurring at a school. It has the responsibility to investigate a crime, conduct crime prevention awareness programs, or provide hostage negotiators or a SWAT team in the event of a violent incident. See Community-Oriented Policing, D.A.R.E., G.R.E.A.T., Hostage Negotiator, SWAT Team.

Liability–The legal exposure a school might face because of a failure to provide a reasonably safe environment or one that is haphazardly developed that results in injuries or loss by those who use the facility. See, Foreseeability, Negligence.

Line-of-Sight–The jeopardy posed by armed perpetrators who have the ability to fire on victims that are within their direct viewing range.

Line Posts–The vertical poles that are spaced equidistant along a fence line on which the fencing fabric is attached.

Line Supervision–A method for protecting an alarm system line that causes an activation of the alarm in the event of tampering with the unit. This is a particularly important feature for a school's intrusion alarm system.

Locking Device–Any mechanical or electronic apparatus that is used to secure a particular point or location from unauthorized access and requires a key, PIN code, combination, or other means for it to be opened. See, PIN Code.

Master Key–A key that will open a certain series or segment of locks within an over-all lock system. The problem with the master key arrangement is that, if lost, the entire series of locks that can be operated with this key can be compromised.

Monitor–The television unit that provides the video imaging for observation of activities covered by a closed-circuit television surveillance system.

Negligence–The legal concept in which there is a failure to exercise the degree of care that a reasonable, prudent person would exercise under the same circumstances or conditions. This standard is applied in security-related litigation in which particular precautionary measures were not implemented to properly safeguard those present in a given situation where known or potential threats to personal safety existed.

Physical Security–The use of security hardware or technology such as locks, alarm systems, closed-circuit television applications, access control systems, and the like to safeguard a school and the people who use the facility.

PIN Code–The acronym for "Personal Identification Number" that is the code number used in conjunction with card access keypads or with push-button mechanical locks.

Plan–The scheduled, orderly progression of events and activities that will lead to the accomplishment of an objective.

Planning–See, Security Planning.

Policy and Procedures–The written statements that outline the functions of the school security program and how it is to be administered for the protection of the school and those who use the facility. The various policy and procedures are the guidelines that proscribe the who, what, when, why, and how the program is to be maintained for the desired level of safeguards.

Preemptive–The act of seizing the opportunity or to strike first before others are aware of the event. This is the one factor of surprise that criminal perpetrators rely on to get the advantage over others for victimizing them.

Prevention–The act of taking the necessary measures to stop or deter an event from happening. Prevention is the central theme of any school security program.

Priority-based Security Planning–The security planning concept that considers the threats that are more imminent and require immediate attention with subsequent countermeasures implemented to address lesser serious protection problems as they are needed or become available.

Proactive–To act in advance of a tragic or criminal incident occurring by taking the advance precautions to prevent or deter it. See, Preemptive, School Security Program.

Pro Bono–Consulting work that is performed free of charge by a security professional.

Protection–The system or methods implemented to provide safeguards for persons, places, and/or things.

Protection-in-Depth–The establishment of a system or series of protective rings that enclose an object, place, or situation that is vulnerable to criminal threat. This design is to ensure more complete security. See, Security Overlap.

Rampage Killers–Criminal perpetrators who suddenly and unexpectedly undertake random murder sprees with the intent of inflicting a maximum amount of death and injury on soft targets such as schools, the workplace, or other settings where such occurrences are least expected.

Rampage Violence–The sudden, spontaneous use of force intended to impart mass killing, injury, and destruction on unsuspecting, innocent victims and their location.

Resource Officer–See, School Resource Officer.

Safeguards–The measures that are incorporated to provide the necessary security.

Scarecrow Effect–The psychological effect created by the presence of security implementations such as a closed-circuit television surveillance system that provides a ready indication to observers that security is active to ward off those who would otherwise want to commit a crime on school property.

School Crime–Criminal acts for which the school security program should be designed to address. Acts of crime and violence within the school setting including, but not limited to:
- Theft of school property, e.g. instruments from band room, athletic equipment from the field house, computers, office supplies, unsecured students' and teachers' valuables
- Unauthorized use of school telephones for long distance calls
- Trespass or loitering on school grounds
- Breaking into vehicles
- Burglarizing the school building after closing
- Theft from vending machines in Commons or other areas
- Assault from fights
- Felonious assault from shootings or knifing incidents
- Drug dealing
- Abduction and/or kidnapping
- Possession of dangerous and deadly weapons
- Illegal substances possession
- Sexual assault
- Larceny of foodstuffs from cafeteria
- Theft of unsecured mail or packages delivered to the school
- Theft of unsecured petty cash funds or money from vending machines
- Vandalism to school property
- False fire alarms
- Bomb threats
- Hostage seizures
- Homicides from violent incidents

School Resource Officer–Law enforcement officers who are assigned to schools to serve as liaison for reducing crime and violence on campus.

School Security Program–A comprehensive program of protective measures that incorporates technology and procedures designed to safeguard persons who use the school facility and prevent loss of school property. See, Protection-in-Depth, Three P's of Protection, School Crime.

School Security Task Force–The team of teachers, students and other staff members who are delegated the task of developing the school security program.

Security–The perception of safety or the state of being free from danger, fear, or harm. The operations and activities associated with the defense or protection of something, someone, or someplace from threat or attack.

Security Audit–A security study conducted on a facility or setting that has a security program to determine the level of integrity and compliance maintained by the program.

Security Cables–High-strength metal cables that are sheathed in plastic and are used to secure computer units and other portable office equipment in place to prevent their easy removal by theft.

Security Consultant–An individual who serves as an advisor that is a protection professional skilled in the study and analysis of an organization and its facilities to determine where threats and vulnerabilities exist and make the necessary recommendations to correct these problems.

Security Overlap–The arrangement of security technology and procedures so that each individual measure is backed up or supported by another to act as a fail-safe in the event the primary implementation malfunctions or is circumvented. See, Protection-in-Depth.

Security Personnel–The use of uniformed security officers to maintain watch inside the school or to patrol school grounds.

Security Planning–The layout and design of a comprehensive security program for a school that is developed from an analysis of the threats and vulnerabilities that confront that particular scholastic setting. See, Priority-based Security Planning.

Security Program–The comprehensive system or process by which protection is undertaken and provided for an organization and its setting.

Security Signage–Signs, placards, or other visual displays that are used to enhance the security program by informing observers of certain conditions or measures that are in place that direct their movements or ward off criminal threats.

Security Survey–The in-depth examination of a school, its setting, and its activities for the purposes of identifying threats and vulnerabilities that pose harm to the facility from which the necessary security countermeasures can be implemented for a comprehensive program of protection.

Set Screw–A tiny screw that secures the pin that fits into the external hinges of a door and prevents its removal and, thus, removal of the door from its hinge, which would then permit unauthorized entry.

Shroud (Lock)–A metal or other protective covering that is placed over a locking device located outdoors and subject to weather conditions that could cause corrosion or other damage.

Signage–See, Security Signage.

Soft Target–A setting, situation, or organization that has minimal or no security with which to protect the premises and persons located there.

SRO–See, School Resource Officer.

Survey Team–A team of school security task force members who have been designated to conduct an in-depth review of the school's facilities to determine where protection shortcomings and problems exist so that specific countermeasures can be implemented for the development of the school's security program.

SWAT Team–A specially trained unit of law enforcement officers who are skilled in the application of special weapons and tactics to be used for the rescue of victims from high-risk situations.

Theft -The criminal act of unauthorized removal of property belonging to the school or to other persons.

Threat–An indication of an impending danger or harm.

Threat Triangle–An illustration of the three elements necessary for a security threat, which are the "opportunity" to commit an act of crime or violence, the "desire" on the part of the perpetrator to commit such an act, and the "target" or the victim of the crime. To eliminate any one of these factors negates the ability to commit a completed crime.

Three P's of Protection–These are the fundamental components of any comprehensive security program, which include people, physical security, and procedures.

Throw–The metal rod or bar that extends from the door locking device into the strike plate of the door frame and shifts into the locked/unlocked position as the key is turned.

Timeline–A graphic representation of the scheduled sequence of events involved in a plan, from beginning to end, that can be a valuable aid to the school security planning process.

Top Rigger–The three-strand barbed wire attachment that is affixed to the top of a chain-link fence and is usually placed at an angle.

Vandalism–The criminal acts of destroying school property, graffiti, or other malicious mischief.

Vendor–One who offers security products or other commercialized security services.

Violence–See, Rampage Killing, Rampage Violence.

Vulnerability–Being susceptible or subject to a weakness in protection from criminal victimization.

BIBLIOGRAPHY

American School & University and *Access Control & Security Systems Integration* Magazines. "Undersiege–Schools as the New Battleground." (Special Supplement) A collaboration of the staffs of the magazines *"American Schools and University* and *Access Control & Security Systems Integration."* 1999.

Barnard, Robert L. (1981). *Intrusion Detection Systems–Principles of Operation and Application.* Woburn, MA: Butterworth.

Bintliff, Russell L. (1992). *The Complete Manual of Corporate and Industrial Security.* Englewood Cliffs, NJ: Prentice-Hall.

Black, Henry Campbell. (1979). *Black's Law Dictionary.* 5th ed. St. Paul, MN: West Publishing.

Bowles, Rice, McDavid, Graff and Love, PLLC. "Violence in West Virginia Schools." Charleston, West Virginia. April 20, 1999.

Broder, CPP, James F. (1984). *Risk Analysis and The Security Survey.* Stoneham, MA: Butterworth. Stoneham, MA: Butterworth, 1983.

Cole, Richard B. (1974). *Protection Management and Crime Prevention.* Cincinnati, OH: W. H. Anderson.

Crowe, Timothy D. (1991). *Crime Prevention Through Environmental Design–Applications of Architectural Design and Space Management Concepts.* National Crime Prevention Institute. Stoneham, MA: Butterworth-Heinemann.

Cumming, Neil (1992). *Security–A Guide to Security System Design and Equipment Selection and Installation.* Newton, MA: Butterworth-Heinemann.

D'Addario, Francis James. (1989). *Loss Prevention through Crime Analysis.* National Crime Prevention Institute. Stoneham, MA: Butterworths.

Department of Justice, United States. (1992-1995). *Community-Oriented Policing and Problem Solving (COPPS) Training Programs.* Charleston, WV: Charleston Police Department.

Fay, John J. (1993). *Encyclopedia of Security Management–Techniques and Technology.* Stoneham, MA: Butterworth-Heinemann.

Federal Bureau of Investigation. School Violence. Volume 68, Number 9. *The Law Enforcement Bulletin.* United States Department of Justice. Washington, D.C. September, 1999.

Fennelly, Lawrence J. (1982). *Handbook of Loss Prevention and Crime Prevention.* Stoneham, MA: Butterworth.

Fennelly, Lawrence J. (1992). *Effective Physical Security.* Stoneham, MA: Butterworth-Heinemann.

Floyd, William R. (1995). *Security Surveys.* Crete, IL: Abbot, Langer and Associates.

Galaxy Control Systems. (1996). *Reference Guide to Access & Security Management.* Walkersville, MD: Galaxy Control Systems.

Gifis, Steven H. (1975). *Law Dictionary.* Woodbury, NY: Barron's Educational Series.

Green, Gion, & Farber, Raymond C. (1978). *Introduction to Security.* Rev. ed. Los Angeles, CA: Security World Publishing Company.

International Association of Chiefs of Police. (1996). *Combating Workplace Violence–Guidelines for Employers and Law Enforcement.* Defense Personnel Security Research Center (PERSEREC). Washington, DC: Bureau of Justice Assistance.

Kurtis, Bill. "Jonesboro Schoolyard Ambush." *A&E Investigative Reports.* September 3, 1999.

Kurtis, Bill. "Teenagers Under the Gun." *A&E Investigative Reports.* September 8, 1999.

McClure, Lynne Falkin. (1996). *Risky Business–Managing Employee Violence in the Workplace.* New York, NY: Haworth Press.

National Crime Prevention Council. (1996). "Not One More–Making Children, Families and Communities Safer From Violence." Publication funded by the Bureau of Justice Assistance (BJA). Office of Justice Programs. Washington, DC: United States Department of Justice.

National Crime Prevention Council. (1998). "Safer Schools." Publication funded by the Bureau of Justice Assistance (BJA). Office of Justice Programs. Washington, DC: United States Department of Justice.

National Crime Prevention Council. (1999). "Stop the Violence–Start Something." Publication funded by the Bureau of Justice Assistance (BJA). Office of Justice Programs. Washington, DC: United States Department of Justice.

National Crime Prevention Council. (1995). *350 Strategies to Prevent Crime–A Resource for Municipal Agencies and Community Groups.* Bureau of Justice Assistance. Washington, DC: Department of Justice.

Newman, Oscar. (1973). *Defensible Space–Crime Prevention Through Urban Design.* New York, NY: Collier Books.

Phillips Business Information, Inc. and the American Society for Industrial Security. *Security Industry 1999 Edition–Buyers Guide.* Potomac, MD: Phillips Business Information.

Powell, John W. (1981). *Campus Security and Law Enforcement.* Woburn, MA: Butterworth Publishers.

Remsberg, Charles. (1996). *The Tactical Edge–Surviving High-Risk Patrol.* Northbrook, IL: Calibre Press.

San Luis, Ed, Tyska, Louis A., & Fennelly, Lawrence J. (1994). *Office and Office Building Security.* 2nd ed. Newton, MA: Butterworth-Heinemann.

Schactsiek, David A., & Post, Richard S. (1986). *Security Managers Desk Reference.* Stoneham, MA: Butterworths.

Schnabolk, Charles. (1983). *Physical Security: Practices & Technology.* Woburn, MA: Butterworth Publishers.

Walsh, Timothy, & Healy, Richard J. (1991). *Protection of Assets Manual.* Volumes I-IV. 9th Printing. Santa Monica, CA: The Merritt Company.

West Virginia University. "Building Safe Schools and Healthy Communities." A Forum Hosted by United States Senator Robert C. Byrd. Morgantown, West Virginia. August 21, 1999.

Winters Communications, Inc. (1996). *Dealing With Anger.* Tampa, FL: Winters Communications.

INDEX

2712 GIFT